RAID ON ENTEBBE

Inside the terminal lounge there was consternation and panic. Most people obeyed the commandos' injunction to lie down, parents shielding their children's bodies with their own, wives clinging to husbands. As soldiers appeared at the terminal windows, one young student leapt to his feet in terror. The commandos were spraying the room with automatic fire at waist to chest height and he fell instantly. It was a scene of utmost terror and confusion, but gradually order emerged from the chaos. The disbelieving hostages could still hear a fierce firefight going on outside, but the dazed realization that a rescue operation was actually in progress was beginning to sink in.

The firing continued for about a quarter of an hour, then gradually died away as those Ugandan troops who had not been killed, fled. Now Israeli soldiers entered the lounge, moving among the hostages, urging them to their feet and outside to the waiting Land Rovers. Other commandos encircled the buildings and the dispersal area in a ring of steel, watchful eyes scanning the darkness outside the brilliance of the terminal lights. On the roof of the buildings, snipers with Galil rifles fitted with night sights sought further targets . . .

*Books in this series published
by Berkley*

THE WORLD'S ELITE FORCES
THE WORLD'S GREATEST GHOSTS

The WORLD'S ELITE FORCES

BRUCE QUARRIE

B
BERKLEY BOOKS, NEW YORK

The publishers wish to thank the following individuals and organizations for their kind permission to reproduce the photographs in this book: Christopher F. Foss 135; John Frost Newspaper Collection 172; Ministry of Defence 58; Photographers International (Peter Jordan) 147; (Terry Fincher) 204; *Soldier* Magazine 17; Topham Picture Library 43, 73, 85, 91, 102, 122, 125, 159, 229, 235, 241. Maps by Eugene Fleury.

This Berkley book contains the complete
text of the original edition.
It has been completely reset in a typeface
designed for easy reading, and was printed
from new film.

THE WORLD'S ELITE FORCES

A Berkley Book / published by arrangement with
Octopus Books

PRINTING HISTORY
Octopus Books edition published 1985
Berkley edition / May 1988

ISBN: 0-425-10852-X

A BERKLEY BOOK ® TM 757,375
Berkley Books are published by The Berkley Publishing Group,
200 Madison Avenue, New York, New York 10016.
The name "BERKLEY" and the "B" logo
are trademarks belonging to Berkley Publishing Corporation.

PRINTED IN THE UNITED STATES OF AMERICA

10   9   8   7   6   5   4   3   2   1

Among the many people who have helped in the writing of this book, I would like particularly to put on record David Rosser-Owen, Martin Windrow and John Frost. Will Fowler was also of great help, as was Terry Gander, and for all their unstinting generosity I give great thanks. In addition, I would like to pay tribute to Sue Forster's painstaking editing work. Alan Smith of the John Topham Picture Agency, Bill Rouse of *Soldier* magazine, Christopher F. Foss and Terry Fincher also deserve a vote of thanks. However, this book is dedicated to Samantha Yvonne Quarrie for her timely arrival . . .

Bruce Quarrie,
Wellingborough, Northants

CONTENTS

I

REGARDLESS OF RISK

THE ROLE OF ELITE FORCES

"Regardless of risk, he charged up the hill and, although mortally wounded, succeeded in eliminating the enemy machine-gun nest so that the other men in his section could advance to take their objective." How bald it sounds, and yet how many citations for the Victoria Cross and other awards for extreme valour read in just this way. Many perfectly ordinary men, faced with a situation which they know will quite probably lead to their own death, find the inner reserves to act with extraordinary courage if the circumstances demand it. The stranger diving into a roaring river torrent to rescue a drowning child, or hurling himself into a blazing building to save the life of an unconscious neighbour, is no less courageous than the soldier who defends his wounded comrade until his ammunition runs out; but there is a difference. Soldiers who have volunteered for their career (rather than being conscripted) know that their choice is one of kill or be killed, and come to an acceptance of the possibility of their death which is foreign to the average civilian. Nowhere is this more true than in the ranks of the élite military forces of the world, volunteers from the word "go," who undertake even more intensive and rigorous training which will lead them in time of war or emergency into the front line wherever the action is hottest.

Since World War 2, the term "élite," as applied to military formations, has come to acquire at least three separate connotations. The traditional and historical meaning goes back to the Praetorian Guard of the Caesars, to the Saxon huscarls at Hastings, to Cromwell's Ironsides, Napoleon's Old Guard or the men who died at Camerone, defending the Alamo or marching to the relief of Khartoum. Today, this tradition is maintained by such formations as the British Brigade of Guards.

Since World War 1, though, and even more so since World War 2, a different type of élite soldier has emerged. In the early days he would have been a member of an *ad hoc* battle group, a small unit of volunteers, often using imaginatively improvised weapons, which would be deployed as a "hit-and-run" assault force during trench raids on the Western Front. By the time of World War 2, more formally structured units were beginning to emerge on both sides. German, British and American paratroops in particular earned a deserved reputation for daring, for toughness and for the use of unconventional methods in the attacks on Eben Emael in Belgium in 1940, Crete in 1941, Normandy and Arnhem in 1944, and elsewhere. The US Marine Corps and Rangers, the British Royal Marine commandos and other allied units received much media attention, as did such élite German units as the Afrika Korps.

Alongside these relatively large formations, however,

there was a parallel development of small, intensely self-disciplined, highly motivated and ruthlessly trained units, whose function was as often covert as it was overt. The Long Range Desert Group and similar semi-official formations led to the birth of today's Special Air Service Regiment and Special Boat Squadron, for example, while, in America, men who trained as both parachutists and underwater swimmers became the nucleus of today's SEAL (Sea-Air-Land) Teams and, in Germany, Otto Skorzeny's brilliantly successful airborne SS commandos showed the way for the type of role this new élite would adopt in the post-war world.

After 1945, however, the face of war changed dramatically—not just because of nuclear weapons. The "cauldron" was no longer confined to Europe. There had been bloody uprisings in China, India, Africa and elsewhere throughout the nineteenth century, but now, in the wake of a five-year conflict which had weakened the major powers, the emergent countries of the so-called Third World discovered nationalism and self-determination, and a rapid balkanization of colonial territories ensued. British, Belgian, Dutch and French authorities in the Far and Middle Easts found themselves faced with growing demands for independence which created a seemingly never-ending succession of guerrilla wars and terrorist attacks in Indo-China, Malaya, India, Indonesia, Palestine, Kenya, the Congo, Rhodesia and many other countries.

Developing skills

Regular troops, as the British learned in North America in the 18th century, have an almost impossible task when fighting an elusive foe who can, chameleon-like, fade into the natural background, and who avoids at all costs any form of traditional set-piece battle. Ambushes and traps, the torture and mutilation of prisoners, the quick hit-and-run raid, the use of hostages and international blackmail, hijackings and the slaughter of civilians who might be in the way or just in the wrong place at the wrong time—all of these became part and parcel of a new form of total warfare which the conventional armed forces of the world are largely unable to cope with.

There have been a few exceptions. The British Army won the only true victory over an indigenous terrorist force in Malaya; it is still trying in Northern Ireland, and the scope of the problem is illustrated when one appreciates that troops not only have to undergo several weeks of special training before a tour of duty in Ulster, but also have to undertake a similar retraining course *afterwards*, before they are fit to go back into the "real" front line in Germany. Many other nations have experienced similar difficulties. The French, and then the Americans, both tried, and lost, in Indo-China/Vietnam. Using similar tactics, but against a largely disorganized opposition, the Jews succeeded in wresting and holding the new state of Israel from their enemies against frightful odds—simultaneously creating a major new trouble spot for the world to watch.

Alongside the emergence of new nations and new power struggles came the international terrorist, the political or religious fanatic who does not care one iota who is killed, how many are killed, or even if he (or she) is killed, as long as a political objective is achieved. Assassination is, of course, nothing new. Organizations such as the Palestinian *El Fatah,* the Japanese Red Army, the German Baader-Meinhof gang and the Provisional Wing of the Irish Republican Army operate, however, on a different level and, in that sense, *are* new. The fact that they so often strike seemingly at random, and at "soft" targets—not necessarily within the boundaries of the country at whose government their demands are aimed—makes them particularly difficult to deal with on a purely military footing.

The "brush wars" of the 1950s and '60s had already accelerated the creation of special counter-insurgency forces in many civilized countries, and it is mainly with these that this book deals. In Borneo, Malaya, Aden and elsewhere, the British Special Air Service Regiment established for itself a formidable reputation, and other countries were not slow in imitating it. Commonwealth countries were the first to develop special units on the SAS model, and American commanders were so impressed with the Australian SAS in Vietnam that they set up special training camps with Australian instructors for their own élite troops, such as the men of the Airborne, Marine and Ranger battalions. West Germany, shocked by the Olympic Games massacre at Munich, formed its own special anti-terrorist commando group, *Grenzschutzgruppe* (GSG) 9. France cultivated the élite paras of the French Foreign Legion. And, after the Israelis showed the way at Entebbe, these units proved themselves at Mogadishu and Kolwezi.

There are many dramatic and exciting tales of adventure concerning the élite forces of the world, some of which have been selected for inclusion in this volume. They include pitched battles, such as Goose Green, as well as rescue operations, such as Princes Gate and Operation "Eagle Claw," and their locations cross the world from the jungles of Vietnam, via the deserts of the Middle East, to the bleak inhospitable terrain of the Falkland Islands. The intention of this book is to show through example what defines an "élite" force, as well as including as much information as is available on organization and weapons.

It is almost impossible to glean reliable information from the other side of the "Iron Curtain." That East German commandos regularly exercise in NATO uniforms and with NATO equipment on the island of Hiddensee in the

Baltic is no secret, nor is the presence of Soviet airborne troops in Afghanistan. But the main Soviet attempt over the last three decades has been in encouraging and supporting—economically, militarily and politically—the independent terrorist movements which are, for their own motives, trying to destroy the fabric of Western society. Well trained, and just as capable of entering battle "regardless of risk," these organizations also have a separate section in this book.

The future

The last five years have seen an increased awareness of the need for extremely tough and well-trained quick-reaction forces in both British and American military circles, and new ready-alert brigades, as well as command structures, are currently being implemented. To what extent other countries will follow suit remains to be seen, but one particularly encouraging sign has been the hardening of attitudes towards terrorism in recent years, with the result that few governments today will accede to blackmail, and potential hijackers know that they will not be allowed to escape alive. However, although the protection of the innocent from terrorist blackmail is an important role for today's special forces, their recent and continuing reorganization must also be seen in the context of their role in time of global war, and the ominous implication for Europe in particular is that strategic planners in the Pentagon and elsewhere may have finally decided that it is not worth fighting a nuclear war over that continent. Even while we pray that such a theory is never put to the test, let us also give thanks for the fact that the men of the American, British and other élite forces stand prepared to lay down their lives, causing as much damage as possible to the enemy in order to buy the world time to reach sanity.

II

GREAT BRITAIN

**THE PARACHUTE REGIMENT • THE SPECIAL
AIR SERVICE REGIMENT • THE ROYAL
MARINE COMMANDOS • THE SPECIAL
BOAT SQUADRON AND RAIDING SQUADRONS**

The British Army has for centuries combined the best military qualities of professionalism and individual enterprise, and nowhere can these be seen more clearly than in Great Britain's spearhead units. None of these formations existed prior to World War 2, but all of them proved themselves in action in the Western Desert, the Greek islands, France, Norway, and on mainland Italy, and later in the numerous campaigns around the world in which the British Army has been involved since 1945. The nation's soldiers have taken part, it will surprise many people to learn, in more than 50 campaigns of one type or another since the end of World War 2: in Greece from 1945 to '47;

7

WEAPONS OF THE BRITISH ÉLITE FORCES

Designation	Type	Calibre	Magazine	Rate of fire	Range	Remarks
L9A1	Browning automatic pistol	9 mm	13 rounds	Single-shot	40 m	
XL47E1	Walther automatic pistol	7.65 mm	8 rounds	Single-shot	40 m	Modern equivalent of the wartime Walther PP
L2A3	Sterling sub-machine-gun	9 mm	34 rounds	550 rpm cyclic	200 m	
L34A1	Sterling Patchett silenced sub-machine-gun	9 mm	34 rounds	515 rpm cyclic	150 m	
MP5	Heckler and Koch sub-machine-gun	9 mm	15 or 30 rounds	800 rpm	200 m	Used by SAS and SBS
L1A1	Self-loading rifle	7.62 mm	20 or 30 rounds	40 rpm	600 m+	The widely used Belgian FN FAL
L42A1	Sniper rifle	7.62 mm	10 rounds	Single-shot	1000 m+	
M16A1	Armalite assault rifle	5.56 mm	20 or 30 rounds	700–960 rpm cyclic	400 m	
XL70E3	Individual weapon	5.56 mm	20 or 30 rounds	700–850 rpm cyclic	400 m	Just entering service
XL73E2	Light support weapon	5.56 mm	20 or 30 rounds	700–850 rpm cyclic	1000 m	LMG version of Individual Weapon
L4A4	Light machine-gun	7.62 mm	30 rounds	500–575 rpm cyclic	800 m	The faithful Bren gun

in India, Palestine and Aden; in Northern Ireland, of course, but also in the former Gold Coast and British Honduras; in Eritrea and Somaliland; in Malaya and Singapore; in Korea, Kenya, Cyprus, Suez and Hong Kong; in Belize, Togoland, Muscat and Oman, Jordan and Lebanon; in Jamaica, the Bahamas, British Guiana and Kuwait; in Zanzibar, Swaziland, Uganda, Tanganyika, Mauritius and the Seychelles; in Libya, Anguilla, Dhofar and Rhodesia; and finally, of course, in the Falkland Islands.

During the post-World War 2 withdrawal from Empire, when Britain was granting independence to so many of its former colonies, one campaign stands out as unique in the annals of war. While the French, and later the Americans and Australians, were involved in the long drawn-out and

Designation	Type	Calibre	Magazine	Rate of fire	Range	Remarks
L7A2	Machine-gun	7.62 mm	100-round belt	750–1000 rpm cyclic	1800 m	The widely used 'Gimpy'
L32A1	Automatic shotgun	12 bore (20 mm)	5 rounds	Single-shot	50 m	
M79	Grenade launcher	40 mm	Single-shot	6–10 rpm	150 m	
L9A1	Mortar	51 mm	Single-shot	8 rpm	750 m	
L16A1	Mortar	81 mm	Single-shot	15 rpm	5800 m	
L1A1	Anti-tank missile	66 mm	Single-shot	Not applicable	300 m	Modern equivalent of the old 'bazooka'
LAW80	Anti-tank missile	94 mm	Single-shot	Not available	500 m	Just entering service to replace the L1A1
L14A1 Carl Gustav	Anti-tank missile	84 mm	Single-shot	4–6 rpm	500 m	
Milan	Anti-tank missile	90 mm	Single-shot	3–4 rpm	2000 m	Became known as the 'bunker-buster' in the Falklands
TOW	Anti-tank missile	152 mm	Single-shot	Not available	3750 m	
Blowpipe	Anti-aircraft missile	76.2 mm	Single-shot	Not available	3000 m +	
Stinger	Anti-aircraft missile	70 mm	Single-shot	Not available	Not available	Used by SAS in the Falklands

ultimately hopeless war of attrition in Indo-China, Laos and Vietnam, the British Army fought and won a successful campaign against communist-inspired guerrilla forces in Malaya. The Special Air Service and Special Boat Squadron played an especially vital role here during the years 1948 to 1960. Operating in the jungle, living off the land like guerrillas for weeks at a time, they used the same tactics that the terrorists were using against them. It was a hit-and-run campaign of hide and seek, with the destruction of the enemy's will to fight being just as important as the destruction of his arms caches and the killing of his soldiers. Similarly, the SAS and SBS waged a parallel "hearts and minds" campaign among the civil population to deny the guerrillas their traditional refuge of hiding among the innocent. As a result, when the Army left Malaya after 12 years, it was able to hand over the government to a democratically established nation.

With the end of the Empire, the British Army's role has in more recent years been increasingly concentrated in Europe, with its commitment to the North Atlantic Treaty Organization (NATO). As discussed in the following pages, the SAS and SBS have a particularly crucial part to play here, since the behind-the-lines sabotage of Soviet and Warsaw Pact tactical nuclear weapons—particularly the mobile, multi-warhead type, such as the SS-20 —will be essential in the early hours and days of a major conflict. Similarly, it must be assumed that the newly formed 5th Airborne Brigade, the spearhead of Britain's quick-reaction forces, will perform an equally vital function in neutralizing Soviet front-line airfields, while the Royal Marine commandos will be first into the fray in Norway if a Soviet offensive ever develops on NATO's northern flank.

All four of these units, which are considered "élite" in the context of this book, have recently proved their capabilities yet again during the recapture of the Falkland Islands; but it must not be forgotten that they also have a peacetime role. This can take the form of the rescue of hostages from terrorists, as happened at Princes Gate in London in 1980; or it can take the form of aid to a country which appeals for help after being devastated by earthquake or flood. Wherever trouble occurs, whether it be a military threat or a natural disaster, a terrorist hijacking or a full-scale war, the officers and men of the Parachute Regiment, the Special Air Service, the Royal Marines and the Special Boat Squadron stand ready and alert for action. Without a shadow of doubt, there are no finer trained troops in the world.

THE PARACHUTE REGIMENT

"Hallo Two, this is Twenty-Three," came the voice of Private "Beast" Kirkwood over the Clansman radio.

"Send, over," came the reply.

"Twenty-Three, for God's sake beam me up, Scotty!" was the heartfelt message.

B Company of the 2nd Battalion of the Parachute Regiment (2 Para) was in a very exposed position on the hillside overlooking the ruins of Boca House, on the west side of the narrow isthmus joining the two main land masses of East Falkland. The company was on the right flank of 2 Para's attack on Argentine positions around the settlements of Darwin and Goose Green, and was coming under extremely heavy fire from enemy 105 mm howitzers as well as mortars. Retreat to the reverse side of the slope, out of direct Argentine observation, was the only prudent course, and the company retired from its precarious position.

It was the middle of the afternoon of 28 May 1982, and the Paras had been in action since 06:35. It was essential that the Argentine positions around Darwin and Goose Green be eliminated as quickly as possible, for they posed a distinct threat both to the beach-head at San Carlos and to the flank of the main troop movement eastwards across the island towards Port Stanley. When the SAS had originally reconnoitred the Argentine positions, and laid down their diversionary attack to keep the enemy's head down while the Marines and Paras landed at San Carlos on 21 May, the Argentine garrison had numbered a single battalion of about 500 men. Unknown to 2 Para's commander, Lieutenant-Colonel Herbert ("H") Jones, however, in the intervening period the Argentines had transferred a further two battalions of the 12th Infantry Regiment from Mount Kent to Goose Green, so that, when his battalion attacked, the enemy outnumbered the Paras by nearly three to one. To put the Paras' achievement in its correct context, it is normally recommended that an assault against prepared enemy positions should take place with a ratio of three attackers to one defender—the reverse of the situation 2 Para encountered.

The Regiment goes to war

The 2nd Battalion, the Parachute Regiment, was to see the heaviest fighting of all during the campaign to recapture the Falkland Islands, and they had watched with chagrin as 3 Para had sailed aboard the *Canberra* on 10 April. Five days later, however, they felt better as they embarked aboard the chartered ferry *Norland* and began the same sort of intensive training which was being carried out on the other troopships of the Task Force. Their landing at San Carlos had not been auspicious, though. Climbing into the landing craft (nicknamed "rubbish skips" by the Paras) was difficult and dangerous, heavily laden as the men were, and one man slipped and broke his pelvis in the gap between the ferry and the landing craft. A Lance-Corporal with the battalion summed it up. "We got into this landing craft. Well, you'd think it would be easy, wouldn't you? But we were carrying these bergens [rucksacks] which weighed about 100 lb. each. It would take two blokes to help you stand up. There were these Blowpipes as well, and the Blowpipes weigh about 50 lb., and we've got them on our shoulders. Unbelievable!"

However, the men of 2 Para had the honour of setting foot ashore first at San Carlos, although they were not pleased at finding that, while the Marines of 40 Commando on their flank had a shallow, shelving stretch of beach, their own was much steeper and meant they had to wade ashore waist-deep in the icy water. Fortunately, there was no resistance. The Lance-Corporal said, "It was utter bloody chaos. In the dark, everyone looks the same in a helmet from behind, and there was no way to distinguish between anybody, and everybody was coming up to you and saying, 'Do you know where so-and-so is?' Basically, if there had been anybody there it would have been the biggest fiasco ever. All you needed there was a hundred blokes, a couple of sustained-fire machine-guns, or even light machine-guns, a rocket launcher, wait until the boats are almost on the beach and just shoot the rockets straight into the men aboard them. They would have killed us all for sure."

As they moved up the beach, everyone expected an Argentine air attack, but all they encountered was a group of tired and unshaven SBS men who directed them. The battalion's first task was to secure Sussex Mountain, overlooking San Carlos water.

"When we crossed the river," the Lance-Corporal continued, "there was an SBS bloke there helping you up, and I can remember someone asking him, 'How long will it take?' It was only 13 km (8 miles) to the actual top of the mountain and the bloke said it would take about maybe five to six hours. We all thought 'rubbish,' but he was right, almost to the minute."

When they reached the summit, the Paras began to dig in on the reverse side of the slope in anticipation of an enemy counter-attack (which never materialized) from the Argentines in Darwin. Then the anticipated air attacks began. The Lance-Corporal continued, "All of a sudden there was this whistling and we all looked round and we could see nothing. Then there was an aircraft. My first thought was for my camera—I wanted to take a photograph. Never mind shooting the damned thing down!"

The aircraft was an Argentine Pucara ground-attack machine, which fired some rockets at both *Argonaut* and *Canberra* and was rapidly engaged by machine-guns and Blowpipe missiles from everywhere in sight. It was soon shot down, having done no damage to the ships. However, this was only a foretaste of what was to come in "bomb alley." By the end of the first day of the landings at San Carlos, HMS *Ardent* had been sunk after no fewer than 17 determined attacks by Skyhawks, Mirages, Pucaras and Aermacchis, while *Argonaut* was seriously damaged, and *Antrim, Brilliant* and *Broadsword* had all suffered hits, fortunately from bombs which failed to explode. In return, the Argentine air force had lost 16 aircraft. Two days later, HMS *Antelope* was destroyed in the spectacular explosion which made newspaper front pages around the world, and on the 25th *Coventry* also was sunk. But the Argentines had made the fatal mistake of waiting until the troops were ashore before attacking, and all the courage of their pilots could not prevent the counter-invasion succeeding.

By nightfall on the day of their invasion, both Para battalions as well as the Marines were well dug-in, supplies were flowing ashore, the Blues and Royals of the Household Cavalry with their Scorpion and Scimitar light tanks were in position, as were most of the artillery and Rapier anti-aircraft missile batteries. For 2 Para, though, it was the beginning of a very uncomfortable night since, although they were 900 m (3000 feet) above sea level on Sussex Mountain, the bottoms of their trenches were awash with water. Warmth and dryness were luxuries which all the troops on the Falklands, regardless of nationality, soon learned to do without.

Within a few days, despite the repeated air attacks on the ships in San Carlos water, sufficient supplies had been brought ashore, and it was time for the Paras to move on: 3 Para alongside 45 Commando on the long "tab" ("tabbing" being the Paras' equivalent of the Marines' "yomping," or forced-marching) to Port Stanley; and 2 Para towards their destiny at Goose Green.

Colonel "H" Jones' battalion was organized along regular Army lines, but with subtle differences. Because it had been earmarked for duty in Belize at the time the Argentines invaded the Falklands, its men were equipped for the jungle fighting role. Although the terrain and climate on East Falkland could hardly have been more different from the tropical forest of Central America, what this meant was that they were not only issued with twice the normal number of 7.62 mm General Purpose Machine-Guns ("Gimpys") but also with a number of M16 Armalite rifles and M79 40 mm grenade launchers (of the type used so effectively by the Royal Marines' M&AW Cadre in the battle for Top Malo house described on page 57). This weight of firepower was to stand them in good stead. In addition, Colonel Jones had established an experimental, and very successful, dual command structure, with two tactical headquarters; this was to prove invaluable in keeping up the momentum of the Paras' attack on Goose Green when Colonel Jones was killed. Other than this, the battalion comprised the normal headquarters company (split into two), a support company with the mortars and Milan anti-tank missiles, and four rifle companies (A to D). C Company had been designated a special Patrol Company and operated in front of the battalion, confirming SAS reports that the isthmus was held in strength, particularly on Darwin Hill which overlooks the settlement from the south.

At 06:35 on 28 May the battalion moved out, with B Company on the right flank, D Company in the centre and A Company on the left. An Argentine platoon in a farmhouse was rapidly evicted by A Company, who were astounded to discover that the civilians inside had survived their attack. With this position secure (albeit under heavy artillery fire by this time), B Company moved up on the right in a pincer movement, enfilading Darwin from the west, while D Company pressed forward to consolidate the centre, eliminating some Argentine positions which A Company had bypassed, and taking several prisoners. It was during the next phase that Colonel Jones was killed. He was an officer who believed in leading from the front rather than directing matters from the rear, in the finest tradition of the Army, and his tactical headquarters was right forward with A Company when it began an assault up Darwin Hill. Colonel Jones led his own men forward at the same time on A Company's right. Murderous Argentine machine-gun fire forced A Company to fall back with two officers killed, and at this moment a burst of fire from another machine-gun raked Colonel Jones, killing him instantly.

"Sunray is down"

The code message informing him that "Sunray" ("H" Jones) was "down"—whether killed or incapacitated was not known at the time—was received by Major Chris Keeble, the second in command, over the radio at a time when 2 Para's main headquarters was itself being barraged by heavy artillery and mortar fire. The situation was perilous, with B Company pinned down on the slope above Boca House and D Company still reorganizing after its mopping-up operations. Following "H" Jones' example, Keeble moved up to the front and ordered A Company into the assault on Darwin Hill again. Perhaps the death of the commanding officer whom the tough Paras idolized provided the necessary spur, because this time there was no stopping them. While 81 mm mortar rounds and Milan missiles rained into the Argentine positions from the Support Company which Keeble had also brought forward, A Company charged up the hill under cover of smoke gre-

Soldiers of the Parachute Regiment bundle their 'chutes together while a second wave descends in the background.

nades, blasting away with every automatic weapon the men possessed. The Argentines crumbled. With 18 of their number dead and another 39 wounded, they surrendered. *Now* Keeble could bring up D Company to outflank the Boca House position which had pinned down B Company. Rockets, grenades and machine-gun fire poured into the Argentine defences from two directions, and the surviving soldiers quickly surrendered.

Lance-Corporal Kevin Lukowiak summed up the Paras' attitude in such a situation: "Your main instinct in a fire-fight is, 'He's trying to get me, I'm going to get him before he does.' A great Army expression is, 'You don't kill things, you destroy them.' So if you go in to take out a bunker, you waste the bunker before you get to it, then you give it some grenades. And then you blast it with your rifle."

The Argentine troops on the Falklands, by and large, did not wait for the Paras to do this, but retreated or surrendered first. However, this does not mean that they did not fight with determination and vigour at the beginning of an engagement, as any soldier who was there will testify.

With both Darwin Hill and Boca House secured, Keeble could continue the Paras' advance on the main Argentine forces at Goose Green. Again, an enveloping manoeuvre was planned, with B Company pressing right around the western coast of the isthmus to come back round upon Goose Green unexpectedly from the south, while D Company performed a less extensive sweep so as to come in from the west, and C Company, the Patrol Company, moved through A Company's position on Darwin Hill to attack from the north. The Support Company was also brought forward on to Darwin Hill to lend its firepower to the action.

Both C and D Companies soon encountered problems. Even at this early stage in the land battle, the Paras recognized the Argentine disposition to surrender when threatened by determined aggression and so, despite the fact that they came under murderous fire from artillery pieces, mortars and even anti-aircraft guns as they descended Darwin Hill towards Goose Green and its airstrip, few were surprised when, as they reached the Argentine trenches, a white flag was waved. What happened next is confused. One British journalist is reported as having said that a British machine-gun opened fire, to which an Argentine gun responded. Lieutenant Jim Barry of D Company, who had walked forward to accept the Argentine surrender, was killed together with two NCOs. Private Baz Graham of 11 Platoon, D Company, remembers things differently. "We were going up the hill and the flag went up. The officer [Barry] called the Sergeant, and they got half-way up the hill. Bang! They let rip into them. Killed them. One guy was hit in the knee and one of the Argies came forward and shot him in the head. He moved forward out of his position and shot him."

Anyone who has ever been on a battlefield will realize that mistakes occur and that things are not always what they seem; moreover, no two witnesses ever give the same account of events. The effect on C and D Companies, regardless, was electrifying. They went in with everything blazing. The schoolhouse behind the trenches which the Argentines had been occupying was blasted with so many grenades and perforated with such concentrated automatic fire that it was afterwards impossible to determine how many defenders it had held. (The Argentine soldiers did not wear identifying metal "dog-tags," so no accurate body count of their casualties was ever possible during the campaign.)

At this stage in the evening of 28 May the air forces of both sides came into action. D Company was attacked by four aircraft, two Mirages and two Pucaras, the latter carrying dreaded napalm containers. This was, however, the only occasion during the whole campaign that these loathsome weapons were used, and there were no casualties among the Paras. In retaliation, three Royal Air Force Harriers struck hard at the Argentine defences with cluster bombs and cannon fire. As darkness fell, helicopters could be seen bringing up further Argentine reinforcements.

During the night, a Para patrol entered Darwin settlement itself, and the information gleaned from the local inhabitants changed Major Keeble's ideas about the following day's action. In order to save the lives of his own troops during what was certain to prove hard street-fighting, he had decided to lay on a concentrated artillery barrage and had ordered up more 105 mm guns, mortars and ammunition. However, the patrol discovered that the Argentines held over a hundred British civilians hostage in the community centre in Goose Green. Whatever form an attack took, innocent lives would be lost. Keeble radioed for permission from Brigadier Julian Thompson to ask the Argentine commander to surrender, or at least to release the civilians (who had, it transpired, been incarcerated since 1 May). Thompson agreed, and preliminary negotiations took place over the radio between two British farm managers, one in San Carlos and one in Goose Green. In the morning, two Argentine senior NCOs emerged under a white flag and Chris Keeble, together with two other officers—one a Spanish-speaking SBS officer, Captain Rod Bell—plus a radio operator and two journalists, accompanied them back to the airstrip, where the Argentine commander, Air Vice-Commodore Wilson Pedrozo, agreed to surrender. Then came the surprise. Instead of the 300-odd men expected as a result of the earlier faulty intelligence reports (allowing for those already killed or captured), Argentine troops emerged in their droves from the buildings in and around Goose Green, most of them very happy with the bloodless end to the battle. The Paras had gone in and won at odds of one to three!

The making of the Parachute Regiment

Britain was a late starter in the development of airborne troops, and it was not until late in June 1940, after the dramatic successes of German paratroops and glider-borne forces during the invasion of Belgium and the Netherlands, that Prime Minister Winston Churchill issued an instruction to begin the formation of an airborne corps of at least 5000 men. Thus was the 1st Airborne Division born, and it proved so successful in Tunisia (where British paras—the "red devils"—met German *Fallschirmjäger*—the "green devils"—for the first time), and later during the invasions of Sicily and Italy, that in May 1943 the creation of a second division, the 6th Airborne, was authorized. (It should be noted that many military formations, particularly those originated during wartime, are deliberately numbered out of sequence in order to mislead the enemy.) The 6th Airborne spearheaded the British assault on Normandy in the early hours of D-Day, 6 June 1944, while the 1st Division was enjoying a well-earned rest after its labours in the Mediterranean theatre of operations. However, it was the 1st Airborne which won undying glory at Arnhem that autumn.

After World War 2, there was a rapid run-down of all the armed services, and the airborne forces were reduced from 17 to only 3 parachute battalions, the 4th/6th, the 5th (Scottish) and the 7th. Together with supporting artillery and cavalry (light armoured) formations, they became 16 Para Brigade, with headquarters at Aldershot. A quarter of a century later, in 1977, further defence cuts caused the disbandment of the supporting units and, at the time of the Falklands crisis, the Parachute Regiment consisted essentially of just three battalions: 1, 2 and 3 Para.

In the wake of the Falklands' operation, however, considerable rethinking has gone into the Para role. Over recent years it had become fashionable to regard the airborne capability as outmoded, and to treat the Paras merely as especially tough infantrymen. What analysis of the battles for the Falklands shows, on the other hand, is that in almost every case, with the exception of the final assault on Port Stanley, *had* a parachute drop capability existed, Argentine positions could have been captured more quickly and with fewer casualties. It is equally true to say that, without the loss of so many troop-carrying Chinook helicopters aboard *Atlantic Conveyor,* the course of the campaign would have been different. In both cases, the answer is speed and mobility—the prime attributes of the airborne trooper, who can get quickly to where he is, hopefully, least expected, or at any rate before the enemy can prepare adequate defences.

What the Falklands also showed was that Britain had, in the Parachute Regiment, the nucleus of a "quick-reaction" force second to none—small, maybe, but in the British Army quality has usually counted for more than quantity. "Small is beautiful" has more than one meaning. The British Army, even allowing for the well-trained members of the Territorial Army, is only half the size of those of France or West Germany and a mere fifth the size of that of America. The closest comparison one can draw is that the British troops in the Falklands proved once more the point Wellington made in the Peninsular War against France: a small, trained, motivated and professional force will defeat a far larger conscript army of reluctant soldiers. The only truly professional force the Argentines possessed was their air force, and they frittered it away. Fortunately, official government thinking has finally reached the same conclusion, with the result that, while these words are written, the old British 5th Infantry Brigade is being reconstituted as the new 5th Airborne Brigade. As during the 1970s, its task remains essentially that of principal reserve for commander-in-chief of United Kingdom Land Forces (UKLF). This means that it is principally entrusted, in time of global war, with the internal defence of the United Kingdom. However, the brigade now includes two battalions of the Parachute Regiment together with an armoured reconnaissance regiment whose Scorpions and Scimitars can be transported by air, together with a helicopter support squadron, an air defence troop equipped with Blowpipe surface-to-air missiles, plus signals, ordnance and engineering units. This gives the new brigade far greater flexibility as well as mobility and, despite its small size, shows that the goverment is not willing to be "caught napping" by another Falklands-type encounter. Had the 5th Airborne

Brigade existed in 1982, it could have been in Stanley before the main Argentine forces arrived. Considering the havoc that the tiny parties of Royal Marines managed to cause, what would the Argentines have accomplished against such an airborne force? And so, today, 5th Airborne, proudly wearing the same maroon beret which meant so much in 1944, stands ready for an almost immediate departure for any one of the world's trouble spots in which British interests or the lives of British civilians may be threatened.

Parachute training

It is common knowledge that the training course for a modern paratrooper is both intense and gruelling. Basic training takes seven weeks and, while principally designed to toughen up recruits physically, it also involves learning weapons use, fieldcraft and rudimentary first aid. The course culminates in a realistic exercise in the Welsh mountains, after which the recruits' performance is examined by a selection committee. Some men are weeded out at this stage as being unsuitable material for the Parachute Regiment (although many of them would be perfectly at home in a regular infantry regiment); others are recommended for further training and a "second chance"; and the best recruits, after a weekend's leave, begin the second stage of their course. The first three weeks of this involves advanced weapons handling with automatic rifles, machine-guns, sub-machine-guns, anti-tank missiles and grenades, but the physical toughening-up process does not stop either. At the end of this period there is a further selection committee to decide which recruits are suitable to go on for parachute training and which must, regretfully, be passed over.

Unbelievably, the next training stage is even more demanding than the preceding two, but by this time the recruits are in peak physical condition and the knowledge that they are on the "final lap" promotes confidence. The initial stages involve crossing obstacle courses some 9 m (30 ft.) above the ground, taking part in a boxing match designed to test aggression, completing a 16 km (10 mile) forced march in full kit in under two hours, a 12 km (7½ mile) "stretcher race" carrying a simulated casualty, a "log race" carrying a simulated box of ammunition, a cross-country steeplechase, and three circuits of the assault course. After the successful completion of all these, the recruit is finally permitted to wear the coveted red beret, but he still has to earn his parachutist's wings.

Following four week's advanced training in fieldcraft and tactics in Wales, designed to make them think and act as part of a military team rather than as individuals, the recruits finally proceed to the RAF Station of Brize Norton in Somerset. Here, they are first taught the correct way in which to fall, then proceed to dummy exits from a mock-up of a Hercules transport aircraft, and controlled drops from the hangar roof on rigging lines whose rate of descent is controlled by gears to approximate the 30 km/h (20 mph) speed of an actual parachute drop. Once he has mastered the art of falling correctly and safely, a recruit goes outside to the tower, where he makes further controlled drops of longer duration and learns how to deal with tangled rigging lines and similar problems. Then comes the balloon jump, and it is at this stage that some recruits balk.

However, refusal to jump is the cardinal sin in the Parachute Regiment and any recruits who simply cannot face it are gently and sympathetically made to leave the Regiment. For most of them, though, that first jump from the balloon, in a silence only broken by the wind, is an exhilarating experience, although the seconds before the parachute is pulled open by its static line (fixed to the balloon

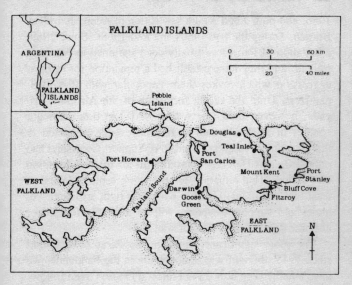

FALKLAND ISLANDS

platform) seem far longer than they really are. Then the recruit is floating gently to earth. He has only a few seconds in which to appreciate the sensation, because the ground is rushing up and it's feet together and hit and roll. I've made it! An incredulous grin. "Feeling nine feet tall and covered with hair," a recruit at this stage regards the final qualifying seven jumps from a Hercules, three of them with full equipment and one of them at night, with relative equanimity. And, at the end, there are those coveted wings to add to the maroon beret.

Paras in action

The Parachute Regiment has seen extensive service around the world since the end of World War 2. 3 Para was instrumental in seizing Gamil Airport outside Port Said during the Anglo-French occupation of the Suez Canal Zone in

1956, and both 2 and 3 Para saw action in Aden, as well as
Borneo, during the late 1950s and mid-1960s. Since 1969,
a battalion of Paras has usually been stationed in Northern
Ireland, and they have established a reputation for ruthless
aggression which makes them unpopular with IRA sympathizers. Until the recent formation of 5th Airborne Brigade, however, their role within NATO in time of major
conflict in Europe would largely have been restricted to
that of ordinary infantry, since RAF Support Command had
only sufficient Hercules transports to air-lift one battalion
into action. That situation is now being remedied, and at
least two battalions, together with their light armoured vehicles and support weapons, will be available for proper
airborne operations in time of war.

The most significant campaign the Paras have fought
since 1945, though, was undoubtedly in the Falklands. We
have already seen how 2 Para fared at Goose Green following the amphibious landing at San Carlos; while they were
making headlines, 3 Para was on the march.

After trudging ashore on 21 May, many of the men
soaking wet because a landing craft had struck an unsus-
pected offshore sandbar, 3 Para entered San Carlos settlement itself to be greeted with joy and hot cups of tea by the
locals. The men then established dug-in positions overlooking the settlement and began sending out patrols to
clear Fanning Head of remaining Argentine troops. On 27
May, as 2 Para was preparing to move on Darwin and
Goose Green, 3 Para was tightening its boots for the long
cross-country "tab" in the company of 45 Commando, via
Douglas and Teal Inlet to Estancia and Mount Kent. Led by
their CO, Lieutenant-Colonel Hew Pike, the Paras completed the march to Estancia House, an isolated building on
the north-west slopes of Mount Kent, in only four days.
The house was packed with local civilians who had left
Stanley to avoid military action and who were astonished

to be awoken during the night of 31 May by a flare bursting overhead and the shouted order, "Open up! It's the British Army."

The Paras rapidly dug in, putting up tents over their foxholes and constructing dug-outs using spare timber and sheets of corrugated iron in order to obtain some shelter from the bitter cold. Defensive machine-gun positions were established using piles of cut peat in place of sandbags, and patrols were sent out. A number of Argentine stragglers (a kinder word than deserters) were brought in, weaponless, and, as dawn broke, the Paras were able to look out over Port Stanley and their next objective, Mount Longdon. However, due both to the acute helicopter shortage and to poor flying conditions, it was another three days before Brigadier Thompson was able to get an artillery battery forward to support them.

The formidable and craggy slopes of Mount Longdon were to prove an extremely tough nut to crack, for not only were they defended by the whole of the Argentine 7th Infantry Regiment, supported by marines and snipers from the *Buzo Tactico* equipped with night sights, but also the mountain approaches had been heavily mined. Because of the minefields, there was just one possible approach for the Paras, and it was on a narrow frontage which permitted the deployment of only one company at a time. Naval gunfire support would be provided by HMS *Avenger,* but Mount Longdon was a veritable fortress, and Colonel Pike knew that he was going to need all the support he could muster.

To begin with the operation went well. A and B Companies moved out to the north and south in a pincer movement at 21:00 on 11 June, while C Company took the centre. Guides were provided by the men of D (Patrol) Company who had reconnoitred the approach routes and minefields over the preceding days. It was a brilliant moonlit night and the men made the best use of whatever cover was available to avoid detection through the Argentine night scopes. However, any element of surprise was lost when a Corporal in B Company trod on an anti-personnel mine only about 630 m (700 yd.) from the first Argentine trenches. The Argentine mortars, machine-guns and artillery pieces opened up immediately, but two Para platoons raced up the slope, covered by a third platoon which had found good cover in some rocks. Hurling grenades in all directions, they took the first objective without loss but unfortunately missed one Argentine bunker, whose occupants opened fire on their rear. Several Paras had died or been wounded before the bunker fell silent.

Advancing from this position, B Company came under severe fire from Argentine positions further up the slope. The Paras used 66 and 84 mm rockets to eliminate the troublesome heavy-calibre machine-guns, but the Argentines seemed to be everywhere and, the moment one position was knocked out, fire opened up from a different quarter. Two Privates ran forward to take out a 0.50 calibre machine-gun nest with hand grenades—something which is easy to say but which in practice demands the kind of courage and determination which defy description. It was while attempting to deal with another such heavy machine-gun that Sergeant Ian McKay won his posthumous Victoria Cross. McKay was the Sergeant of 4 Platoon, commanded by Lieutenant Bickerdike. As his platoon came under sustained fire from a 0.50 calibre heavy machine-gun, two lighter 7.62 mm machine-guns and a 105 mm recoilless gun, both Lieutenant Bickerdike and his signaller were wounded, the former in the leg and the latter in the mouth. McKay took charge and decided that the heavy machine-gun was the main problem. Gathering a four-man section of 4 Platoon around him, he led the way up the slope towards the well dug-in Argentine position, which was further protected by numerous riflemen in well-sited trenches.

The four riflemen with McKay were all hit and fell, but the Sergeant continued alone. As he leapt over the parapet, he was hit by a sniper and was killed instantly. However, in falling he blocked the machine-gun's fire and 5 and 6 Platoons were able to take advantage of the momentary lull to retire.

As the men regrouped and casualties were brought to the rear, a rain of fire fell on the Argentine positions from the Royal Artillery's 105 mm guns and 81 mm mortars. Then B Company moved forward again. 4 and 5 Platoons were merged into one and started forward along the ridge they had so recently evacuated. As they neared the Argentine position, they came under heavy fire from point-blank range and fired a 66 mm rocket at the enemy gunners. Charging forward with their rifles blazing, they discovered several dead Argentine soldiers—but by this time the rest of the company was in trouble, having come under fire from two flanks as they advanced. Once again they were forced to retire, and Colonel Pike decided that their casualties had been so heavy that he would have to pull the survivors back and replace them with A Company.

A Company had its own problems, having come round the northern flank of the mountain to find itself on open ground with little cover, and also under heavy fire. Colonel Pike brought the men back and redirected them up through B Company's position. This time the Paras moved forward painfully on their stomachs, firing as they crawled and launching a barrage of grenades and 66 mm rockets to add to the artillery shells which were still pounding the Argentine strongpoint. As they reached the crest, the artillery fire was called off, but some Argentine soldiers could now be seen fleeing. Fixing bayonets, the Paras grimly began clearing the trenches with brutal efficiency. More and more Argentines began to withdraw, harassed by artillery fire, and, after a battle lasting ten hours—the most costly in the

whole campaign—Mount Longdon was finally secured by
3 Para. Twenty-three men had been killed and twice that
number wounded, but the Argentine casualties were at
least double; once more, due to the lack of dog-tags, it was
impossible to make an exact count.

The final battle

While the Paras and Marines consolidated their positions
on Mount Longdon, Mount Harriet and Two Sisters, 5 Infantry Brigade moved up so that the Scots Guards and
Gurkhas could take Mount Tumbledown. Meanwhile, 2
Para was assigned Wireless Ridge, defended by the Argentine 1st Parachute Regiment and the 7th Infantry Regiment,
which had withdrawn from Mount Longdon. Unlike earlier
attacks during the campaign, when the Paras and Marines
had tried to close with the enemy positions by stealth, it
was decided to make this a "noisy" assault, with a heavy
preliminary bombardment, and accompanied by the Scorpion and Scimitar light tanks of the Blues and Royals.

During 13 June the battalion marched around 3 Para's
hard-won positions on Mount Longdon in order to approach Wireless Ridge from the north. D Company was to
anchor its attack on Mount Longdon, with B Company to
its left in the centre position and A Company on the far
left, or eastern flank. All the artillery and mortars of both
Para battalions would support the attack. C Company
would follow behind the main assault and proceed eastwards along the bank of the Murrell River to outflank the
far right of the Argentine positions.

The battalion moved up to its start line at 22:30 that
evening and moved out just before 01:00 on the 14th, after
the Argentines had been subjected to a full half hour's intense artillery fire. The Paras watched the "firework dis-
play" with intense satisfaction as they trudged forward, and

the night was not without its element of farce for, as an Argentine 155 mm gun began shelling the advancing Paras, two men dived for cover, only to find themselves at the bottom of an abandoned Argentine latrine! As A and B Companies advanced, they were accompanied by two Scorpion light tanks with 76 mm guns and two Scimitars with quick-firing 30 mm Rarden cannon. The Blues and Royals, commanded by Lieutenant Robin Innes-Ker, were anxious to show what they could do, because so far in the campaign they had not been engaged in a proper battle. They soon proved their usefulness, however. As soon as an Argentine bunker was identified, they would open fire with their main armament and then pursue any Argentine soldiers who tried to escape with their co-axial machine-guns. As one observer commented, "The Paras loved it!" But it was not all to be so easy.

As A and B Companies advanced in the centre, the supporting artillery fire was switched to the front of D Company on the right flank. Unfortunately, the gunners got the range wrong to begin with, and the Paras cursed as their artillery fire landed among their own ranks. Soon, however, the night was lit up by shell bursts from both directions, the sparkle of flares and the red arcs of tracer. An Argentine attempt at a counter-attack was soon beaten off, pursued by mortar fire. 2 Para's determination had never been grimmer. Even the cooks and clerks came along to help out, acting as stretcher bearers and carrying ammunition. By the early hours of the morning, Wireless Ridge was virtually in the Paras' hands, and they could look down at the old Marines' barracks which Argentine troops had stormed on the first day of the invasion. Argentine artillery in Stanley was still active, but following a second attempt at a counter-attack by men of the 1st Parachute Regiment which was broken up by artillery fire, the heart seemed to go out of the resistance. More than a hundred

Argentines had been killed in the attack; 2 Para had lost just three men.

As the daylight grew stronger on the morning of 14 June, the enemy's position was revealed as hopeless. The Argentines were completely surrounded by eager troops on all the high ground around Stanley, and their men were demoralized. Brigadier Thompson flew in to Wireless Ridge by helicopter to observe the situation for himself, and gave his approval for 2 Para to continue down the hill, past the Marines' barracks, into Stanley itself. After having been first ashore at San Carlos, and following Goose Green and Fitzroy, it seemed only just that 2 Para should be first into the islands' capital. Jauntily, the men strolled, sauntered or ran down the slopes, many of them yelling at the tops of their voices. Most of the Argentine troops just stood and watched them, making no attempt to stop the Paras as they started climbing over the Panhard armoured cars and removing souvenirs. At last the guns were silent.

THE SPECIAL AIR SERVICE REGIMENT

At 04:15 on 15 May 1982, Griff Evans, a sheep farmer in the small community on Pebble Island, and his wife Gladys, were awoken by the sound of explosions. Peering through their farmhouse windows, they saw the whole night sky brilliantly illuminated by exploding flares, ammunition and oil drums from the nearby airstrip which the invading Argentine forces had been building as an alternative to Stanley airfield. As Griff and his wife made a cup of coffee and tried to reassure each other, they were unaware of the fact that the darkness outside concealed a troop of men from the Special Air Service Regiment who had been detailed to protect the settlement in case of an Argentine counter-attack. A second troop, led by Captain John Hamilton (who was later to be killed in circumstances of great personal valour), was busy placing charges of plastic explosive in the 11 aircraft on the strip—Pucara ground-attack aircraft, Puma helicopters and a Shorts' Skyvan utility aircraft.

Apart from Port Stanley airfield itself, Pebble Island, lying on the north coast of West Falkland, is the only place in the rocky and mountainous island group where there is a sufficiently long stretch of level ground to accommodate large aircraft. Both the Argentines and the British Task Force commander, Rear Admiral "Sandy" Woodward, appreciated the strategic value of Pebble Island, and the airstrip had been reconnoitred during the night of 13 May by an eight-man SAS patrol. Landed on Keppel Island the previous night, they had carried their lightweight Klepper canoes down to a sheltered cove from which they were able to observe their objective. As darkness fell, they paddled across Keppel Sound and landed on the south-west shore of Pebble Island. Moving stealthily through the darkness, they established a hidden observation post on First Mount Hill, 290 m (960 ft.) high, overlooking the Argentine airstrip with its accompanying radar post and fuel dump. They radioed their observations to the Task Force flagship, *Hermes,* and marked out a landing zone for the Sea King helicopters which would bring in Captain Hamilton and the men of D Squadron, 22 Special Air Service Regiment, plus a Naval Gunfire Support Forward Observer, Captain Chris Brown of 29 Commando Regiment, Royal Artillery. Offshore lay the "County" Class destroyer *Glamorgan,* whose 4.5-inch guns would soon be brought into play.

The Sea Kings landed after dark on the night of 14 May, and John Hamilton and his men disembarked. They were heavily laden down with machine-guns, 2-inch mortars, bombs, grenades, and plastic explosive charges and detonators, and a strenuous cross-country march lay ahead of them. Eventually, they reached the site that the earlier patrol had selected as a mortar position, and thankfully dropped their loads. Splitting into three groups now—one with the mortars as a support section, one to cover the civilian settlement, and one to sabotage the Argentine aircraft—they were ready to tackle the Argentine air force personnel guarding the airstrip.

As the SAS men settled into position, Chris Brown started relaying target information to *Glamorgan* and the shells began to arrive.

For a soldier, naval gunfire support is terrifying. The ship or ships are lying well offshore, outside the range of normal infantry weapons. With an observer on the ground, as in the case of Chris Brown, the accuracy is point-blank. *Glamorgan*'s 20 kg (46 lb.) shells appeared to come from nowhere and were unstoppable. Blast after blast scoured the Argentine positions, carefully timed at one-minute intervals. Nowhere was safe. Ammunition and fuel began exploding, awakening Griff and Gladys Evans and sending the 200 men of the Argentine garrison scurrying to hide from the fury in their dug-outs. Into the confusion slipped the dark shadows of John Hamilton's troopers, festooned with plastic explosive charges, wire and detonators. Working their way, without spoken orders since each man knew exactly his job, from aircraft to aircraft, they placed their charges and detonated them. When daybreak dawned, the Argentine officers surveyed 11 heaps of scrap metal where 11 vital aircraft had been the preceding day. The SAS, meanwhile, had slipped back to their landing ground, picking up the mortars *en route*, and had been flown back to *Hermes*.

"Who Dares Wins"

The Special Air Service Regiment ("Ess-Ay-Ess" to most people, but "Sass" within the Army) had led a largely secret life from the time of its official post-war establishment in 1950 until that never-to-be-forgotten day in 1980 when the black-garbed figures of SAS men were photographed on the balcony of the Iranian Embassy in London by the eagerly awaiting press and television cameras of the world. "Sass" is a military organization which has always shunned the glare of publicity, but the rescue of hostages from a group of fanatics in the centre of one of the world's principal cities focused the limelight on them long before the Falkland Islands' confrontation. Suddenly, their motto was on everyone's lips, and at least one fortunate book publisher made a small fortune through having a manuscript on the regiment's history already in production! From the obscurity of the campaigns in Malaya, Aden and elsewhere around the world in which they had won their spurs, suddenly the men of the SAS were exposed to the public gaze.

This exposure has not been welcomed by the Army; the role of "Sass" is clandestine. The regiment's exact strength and order of battle are not discussed in public, nor will a list of the officers and men in its ranks be found in any published gazetteer. It is officially forbidden to take a photograph of a member of the regiment unless he is sufficiently camouflaged as to be unrecognizable, and even then the practice is frowned upon. The reasons are obvious and understandable. In time of global war, the regiment's duties include the kind of behind-the-lines reconnaissance and sabotage which it accomplished with such panache in the Falklands. In time of "peace," the regiment is responsible for intelligence gathering and the setting of ambushes against the Irish Republican Army in Ulster, while all of its troopers are specially trained in anti-terrorist duties—specifically, the safe rescue of hostages in a hijack situation. Officers and NCOs of the SAS act as advisers to most of the free world's special forces, and, from America to Australia and back, the crack troops of all the western and aligned nations are organized and trained on the SAS model.

The men who join "Sass" are an élite even before their special training. For the most part, the regiment recruits from the Brigade of Guards or the Parachute Regiment, although the officers and men of other regiments are entitled to volunteer (Captain John Hamilton, for instance, came from The Green Howards). The SAS is the only remaining regiment in the British Army which does not recruit directly from the general public, and its standards are so high that by no means all of those who apply, even after the gruelling physical and aptitude tests and training needed for their parent regiment, are accepted.

Volunteers, after passing preliminary interviews, have to undertake the SAS's even more rigorous four-week selection course. This not only embraces the "ordinary" skills of the Para or Commando units, such as rock-climbing, parachuting, skiing, canoeing, swimming and prolonged forced marching in full kit, but a wide variety of psychological tests to ascertain a recruit's ability to respond intelligently and quickly under the most difficult circumstances imaginable. Sensory deprivation tests, in which recruits are spun in a chair similar to those used to train astronauts, but in complete darkness and wearing earplugs, are just one of the many trials a volunteer must endure. At the end of the test, he has to be able to aim and fire at a target which suddenly springs up. In other, Houdini-style tests to judge nerve and susceptibility to panic, recruits are released into darkened swimming pools, laden down with chains, and must release the combination locks on these chains before they can surface to breathe. There *are* casualties during SAS selection and training, and once in a while they hit the headlines, but the effect is to ensure that a man is not admitted to the regiment unless the selection officers are as certain as they can be that he is not only at a peak of physical fitness, but also alert, intelligent and self-motivated.

Once a soldier has passed this initial selection process, which is deliberately made extremely tough in order to weed out as many unsuitable candidates as possible before the more expensive phases of advanced training begin, he enters a two-year training programme. As described by Tony Geraghty in his fine book on the history of the SAS, *Who Dares Wins* (Arms and Armour Press), this training is divided into six phases. The first is a continuation of the basic toughening-up process, which even Paras find strenuous. Route marches of ever-increasing length, with heavier and heavier loads, together with instruction in map-reading and navigation, are accompanied by continuous psychological testing and training in basic security, such as memorizing information instead of writing it down. Phase 2, which lasts three weeks, involves the men being taken to somewhere in the Welsh mountains, or a similar piece of inhospitable terrain, and being given the task of finding their way to a particular rendezvous within a time limit. During this phase a candidate gets very little sleep—another test of stamina and determination—being awoken at 04:00 every morning and having to attend a briefing for the following day's activities at 22:30. Phase 2 ends with a march of 65 km (40 miles) over mountainous terrain, which has to be accomplished within 20 hours.

Candidates who have survived the course to this point now enter Phase 3, which involves both a three-week combat survival course on Exmoor, during which they learn to live off the land, improvise shelter and avoid detection—all vital elements in the training of a soldier who will be expected to operate behind enemy lines in time of war. Phase 3 also includes highly realistic exercises during which candidates are interrogated by experts in just the same way that they would be if captured by an enemy. Having a hood placed over one's head in a bleak cell and not being allowed to sleep because of blaring loudspeakers, or being forced to squat for hours on end in ice-cold water, are just two of the basic techniques. Others include being blindfolded and having to listen to the apparent sounds of a colleague being beaten up, as well as other even more unnerving experiences such as being manacled, blindfolded, to a railway track. The few candidates who survive Phase 3 are judged worthy of entering the SAS and are thereafter entitled to wear the regiment's beige beret and winged-dagger badge.

During Phase 4 the new SAS men can opt for one of four specialist training courses (although many men go on to complete them all, in due course). Each of the SAS's four Sabre squadrons is specially trained for particular duties: one is high-altitude free-fall parachuting; the second, which the SAS shares with the SBS (Special Boat Squadron), is marine operations, including canoeing, landing on a hostile shore at night either from a dinghy or by swimming from a submarine, and sub-aqua work; the third, where training is shared with the Royal Marines' Mountain & Arctic Warfare Cadres, is in their skills; and the fourth, harking back to Long Range Desert Group days, is cross-country mobility, particularly in desert terrain. Once an SAS man has completed his specialist training, Phase 5 begins, which is the all-important counter-terrorist course. Many details of this are necessarily secret, but the use of explosives, stun grenades and the setting (and detecting) of booby traps; planning how to break into a house, airliner or train and kill terrorists while minimizing risk to their hostages; and the use of non-regulation firearms from many countries, all form part of this course.

Finally, the SAS trooper will be allocated to one of the four Sabre Squadrons to begin his work in earnest. Because the regiment may be called upon at any time to go anywhere in the world, and because its men have to act intelligently in the face of a wide variety of possible situations, their training is as broad as possible and never really ends. Numbers of SAS officers and NCOs, for example, learn to fly with the Army Air Corps. Britain's AAC pilots are the most highly trained in the world and, although an SAS trooper escapes their basic training, he still has to do the preliminary ten-week course which covers aerial map reading, aerial observation post duties, the direction of artillery fire, flight servicing, and other essential skills. Within the AAC, a soldier has to spend a minimum of two years acting as an aircrewman/observer before he can apply for pilot training, but for the SAS this is reduced to four weeks. A five-week pre-flying course is followed by a minimum of 60 hours on fixed-wing trainers—Chipmunks and Beagles —before the trainee goes to the civilian Basic Helicopter Flight for a further 60 hours on Bell 47 helicopters. Another week is spent learning aero-medical and ditching procedures before the recruit finally passes to the Advanced Rotary Wing Squadron at the Army Air Corps headquarters at Middle Wallop. A further 115 hours' inflight instruction on the fast and versatile little Aérospatiale Gazelle follows before the soldier finally gains his wings as a fully qualified helicopter pilot; even more experience is required if he wishes to qualify on the Lynx, Puma or Chinook.

Many SAS officers, because of their behind-the-lines infiltration and intelligence-gathering role in time of war, also spend some time learning intelligence skills with "I" Corps (the "MI6" of popular fiction) at its Ashford headquarters. Their studies here include not only photography and photo reduction (to make microdots), but also specialized signals training, surveillance techniques, the use of codes and ciphers, and even lock-picking. Finally, because an understanding of the language in an overseas operation is always an asset, many officers learn German, Russian,

Chinese and other languages at the Army School of Languages at Beaconsfield. Within the SAS, indeed more than in any other branch of the Army, learning is something which never ceases, as the highly motivated officers and men in the regiment would chafe at the restrictions of normal Army life.

In Northern Ireland

As a result of this highly specialized training, "Sass" is much in demand in the constant fight against terrorist outrages in Northern Ireland, and between 120 and 160 members of the regiment are normally stationed in the province. Just as when on duty elsewhere, whether with the British Army of the Rhine, in Hong Kong, Cyprus or Belize, the soldiers of the SAS rarely wear their famous winged-dagger badge or beige beret, but rather the insignia of the regiment to which they are temporarily attached, or something fairly innocuous such as Royal Army Ordnance Corps or Royal Corps of Transport badges. Frequently, only the commanding officer and intelligence officer of a regiment will know the identities of any SAS men in their ranks.

The Army's task in Northern Ireland is neither an easy nor a pleasant one, but it is vital if the province is not to erupt into total civil war. Even before the present troubles began in 1969, the British government maintained a peacetime garrison in Northern Ireland in support of the Royal Ulster Constabulary. As the bombings and shootings increased in frequency and intensity, the Royal Ulster Constabulary was disbanded under political pressure and a new Army regiment was formed to replace it—the Ulster Defence Regiment which, although currently the strongest regiment in the British Army with more than 7000 men and nearly 1000 women in its ranks, is also a part-time regiment, being organized along Territorial Army lines from civilian volunteers. The SAS work closely with the UDR and other Army regiments which are stationed in the province as peace-keeping forces, but particularly closely with the UDR because its members, being local to the area and with friends and relatives all over the province, have their ears more closely to the ground than any mainlander could hope to have, and are vital in securing intelligence.

The SAS's role in Northern Ireland is largely concerned with intelligence gathering and implementing direct action as a result of information gathered. This can involve the setting up of ambushes, especially along the Border, the pursuit of terrorists after an attack, the rescue of Protestant hostages from the IRA, and the tracking down and capturing of hidden arms caches. In this work the SAS liaises closely with the Marines of Commachio Group and the Special Boat Squadron, as well as with the Customs and Excise and the coastguards, and they have become very successful in intercepting smugglers attempting to bring arms and ammunition into Northern Ireland.

As a result of its 15 years of experience in the province, the SAS, and the Army in general, have become highly experienced in dealing with terrorists and terrorist methods, and this has led to SAS officers being in great demand in many other countries, both inside and outside Europe, as instructors for indigenous commando and anti-terrorist units. Of course, the Special Air Service Regiment has a long tradition in this role. In 1940 Winston Churchill called for the establishment of special commando-style units capable of hitting back at objectives inside Nazi-occupied Europe, and in November of that year 11 Special Air Service Battalion was formed from No. 2 Commando. Three months later the battalion made its first attack, destroying an aqueduct in Italy, and from then until the end of the war was constantly in action, one of its main tasks being to help equip and train resistance groups in France and Italy. At the same time, in North Africa, an unconventional officer, Colonel David Stirling, was organizing hit-and-run forces for operations behind Rommel's lines, and for many years the bearded men of the Long Range Desert Group, with their jeeps and trucks festooned with machine-guns, became the epitome of the Special Air Service Regiment in the popular imagination. That image has long since disappeared, but the regiment's success at Pebble Island was foreshadowed 40 years earlier in the Long Range Desert Group's destruction of German aircraft and fuel and ammunition dumps in the desert.

By 1942 the SAS had been expanded to the strength of a regiment with the addition of French and Greek battalions. Two years later it was the size of a brigade and comprised one British regiment, one Commonwealth regiment formed from Australian, New Zealand, South African, Rhodesian and Canadian volunteers, two French regiments and a Belgian squadron. At the end of World War 2, the brigade was disbanded, but in 1947 a territorial SAS regiment was raised in London as 21 SAS (which still exists) and, as a result of its success in Malaya during 1948 and '49, in 1950 a regular Army regiment was formed, 22 SAS, which remains to this day.

During the 1950s and '60s, 22 SAS played a vital part, not just in the continuing war in Malaya which finally ended in 1960 (the first time in history a terrorist force operating on its own territory—like the IRA in Ulster—has been so totally defeated), but also in Korea, in Kenya against the Mau-Mau, in Cyprus and Aden, at Suez in 1956, in Muscat and Oman, Jordan, Kuwait, Belize and many of the world's other trouble spots where the SAS's experience and techniques have been welcomed by the governments or rulers of several countries. With the exception of Malaya, Cyprus and Oman, SAS operations re-

Black-garbed men of the Special Air Service Regiment on the front balcony of the Iranian Embassy in Princes Gate.

ceived little publicity and the regiment remained largely an unknown quantity to the general public until 1980 and the Princes Gate siege.

Princes Gate

On Monday, 5 May 1980, concealed television cameras, whose presence was not even suspected by the SAS, revealed to an enthralled audience a spectacle which would have done credit to a thriller film. On the balcony, and in the street outside the white, colonnaded façade of the Iranian Embassy in Princes Gate, London, suddenly materialized the sinister figures of a number of armed men carrying automatic weapons and tear-gas grenade launchers. Since the previous Wednesday, 24 men and women, mostly Iranian Embassy staff but including three Britons, had been held hostage by six masked gunmen who were demanding the release of 91 political prisoners held under the Ayatollah Khomeini's administration. Many people sympathized with their aims, especially since American Embassy staff in Tehran were, at the time, being held prisoner by that same evil regime. But when the gunmen began shooting their hostages, there was only one answer—send in the SAS.

Up until this point, at 19:00 on a warm, early summer's day, the normal siege tactics practised by the Special Branch of the Metropolitan Police had seemed to be working well: establish contact with the terrorists, discover their aims, and do everything possible to take the tension out of the situation. Little was known about the gunmen inside, except that they had come from Iraq and were believed to be Arabs from Khuzestan, the southern region of Iran which contains the main oil installations, and yet whose people appeared to be benefiting least from the new government's policies. It gradually emerged that there were five or six men, all with their features concealed by Arab head-dress; five were to die.

In the beginning, the police allowed the terrorists free access to the outside world, laying on telephone and telex links so that they could communicate their demands not only to Tehran but also to the rest of the globe. In response, the terrorists released one of the hostages, BBC reporter Chris Cramer, who was suffering from acute stomach-ache. Later, these facilities were cut off to build up the psychological pressure on the gunmen. Similarly, food and cigarettes which to begin with had been provided on demand were discontinued, and the terrorists were told that they would have to make do with what they had. The reasons were simple: it quickly became clear that the terrorists' demand for the release of unnamed hostages in Iran was something which the Ayatollah's government would not countenance, and, in any case, the British government had no influence with the Iranian authorities. The inescapable conclusion was that the gunmen were purely seeking publicity for their cause rather than tangible results. This changed the whole complexion of the affair, because normal police tactics would not work unless there was a negotiable objective. Thus, although it is quite likely that the SAS had been called in as observers and advisers even before the third day of the siege, there is no doubt that they were involved by this time. However, the "hard" decision was not going to be taken unless, or until, the terrorists began carrying out their threat to shoot the hostages.

So the seemingly endless, and ultimately pointless, talks dragged on through the weekend. There were 18 men and 6 women held hostage inside the embassy, in different rooms; the men at the front and the women at the rear. Planning for the eventuality for which they had been trained, the SAS Troop of 18 men decided that any assault would have to be made from front and rear simultaneously. Climbing over the rooftops from an adjoining block of flats, the SAS made their preparations, securely attaching ropes to the chimneys at the rear of the embassy down which two sections of four men each would abseil into action once given the word. Around the embassy, other members of the troop mingled anonymously with the police and onlookers.

Inside, a curious rapport was growing up between captors and captured and, when the terrorists were informed on Saturday that their message would be broadcast in full by the BBC, they allowed two hostages to go free—a pregnant woman and a Pakistani journalist. Gunmen and hostages celebrated together as the police sent in a meal for them all; it was the first since Thursday. On the Sunday morning the hostages were even allowed a bath. However, what the terrorists took to be the sounds of preparation for an attack—the noise of pneumatic drills—soured the increasing *détente* inside the embassy. The gunmen became more tense and moved the male hostages to a lower room in the front of the building. They had reason to worry. Two demands—one for a meeting with Arab ambassadors from other countries in London, and a second for a safe-conduct by coach to an aircraft at Heathrow—which the terrorist leader "Oan" had made by telephone the previous day, remained unanswered.

By Monday, therefore, the tension was becoming unbearable and something had to snap. It did. The Iranian assistant press attaché, Abbas Lavasani, had been pleading with the gunmen since Friday that they kill him and let the other hostages go. He had been particularly incensed when the terrorists scrawled "Death to the Ayatollah" on the wall of the room in which the male hostages were held. Late on Monday afternoon, Lavasani asked to go to the toilet, and somehow got hold of the terrorists' radio-telephone. He began calling the police and "Oan" cut him down with three shots. The leader of the gunmen then picked up the telephone to inform the waiting world that he had just executed one of the hostages and that he would not speak again until he heard news about the requested meeting with the Arab ambassadors.

A personal message from the Commissioner of Police, Sir David McNee, brought the senior Iman of the London Central Mosque to the scene. He pleaded over the radio-telephone for patience, but the leader of the terrorists shouted, "Why should we wait any longer?" The sound of further shots was heard and the line went dead. When, a few minutes later, a body was pushed out of the front door of the embassy, it was believed, quite naturally, that a second hostage had been shot. In fact, the firing was a bluff, but nobody outside the building could have been expected to know that. It was time to send in the SAS.

The two sections with the trickiest task crossed the roof from an adjacent skylight at 19:20 and clipped their abseiling clamps to the ropes which were already affixed to the embassy chimneys. Each pair of troopers was equipped with a specially tailored frame charge—a rectangular frame designed to fit the embassy windows exactly and blow them in. Timing is of the essence in any military operation, but most especially in a situation where innocent lives are at stake. Hearts stopped as the first pair of men began abseiling down to the ground floor terrace, and one trooper's flailing boot smashed an upper storey window. Inside the embassy, one of the gunmen asked a hostage what was happening, and received the reply, "Don't worry. They wouldn't try anything in daylight."

As the first pair of troopers reached the terrace, the second two abseiled down to the first-floor balcony. Then came a hitch—literally. One of the third pair of troopers managed to get entangled in his rope and was dangling helplessly outside the second-storey room where the female hostages were held. The men on the floors below could not now use their frame charges without risking serious injury to him, so they kicked in the windows and hurled stun grenades (known as "flash-bangs" in the trade) into the rooms. These grenades are encased in stout cardboard but produce such a concussion shock-wave that, in an enclosed space, they literally paralyse their victims for what can be vital fractions of a second.

As the second pair of troopers swung into the first-floor room, "Oan," the terrorist leader, ran to the landing and raised his automatic pistol. Only prompt intervention from an unlikely source saved the life of the leading SAS trooper. Police Constable Trevor Lock, a 41-year-old member of the Diplomatic Protection Group, had been on duty at the embassy when it was seized, and had been held hostage ever since. He and a BBC sound engineer, Simeon Harris, had been talking to "Oan" as the SAS troopers broke in. Now he hurled himself on the terrorist leader and grappled with him until the SAS man shot the Arab. Harris fled towards the front of the building where, little did he know it, the third SAS section had now placed a frame charge and were about to enter. He threw open the curtains and was confronted by what he thought was a frogman on the balcony. In fact, it was an SAS trooper wearing a black balaclava helmet, urgently gesturing for Harris to take cover. Moments later the frame charge exploded and four more SAS troopers entered the embassy through clouds of smoke.

On the second floor, above Harris, the 15 male hostages were listening with horror to the sounds of shooting and explosions. When the attack began, they were guarded by only one man, but now two more ran in and began shooting. Samad-Zadeh, another press attaché, was killed and two other men were wounded. At this point, as if realizing what they had done, the terrorists started throwing down their guns, but it was not to save them. The SAS shot them anyway, in two cases by holding pistols to their heads. Within minutes, only one of the terrorists was still alive— the man who had been guarding the women in a back room.

By this time the embassy was ablaze, and it was only with difficulty that the third SAS section managed to rescue the stranded trooper at the back, who was still dangling from his rope. The wounded were quickly loaded on to stretchers and bustled out to waiting ambulances, while the hostages were hurried out of the building into a waiting coach. As firemen outside tried to control the blaze, guarded by some Special Branch officers with tear-gas dischargers (not least from the howling crowd of Khomeini supporters who had gathered outside the embassy), the SAS teams inside hastily combed the building for any further survivors.

Despite a certain amount of vilification which they received from some sections of the Press for killing at least two of the terrorists while they were apparently trying to surrender, the SAS men rightly received a verdict of "justifiable homicide" at the inquest, which ended the following February. The coroner, Dr. Paul Knapman, said, "I think it is important to consider the implications to this country if a verdict of unlawful killing were to be recorded, if soldiers were sent in to do a specific job."

The SAS had been called upon and had done its job. Only one hostage died directly as a result of the assault, but who knows how many others might have perished if "Oan" had carried out his threat, delivered earlier that evening, to shoot another hostage every half hour if his demands were not met.

Two years later, a different enemy was holding a different community of civilians prisoner, and once again the SAS was to play a vital role in the rescue mission.

To the South Atlantic

When it became obvious, in March 1982, that the Argentines seriously intended invading the Falkland Islands, it was inevitable that the SAS should be one of the first units involved, and it was appropriate that an SAS man should have been the first to run up the Union Jack again on South Georgia. However, victory was preceded by near disaster.

After the Argentine forces, under the command of Lieutenant-Commander Alfredo Astiz, had taken control of

South Georgia (see page 67), their garrisons were established at the former whaling stations of Leith and Grytviken. Within days some 60 men of the Mountain and Boat Troops, D Squadron, 22 SAS, together with 2 SBS, were joined on Ascension Island by M Company of 42 Commando. On 10 April they embarked on HMS *Antrim*, accompanied by the Royal Fleet Auxiliary *Tidespring*, for a rendezvous two days later with the ice patrol and research vessel *Endurance*. On board *Endurance*, British Antarctic Survey scientists briefed the SAS and SBS on the conditions they could expect to meet on South Georgia, which were hostile to say the least.

The final attack plan was for the Mountain Troop of D Squadron, 22 SAS, to be landed by helicopter on the Fortuna Glacier, thence to make their way overland to Leith, while the SBS and Boat Troop would land in Gemini inflatable assault boats in Hound Bay and proceed to Grytviken. M Company of 42 Commando would be held in reserve as the main force for the principal attack on Grytviken. The scientists had warned that weather conditions on the glacier could be extreme in the Antarctic autumn, but nobody expected the hell which lay ahead.

At dawn on 21 April a Wessex helicopter took off from HMS *Antrim* in order to reconnoitre the glacier. High winds and driving rain were observed, but these did not deter the SAS. The chopper returned to the ship to pick up the advance party of four men but, by the time it returned to the island, low cloud in addition to the wind and rain made a landing impossible. A few hours later the cloud lifted and a second attempt was made, despite violent changes in wind direction caused by the glacier, and heavy gusts of sleet and snow which obscured visibility. This time the Wessex succeeded in landing, and was rapidly followed by two others which disgorged the remaining 11 men of the Mountain Troop. The helicopters then hurriedly set off back to the ship, flying low to avoid radar detection from the Argentine garrison. Even midwinter in Norway had not prepared the 15 SAS men for the night which followed, however. The barometer fell by over 50 millibars to 960 mb—a decrease in atmospheric pressure which in itself causes the temperature to drop—while at the same time the wind speed picked up to Force 10 (storm) on the Beaufort scale, carrying snow and ice spicules in gusts of up to 130 km/h (80 mph) across the glacier. Since the effective temperature drops by one degree centigrade for every mile per hour of wind strength once the ambient air temperature falls below zero (the so-called "wind chill factor"), the SAS patrol had to spend the night in over 55°C (68°F) of frost. Moreover, the blizzard blew away their tents.

By 11:00 on the following morning John Hamilton was forced to radio the ship with the news that, not only had the SAS patrol been unable to move off the glacier, but also that, unless they were picked up within hours, they would perish from frostbite and exposure. The same three Wessex helicopters which had landed the party the previous day took off immediately, but were unable to land because the wind was gusting so violently, from a full gale one moment to virtual calm the next. After three attempts, the helicopters had to return to *Antrim* to refuel. Then they set off again. This time luck appeared to be on their side. They spotted the smoke flare ignited by the desperate men on the glacier and, taking advantage of a momentary lull in the wind, succeeded in landing. However, as the SAS men emplaned, the wind rose again and the driven snow created a total "white-out." One Wessex lifted off regardless but, blown sideways by the ferocious wind, tilted. A rotor touched the ice and the helicopter crashed on to its side. Miraculously, no one was seriously hurt. The other two helicopters landed alongside and the troops from the first piled into them while the pilots dumped fuel to accommodate the additional load.

They took off into a roaring white hell, visibility being

effectively nil, and flew on radar and compass alone back down the glacier until tragedy struck again. Cresting a ridge, the leading Wessex lurched under a sudden and unexpected gust of wind and struck the ground, rolling on to its side. Its radio was damaged and the pilot of the third helicopter, Lieutenant-Commander Ian Stanley, could not make contact to ascertain the extent of the damage. Undaunted, he flew his overloaded Wessex back to *Antrim* where his passengers were helped out, wrapped in blankets and hustled to sick bay for a hot drink and medical attention. Ian Stanley had not finished yet, however. After refuelling and packing his helicopter with spare blankets, he took off some 30 minutes later to return to the crash site. Miraculously, once again, there had been no serious casualties, and the 17 SAS and Fleet Air Arm personnel piled hastily into Stanley's Wessex. Just over half an hour later they, too, were safely aboard *Antrim*.

The attempt to land SAS and SBS men by Gemini boats fared little better than the Fortuna Glacier venture. Five Geminis were launched, each carrying three men. The engine of one failed almost immediately, and it disappeared helplessly into the blizzard. Somehow, however, it stayed upright and its crew was later rescued by helicopter. A second boat was swept away and just succeeded in landing on the last toehold of South Georgia before being lost forever in the wild, dark wastes of the South Atlantic. The remaining three boats landed safely, but needle-sharp splinters of blown ice from the glacier rapidly punctured the tough rubber hulls, and their crews had to be evacuated by helicopter.

The landings could not have gone worse for the SAS and SBS, and from this point onwards matters could only improve. However, theirs were not to be the only British landings on the island. Knowing of the presence of British warships off South Georgia, the Argentine commander,

Astiz, had requested reinforcements, and a party of 40 marines had been dispatched aboard the ex-US Navy Guppy Class submarine *Santa Fe*. Even as John Hamilton's men were being ferried back to Fortuna Glacier during a lull in the blizzard the day after they had been evacuated, the Argentine submarine was detected. *Antrim* went on full alert and, on 25 April, her crew's vigilance was rewarded, for the *Santa Fe* was spotted on radar by one of her Wessex helicopters. Amazingly, the submarine was running on the surface, having dropped her marines at Grytviken, and she was promptly depth-charged by the hovering helicopter. Damaged on her port side and apparently unable to dive, she turned back towards the whaling station, harassed by machine-gun fire from the helicopter and anti-tank missiles from *Endurance*'s Wasp helicopters, which arrived to join the fray. Leaking oil and listing badly, the damaged submarine made a sorry sight as she limped back to Grytviken. The effect on the morale of the Argentine troops on South Georgia was understandable, and Major Cedric Delves, commanding D Company, 22 SAS, was determined to take advantage of it. Thus it was that Major Guy Sheridan assembled his *ad hoc* assault group and landed by helicopter, while *Antrim* and *Plymouth* poured down an intense naval gunfire barrage—not *on* the Argentine positions but 725 m (800 yd.) beyond them (at this point, the cruiser *Belgrano* had not been sunk and it was the British government's policy to try to preserve as many lives as possible).

However, after their earlier epic on the glacier, John Hamilton was determined that the SAS should be in at the kill. Even while Guy Sheridan was establishing his positions, Hamilton was leading his men through an Argentine minefield on the outskirts of Grytviken. Walking into the centre of the settlement, he had the Argentine flag hauled down and the Union Jack raised in its place. The thoroughly demoralized Argentine troops began waving white flags and all resistance, or even thought of resistance, ended. Hamilton, who was later to be described by an Argentine Colonel who witnessed his death as "the most courageous man I have ever seen," had well and truly vindicated the SAS motto.

Ashore on the Falklands

Even before the Marines and Paras landed at San Carlos on 21 May, SAS and SBS patrols, usually of four men apiece, had been landed by boat or helicopter to scour the land, reporting on Argentine positions and troop movements. Following the success of John Hamilton's Pebble Island raid on 15 May, numerous diversionary attacks were made in order to delude General Menendez into thinking that these were going to be the style for the British campaign, and to distract Argentine attention from San Carlos. Similarly, while the San Carlos landings were actually taking place, three SAS Troops engaged the Argentine garrison (at odds of roughly one to ten!) in Darwin to prevent a counter-attack across the Sussex Mountains. The 40-plus SAS troopers were armed with the heavy mixture of machine-guns, rocket launchers and mortars which characterized so many of the Falklands' operations, and kept up such a barrage of fire that, in the darkness, the 500 men in Darwin imagined they were faced by at least a battalion. In this instance, however, it was not the SAS's intent to capture the objective, merely to keep its inhabitants' heads low so that 3 Commando Brigade and the two battalions of the Parachute Regiment could get ashore safely. A full assault on Darwin and Goose Green would have to wait a few days—fatal days, as it turned out for, when 2 Para went in during the night of 27 May, they found the Argentine garrison reinforced to three times its original strength.

Ironically, one of the reasons for the strong resistance

the Paras encountered was SAS activity further east, on the slopes of Mount Kent—the highest point overlooking Port Stanley. Here, the SAS Troops (each consisting of 15 troopers and NCOs plus 1 officer, a pattern which is now being adopted throughout the Army) had already established a strong presence in front of, and often among, the well dug-in positions of the Argentine 12th Infantry Regiment. This was a conscript regiment, full of raw troops who did not know enough to avoid presenting silhouettes against the rocks of the mountain slopes, and who were sufficiently ignorant to allow their cooking fires, torches and cigarettes to burn unshielded at night. As a result, men began disappearing, or were found with broken necks as the result of an apparent fall, while the Argentines' sleep was further disturbed by constant alerts and strange noises. This stealthy attrition made morale-sapping inroads into the Argentines' confidence, and many of them must have greeted with relief the news that they were to be ferried by helicopter to Goose Green. Under some circumstances, the prospect of a pitched battle can seem healthier than another night in a dark bunker with an unseen enemy stalking outside.

By the end of May, Mount Kent was effectively in the SAS's hands, but they were insufficiently strong on the ground to have held out against more determined Argentine opposition or counter-attack. 45 Commando were on their way, footslogging across the bleak terrain together with 3 Para, but the SAS needed urgent reinforcements. On 31 May, an attempt to fly in 42 Commando by helicopter was aborted due to the weather, but another attempt the following night was successful. Cedric Delves and John Hamilton were looking out for them, but were distracted by movement in the darkness. An Argentine patrol was approaching the helicopters' landing zone. Once again the SAS troopers went into action, and the deceptively slow-moving streaks of red machine-gun tracer lit the mountainside as the first Sea King arrived, containing 42 Commando's CO, Nick Vaux, and the Special Air Service Regiment's own CO, Lieutenant-Colonel Mike Rose. The Argentine patrol was wiped out and the Marines occupied Mount Kent.

The SAS continued to play an important role in the capture of the other hills around Port Stanley, operating ahead of the main British lines to scout enemy positions and call in artillery fire or naval support, and Mike Rose was involved in the final surrender talks with General Menendez, under the pseudonym "Colonel Reid." Before these took place, however, tragedy was to befall the regiment. John Hamilton, having survived the ordeal on Fortuna Glacier, having run up the Union Jack in Grytviken, having assisted in the diversionary attack on Darwin and having survived the Argentine artillery fire on Mount Kent, was on West Falkland—where he had first gone ashore for the Pebble Island raid—observing troop movements in Port Howard. With him was a signaller. Somehow they were detected and Argentine troops moved forward to try to surround them. Both sides opened fire and Hamilton was hit in the back. Knowing he could not escape, he ordered his signaller to "get the hell out" while he covered his escape. As the signaller crawled away to safety, Hamilton drew himself up and, firing on the run, charged straight at the Argentines. He was hit again, and got up. And again. And again. The fifth time he was hit he did not get up. Among the many awards for gallantry awarded to the soldiers, sailors and airmen involved in the Falklands campaign, Gavin John Hamilton's Military Cross must be one of the most deserved.

Thus ended the SAS's war in the South Atlantic, but not elsewhere, because they still have a vital role to play in Northern Ireland and a potentially even more crucial role to play alongside the newly formed 5th Airborne Brigade which, in 1985, spearheads Britain's quick-reaction force. While there is the possibility of major global confrontation, while there are still terrorists, while there are still "small" wars like that in the Lebanon, there will still be a place for the SAS and honest citizens can rest more safely in their homes for the presence of these fearless men.

THE ROYAL MARINE COMMANDOS

The twenty-sixth of May 1982 is a date which Sergeant Derek Wilson will not soon forget. As a member of the Royal Marines' crack Mountain and Arctic Warfare Cadre, he had been one of the first ashore during the re-invasion of the Falklands, and had spent the previous 12 days in deep-probing reconnaissance patrols. On this particular day, which dawned dull and snowing but which later cleared and brightened, observers had spotted an unknown number of Argentine soldiers in the isolated Top Malo House, in the middle of the valley to the south of Teal Inlet. As it turned out, there were in fact 16 Argentine soldiers present, all members of 602 Marine Commando Company.

Captain Rod Boswell, commanding the M&AW Cadre on the spot, tried to call up a Harrier strike but no aircraft were available at the time so he decided to launch an assault on foot with the 19 men at his disposal. Shortly after first light, the Marines embarked in a Sea King helicopter which flew them at virtually zero height, hugging the contours of the ground, and dropped them into a partially frozen bog about 1.5 km (1 mile) from the house. The landing was unobserved because the Argentines had posted no sentries during the bitterly cold night. They were shortly to pay a heavy price for this oversight.

Deploying into two parties on either side of the house, a

Mountain and arctic warfare training in the bleak Norwegian winter; the helicopter is a Wessex.

fire section of six men on the left and an assault group of 13 on the right flank, the Marines moved quickly into position, still unobserved. Sergeant Wilson, armed with an American-made M79 40 mm grenade launcher, was with the latter group. As Captain Boswell fired a green flare, the fire section opened up with four L1A1 66 mm rocket launchers (the modern equivalent of the World War 2 "bazooka") which had no trouble in penetrating the walls of the house. Further 66 mm rounds followed, supported by a barrage of 40 mm grenades from the M79s and a withering fusillade of automatic fire from a mixture of SLR and Armalite rifles plus one L42 sniper rifle.

As the Argentines came tumbling out of the house, firing back with vigour, the fire section continued shooting while the assault group charged in on the flank. Within

seconds there were two casualties—Sergeant Chris Stone
was hit in the chest by a 7.62 mm armour-piercing round
which fortunately missed his lung, while another bullet
shattered Terry Doyle's upper arm, an injury which still
gives him a great deal of pain today. However, realizing
they were outnumbered and outgunned, the Argentine soldiers began throwing down their weapons and raising their
hands, and the British Marines moved in to encircle, blind-
fold and search them. The Argentine commander had been
killed along with two of his men, and seven others were
wounded. Ironically, one of the captured Argentine officers
turned out to be married to an English girl, and had been
on training courses in Great Britain. This brought caustic
comments from the Marines, who told him that if that was
the case he should have learned enough to know to post a
sentry!

Short and sharp though it was, the attack on Top Malo
House well illustrates the calibre of the men in the M&AW
Cadre.

Commando organization

The illustrious history of the Royal Marines goes back to
1664, when the first soldiers to be specially trained to fight
at sea were formed into the Duke of York's Regiment (later
the Lord High Admiral's Regiment), and they have given
sterling service to the nation ever since. The first Commandos were trained during World War 2 for amphibious
assault operations, but today's organization really dates
back to 1956, when the value of helicopters in both the
assault and the casualty evacuation roles became apparent
during the Anglo-French attempt to seize the Suez Canal.
The aircraft carriers *Albion* and *Bulwark* were converted to
helicopter-carrying Commando vessels and soon showed
their value. In 1961, fearing invasion by Iraq, the Ruler of

Kuwait made an urgent plea to the British government for assistance. HMS *Bulwark,* by chance, was in the Gulf of Oman at the time and was able to arrive off the coast of Kuwait within hours. Men of 42 Commando were disembarked in Whirlwind helicopters and the Iraqis backed down.

Since World War 2, all Royal Marines with the exception of the Band Service have been trained as commandos and, indeed, their training today is the toughest and most rigorous in the world, for they are not only expected to be landed by sea, whether from assault boats or helicopters, but may also have to qualify as parachutists.

Commando forces are organized and equipped very much along Army lines but maintain many naval customs and traditions. Their Commandant is a Lieutenant-General, whose office is in Whitehall, but the main Royal Marine establishments are all found in the west of England. Headquarters, Commando Forces, are at Mount Wise, Plymouth, and the Training, Reserve and Special Forces are administered from Eastney, near Portsmouth. Most training is actually carried out at Lympstone, near Exeter, but amphibious assault work is taught at Poole, in Dorset, and airborne training is given at Royal Naval Air Station Yeovilton.

Royal Marines operational units are controlled by Headquarters, 3 Commando Brigade, and comprise Nos. 40, 42, and 45 Commando Groups, each equivalent to an Army battalion, and having some 650 men apiece. In addition, there is an air squadron, a signal squadron, an air defence troop, a raiding squadron and a logistics regiment, while three Army units provide additional support. These are 29 Commando Regiment, Royal Artillery; 59 Independent Commando Squadron, Royal Engineers; and a Territorial Army unit, 131 Independent Commando Squadron, RE.

In time of war, it is expected that the main role of the Commando Forces would be on NATO's northern flank, in

Norway, and to this end British Commandos train and exercise regularly with two companies of the Royal Netherlands Marine Corps, who would come under British command: these are No. 1 Amphibious Combat Group and Whiskey Company, both based at Doorn. The combined force trains for three months of every year, from January to March, in the atrocious weather conditions prevailing in northern Norway, with temperatures often falling as low as $-46°C$ ($-51°F$). For this they are remarkably well equipped, normal disruptive pattern material (DPM) combat clothing being enhanced by the addition of string vests, "long johns," quilted under-jackets and -trousers, thick parkas and special boots with thermal insoles. (Lack of availability of these for the majority of the troops in the Falklands caused considerable problems due to the continuously damp and cold conditions, and the old World War 1 medical condition known as "trench foot" became quite prevalent.) Rucksacks, originally designed for the SAS and weighing only 1 kg (2 lb. 3 oz.), hold everything needed for at least three days in the field under these extreme conditions, including the special arctic, waterproof and down-filled sleeping bag, which is barely heavier than the general service issue. Arctic tents are also provided and, in Norway, Commandos can alternatively sleep in the powered, tracked trailers attached to Volvo Bv202E over-snow tractors, which can each accommodate eight men. In the Falklands, more widespread use was made of the waterproof poncho, which has press studs along its reinforced edges and can be clipped to service sleeping bags to provide a miniature weatherproof tent.

Comacchio Group

Operating independently of 3 Commando Brigade, this company-sized unit is specially trained in the anti-terrorist role, and has a unique task in the protection of Britain's offshore oil rigs against attack or capture. Formed in May 1980 and based in Arbroath, Scotland, the unit was named after a battle fought near Ferrara, in Italy, in 1945. Its techniques and tactics are of necessity secret, but Comacchio Group's personnel are trained in underwater swimming and canoeing in addition to their normal Commando tasks.

All Royal Marines recruits undergo a basic 26-week training course at Lympstone, extended to a full year for officers, who are expected to be able to do everything their men can do, but better and faster. Only at the completion of basic training is a recruit entitled to wear the green beret.

To begin with, training is much the same as in any army today—physical exercise with long cross-country marches and runs to build up muscles and stamina, weapons instruction, and both classroom and field training in tactics and communications. By halfway through the course, the recruits are ready for more advanced instruction, and spend more and more time in practising getting into and out of helicopters and landing craft, and in learning rock-climbing and mountaineering techniques. All this is rounded off with a four-day series of tests involving cross-country runs and hikes, traversing various assault courses, and demonstrating proficiency in weapons use and in swimming.

When basic training is finished, the Royal Marine Commando continues to learn such skills as skiing, diving with both aqualung and oxygen re-breathing equipment (which avoids any tell-tale trail of bubbles to the surface) and parachuting. Those who successfully complete all aspects of this advanced training become qualified swimmer/canoeists and are eligible to volunteer for the Special Boat Squadron or Comacchio Group.

This training was to stand the Royal Marines in good stead in the Falkland Islands.

April Fool's Day recall

Lieutenant Henk de Jaeger was on leave and enjoying his own wedding reception in New York when he received a telegram recalling him to his post as Intelligence Officer with 42 Commando at Bickleigh Barracks, Plymouth. Along with many others in the British armed forces, he was making the best of the Easter break and, when he received the telegram, his first thought, like that of so many others, must have been, "Come on! April Fool's was yesterday." What his new wife thought is not on record . . .

The decision to recall all troops on leave and put the Royal Marines on standby alert had been taken by the Cabinet during the evening of 1 April 1982 and Brigadier Julian Thompson, of 3 Commando Brigade, received his orders from Major-General Jeremy Moore at 03:15 on the 2nd, five hours before the Argentines landed. Within minutes RM Poole was on standby, and the following day British railway stations were flooded with posters and announcements recalling troops on leave. Several officers were in Denmark for a NATO planning conference and a couple of dozen others were also abroad on holiday. Admiral Sir Henry Leach, First Sea Lord at the time, had assured Prime Minister Margaret Thatcher that the Task Force would sail five days later.

In a remote outpost in the South Atlantic, however, two groups of Royal Marines were to see action even more rapidly. On East Falkland itself, Major Mike Norman assumed command of Naval Party 8901, relieving Major Gary Noott, at 09:00 on 1 April. Under his command were 80 men, including 12 sailors from the ice patrol vessel *Endurance*. At 15:15, Norman and Noott were summoned by the Governor of the Falkland Islands, Rex Hunt, who showed them a telex from Whitehall advising that an Argentine invasion was imminent. Despite the obvious impossibility of withstanding an invasion attempt, Mike Norman began issuing orders for his troops' dispositions immediately, concentrating on likely landing areas around Port Stanley airfield and to the east of the town itself. The Marines were lightly armed, possessing only two of the 84 mm Carl Gustav anti-tank missile launchers and a few of the lighter 66 mm L1A1 "bazookas."

Spearheading the Argentine invasion were 150 men of their own special forces, the *Buzo Tactico*, supported by a further 1000 marines and other élite troops. Unfortunately for Mike Norman, the *Buzo Tactico* landed in their helicopters to the *west* of the town and at 06:15 on 2 April were observed attacking the Marines' barracks with automatic weapons and grenades, obviously hoping to catch them still asleep. Mike Norman hastily recalled his troops to Government House, where they managed to beat off the first attack. However, by this time the support troops were beginning to pour ashore, and American-built LVTP-7 Amtrack armoured personnel carriers, which had been landed at Yorke Point, were heading towards Port Stanley. Two were stopped by direct hits fired by Lieutenant Bill Trollope's No. 2 Section using one of the Carl Gustavs and an L1A1 but, as the remaining 16 vehicles started deploying and firing their machine-guns, Trollope ordered a prompt retreat to Government House.

The Amtracks were the Marines' biggest problem, because they could stand off outside the British troops' range and blast Government House to pieces. After telephoning various people in Port Stanley to ascertain the outside situation, Governor Hunt reluctantly agreed to see the commander of the Argentine forces present, Admiral Busser. When Busser declined Rex Hunt's invitation to leave the island, and told him that he now had 2800 men ashore and a back-up force of another 2000 on the ships lying off the coast, the Governor instructed the Marines to lay down their arms. It was 09:15 on Day One of the invasion.

South Georgia scrap

South Georgia is even more bleak and inhospitable than the Falklands. Lying 1300 km (800 miles) to their south-west, it is a windswept, mountainous speck in the middle of a vast ocean, and would probably never have been settled were it not for the fact that it was the ideal location for a whaling base. By the mid-1960s, however, the base was no longer viable, and large numbers of abandoned and rusting ships and other debris cluttered the shore. Ninety per cent of the world's population had never even heard of South Georgia before March 1982, when an Argentine scrap-metal dealer with the unlikely name of Constantio Davidoff arrived with a group of workmen, ostensibly to begin a salvage operation. What caused the British government to protest was his running up of the Argentine flag and, after a week of futile arguing with the junta in Buenos Aires, the ice patrol vessel *Endurance* was ordered to proceed from Port Stanley to South Georgia to evict the scrap merchants. On board were the ship's normal complement of two dozen Royal Marines, plus nine men from Mike Norman's NP8901, all "armed to the teeth" according to a journalist on board *Endurance*. They were landed at Grytviken under the command of Lieutenant Keith Mills, and prepared defensive positions at the site of the British Antarctic Survey installation on King Edward Point, which was considered the most likely location for a landing from the two Argentine warships known to be heading into the area.

Early in the morning of 3 April, the Argentine ice patrol vessel *Bahia Paradiso,* accompanied by the corvette *Guerrico,* entered the bay. Keith Mills informed the ships, by radio, that South Georgia was occupied by British troops and that any attempt to land would be resisted. Having conveyed this message, he strolled down to the harbour jetty, expecting one of the Argentine vessels to lower a boat containing a negotiator. Instead, an Argentine Puma helicopter landed on the shore behind him and began to disgorge troops, who first pointed their guns at him and then began to open fire. As other helicopters landed, Mills sprinted to cover while his own small force gave covering fire, disabling both a Puma and one of the smaller Gazelle helicopters.

The *Guerrico* now opened fire with its 40 mm guns, the whole episode giving further emphasis to the junta's lie that they did not want to take British servicemen's lives, and Mills' troops retaliated spiritedly, holing the corvette below its waterline with an anti-tank missile and disabling one of its guns. The ferocity of this response forced the ship to withdraw out of range, but Mills and his men were now encircled by the Argentine marines from the helicopter and discretion became the better part of valour. Mills had, in any case, been instructed to put up only a "token defence." By this time he had not only made the Argentines' eyes water, but had also given them bloody noses: and they were soon to learn that this was but a foretaste of what the Royal Marines could dish out!

While the main strength of 42 Commando, hastily recalled from leave back in Britain, was preparing to embark aboard the equally hastily converted passenger liner *Canberra*, the 110 men of M Company, under the command of Major Guy Sheridan, were detached to be flown south to join 60–70 SAS and SBS men on Ascension Island: their objective—to recapture the other island Lieutenant Keith Mills had surrendered so reluctantly. As the first piece of British territory to have seen the Argentine flag hoisted, it was only appropriate that South Georgia should also be the first to see it torn down.

South Georgia recaptured

Lieutenant-Colonel Alfredo Astiz had an appalling record on human rights. The presence of such men under the rule of the savagely right-wing junta during the 1970s was hardly surprising. Known as the "blond angel," he was wanted for questioning by both the French and Swedish governments concerning the disappearance of young women, including two nuns. Yet this was the man appointed by the junta to command the Argentine garrison on South Georgia. He was soon to meet more than his match.

Landing on Ascension Island, the Marines linked up with the Mountain and Boat Troops of "D" Squadron, 22 SAS, and 2 SBS, and were embarked aboard the old "County" Class destroyer, HMS *Antrim*, and the Royal Fleet Auxiliary *Tidespring*. As recounted on page 50, several men of the SAS and SBS trans-shipped to HMS *Endurance* when the ships rendezvoused on 12 April, and the epic saga of Fortuna Glacier ensued. However, the Marines were to be in at the kill when Guy Sheridan formed a scratch force of all the available troops aboard *Antrim*—75 Commandos, SAS and SBS, including headquarters and administrative personnel—to take advantage of the morale-sapping disablement of the Argentine submarine *Santa Fe*.

Landing in Wessex helicopters, during the afternoon of 25 April, Sheridan's mixed force moved in on the Argentine positions, which had been extended beyond those occupied only a few days earlier by Keith Mills' valiant garrison on King Edward Point. Naval gunfire from HMSs *Antrim* and *Plymouth*, even though aimed deliberately to avoid the Argentine positions, clinched the day and Astiz' troops surrendered. Raised by the SAS, the Union Jack flew over South Georgia on 26 April, barely a month after a belligerent scrap merchant had taken it down.

Astiz, after signing the surrender document aboard HMS *Plymouth,* was later returned to Argentina as a prisoner of war and has since been put on trial by the new Argentinian government.

Aboard the "Great White Whale"

With the exception of Sheridan's small force, the bulk of 42 Commando, together with 40 Commando, a company of 45 Commando, and 3 Para, embarked aboard the Cunard passenger liner *Canberra* which, with her white paint scheme, was quickly re-christened "the Great White Whale" by the troops of the Task Force. The remainder of 45 Commando shipped aboard the Royal Fleet Auxiliary *Stromness* and the carrier *Hermes.* On all three ships, a rigorous training programme designed to bring the Marines to a peak of physical and mental preparedness was instituted immediately. Aboard *Canberra,* the troops exercised around the Promenade Deck, six circuits of which constituted approximately 1.5 km (1 mile), while lectures—on the geography of the Falkland Islands, on the known capabilities of the Argentine troops, on their weapons and probable dispositions, and on the Marines' own anticipated tasks—were given daily.

Weapons drill was also intensive, particularly in the use of the Marines' Milan anti-tank missiles. Manufactured under licence by British Aerospace, Milan is a French-designed, second-generation wire-guided missile which is capable of destroying all known main battle tanks at up to 2000 m (2200 yd.) range. The Falklands would see its first use in anger by British troops, and it was to prove particularly effective in destroying Argentine bunkers. Each Commando Support Company includes an anti-tank Troop of 48 Marines equipped with 14 Milan launchers.

Training did not stop when *Canberra* reached Ascension

Island on 20 April. The Army and RAF personnel already
on the island had constructed several firing ranges, and the
Marines practised intensively for the two weeks they were
there, being dropped by helicopter at Wideawake airfield
and then marching—or, more often, running—several
miles in full kit to the ranges. When you consider that a
man carrying his personal equipment, including rifle and
ammunition, plus a Milan missile or launcher, or one of the
various other support weapons, was laden down by 54 kg
(120 lb.), the necessity for the intensive physical training
becomes obvious.

Suddenly the training was over. On 1 May huge delta-
winged Avro Vulcan bombers attacked Port Stanley airfield, the intention being to damage the runway sufficiently
to prohibit Argentine air movements. They were followed
by Royal Navy Sea Harriers from the two British carriers,
Hermes and *Invincible*. The following day the Argentine
cruiser *Belgrano* was torpedoed and sunk by the submarine
Conqueror. To the Marines, as to the rest of the world,
came the shocked realization that a real state of war existed
in the South Atlantic. Two days later the British destroyer
Sheffield was hit and mortally damaged by an AM39 Exo-
cet missile launched by an Argentine Super Etendard naval
strike aircraft.

While plans for reinforcing the Task Force were hurriedly being implemented back in Britain, including the
commissioning of the liner *QE2* as a troopship for 5 Infantry Brigade and the Ghurkas, the men of 3 Commando
Brigade and 2 and 3 Para embarked at Ascension on the
amphibious assault ships *Fearless* and *Intrepid*. On 10
May, following Task Force commander Rear Admiral
"Sandy" Woodward's decision that the main attack would
go in at San Carlos, the Royal Marines' commander, Brigadier Julian Thompson, briefed his own unit commanders.

The San Carlos decision had not been an easy one.
Many officers favoured a frontal assault on Port Stanley

using landing craft supported by troop-carrying helicopters, but this was abandoned because of uncertainty as to whether the harbour had been mined by the Argentines. There was even a plan for an Entebbe-style raid by the SAS to eliminate the Argentine headquarters in Stanley. Eventually, however, San Carlos was chosen for two reasons. One of the officers with the Task Force, Major Ewen Southby-Tailyour, was a keen amateur yachtsman who had spent most of his leisure time sailing round the coast of the Falkland Islands when he had commanded Naval Party 8901 there four years previously. He reported to Rear Admiral Woodward that San Carlos, 100 km (65 miles) from Port Stanley, was both sheltered and dominated by high ground, giving good positions for observation posts. SAS teams and men of the Royal Marines M&AW Cadre, who had been landed secretly by helicopter on the islands to reconnoitre, not only confirmed Southby-Tailyour's report, but also discovered that there were no Argentine troops in the immediate vicinity, although there were strong Argentine garrisons within 20 km (13 miles), at Darwin and Goose Green.

On 18 May the assault ships rendezvoused with *Hermes,* which had been reinforced by a dozen Harriers from the ill-fated container ship *Atlantic Conveyor* and by a further four RAF GR Mark 3s which had made the long flight all the way from Britain, via Ascension Island. The Task Force steamed steadily towards East Falkland, and during the night of 20 May entered Falkland Sound. It was a crisp, clear night after the evening's mist, and the sea was calm.

D-Day at San Carlos

After a delay of about an hour, caused partially by a casualty in 2 Para who missed his footing while climbing into his landing craft and smashed his pelvis, and partially by a pump failure aboard *Fearless* which prevented her well deck from being flooded, it was 04:00 on 1 May when the troops began swarming ashore. (The normal landing procedure is to fill the well deck with water, as in dry dock. Since this proved impossible, the captain of *Fearless* simply ordered the forward ramp to be lowered, allowing the sea to flood in.) The first wave comprised 40 Commando, 2 Para and 4 Troop of the Blues and Royals—Household Cavalry equipped with Scorpion and Scimitar light tanks which have an armament of a 75 mm gun and a 30 mm quick-firing cannon, respectively. As expected, there was no opposition to the main landing, although the SAS encountered more trouble than they anticipated from a small Argentine garrison on Fanning Head (overlooking San Carlos water) whose presence had been detected only hours before.

While HMS *Plymouth* bombarded Argentine positions at Goose Green, and other diversionary attacks were taking place elsewhere in the islands, the men of 40 Commando, flanked on their right by 2 Para, waded ashore from their landing craft across the gravel beach and headed up the hillside to begin digging in. The only sign of life so far was a group of Special Boat Squadron Marines who stood leisurely watching the landing craft move in and who gave directions for moving off the beach. However, this was just the lull before the storm.

As the men ashore pushed inland and consolidated their positions, the landing craft returned to the ships to bring in the second wave—45 Commando on the right of 2 Para in Ajax Bay and 3 Para on the left of 40 Commando on Fanning Head. Meanwhile, helicopters had been busily ferrying in the 105 mm light guns of 29 Commando Regiment, Royal Artillery, and the Blowpipe and Rapier anti-aircraft missiles of the Air Defence Troop, 3 Commando Brigade

HQ, and "T" Battery, 12 Air Defence Regiment, Royal Artillery. They were none too soon. The first attack by a solitary Argentine Pucara ground-attack aircraft, which was shot down after unsuccessfully firing rockets at *Canberra* and HMS *Broadsword,* was followed half an hour later by a strike delivered by a pair of Mirage supersonic fighters.

Few of the troops ashore recognized the air raid warning for what it was. "The first air raid was quite frightening," said one Marine afterwards. "It became apparent after a while that they were after the boats. As they flew over, everyone opened up on them with everything from Gimpys [General Purpose Machine Guns] to pistols and SLRs [rifles]. Of course, in the excitement, we didn't realize we were firing towards the ships and they were firing back towards us. It really was quite something to see."

Another man commented, "We hadn't been told that that was a signal to notify that an air attack was coming in, and we all stood around looking at each other. This 'plane suddenly rolled over the top [of the hill] and everyone just dived for cover. I think he [the pilot] must have been as surprised as we were!"

As the air attacks intensified, the troops became accustomed to them and would let fly with the nearest weapon to hand. The American Stinger anti-aircraft missiles used by some of the SAS proved particularly valuable during the early part of the campaign, as the long voyage and salt air had affected the guidance systems of the normally very effective Rapier missiles. Of the first ten Rapiers fired at attacking aircraft, only three scored hits, but thereafter the "kill" rate soared and Rapiers accounted for at least 14 Argentine aircraft during the course of the campaign, plus six "probables."

What is really surprising is that the Argentines delayed so long before sending in their first air strikes. One of their

Royal Marine Commandos dig in on the steep slopes overlooking San Carlos Water in anticipation of a counter-attack.

Canberra high-altitude reconnaissance aircraft had observed the Task Force manoeuvring in Falkland Sound during the evening of 20 May, and it would have been logical for them to have launched an attack at dawn, while the vulnerable landing craft were still coming ashore and before the ground-based anti-aircraft systems were established. Despite the success of their later efforts, and the unquestioned courage and skill of their pilots, by allowing the British Task Force to establish itself ashore the Argentines had effectively lost the campaign.

Casualties mounted over the next few days. HMS *Ardent* was sunk on 21 May, *Antelope* on the 23rd, *Coventry* on the 25th, together with *Atlantic Conveyor,* while other ships were damaged, including *Broadsword* and *Glasgow.* Ashore, the three Commando and two Para battalions dug into the peaty soil and waited. They had established their beach-head and could do nothing but wait for reinforcements before beginning the long slog to Stanley. Brigadier Thompson had intended to leapfrog his units across East Falkland using the heavy-lift Chinook helicopters which were on their way aboard *Atlantic Conveyor*. Their loss caused a complete change in strategy and, on 26/7 May, while 2 Para headed towards their epic battle at Goose Green, 42 and 45 Commandos and 3 Para prepared for the long cross-country march to the other side of the island and the final goal, Port Stanley. 40 Commando remained at San Carlos to secure the bridgehead against counter-attack.

The long march

A backpacking holiday in one of the moorland and mountain beauty spots of the world is one thing; a forced march carrying some 50 kg (100 lb.+) of gear across similar terrain, treacherous rock outcroppings alternating with bogs, streams and ravines, in the cold of the late South Atlantic autumn, is a different matter entirely.

The brunt of the three-day march was borne by 45 Commando and 3 Para who had to "yomp" (the Marines' name for a forced march) around the northern side of the island, via Douglas and Teal. 42 Commando were luckier, and were in fact the first troops—with the exception of the SAS—to get within sight of Port Stanley. The SAS, as recounted on page 55, had established an observation post on Mount Kent, overlooking Stanley, some days earlier, and by 27 May the mountain was effectively in their hands. Brigadier Thompson's problem was how to reinforce them quickly with the helicopters—already stretched to their limit—at his disposal. After two days' planning it was resolved to fly in one Commando company first, to secure the position, and to fly in the rest of 42 Commando in batches.

The first attempt, on the night of 31 May, failed because a blizzard forced the helicopters to return to San Carlos shortly after taking off. On the following night, however, K Company, commanded by Lieutenant-Colonel Nick Vaux and accompanied by Lieutenant-Colonel Mike Rose of the SAS, took off in their Sea King helicopters which flew virtually "on the deck" (at or below 6 m [20 ft.]) towards their objective. As the evening darkened, passive night sights (light intensifiers) were used by the helicopter pilots to enable them to see where they were going without giving their position away to the enemy. However, when they arrived at their landing zone some 3 km (2 miles) behind the ridge of the mountain, the Marines were surprised to see the flashes and lines of red tracer ammunition of what was obviously a fierce firefight taking place a few hundred metres away. The SAS had intercepted an Argentine patrol, which they eliminated.

K Company swept up the ridge and started digging in. A couple of hours later, an RAF Chinook helicopter brought in a 105 mm light gun, and the Sea Kings began ferrying the rest of 42 Commando. With Port Stanley in sight, they settled in to endure the cold, the wet and the occasional Argentine artillery barrage. Meanwhile, 45 Commando had started their heroic "yomp" around the other side of the island, an exploit which was to make newspaper headlines and add this new and expressive word to the English language. Charles Lawrence, a distinguished journalist with the *Sunday Telegraph*, marched with them. He found it "punishingly hard," partly due to the terrain with its coarse tussocks of grass and soft mud, but largely to the enormous weight of equipment everyone had to carry.

After an early morning brew of tea, the men of 45 Commando tightened their bootlaces and marched down to Ajax Bay, where landing craft ferried them to the opposite side of the water. Then they began walking, their leather boots soon becoming soaked through, the weight of their equipment appearing to treble. Breathing hard through open mouths they pressed on, accompanied by Volvo Bv202 over-snow vehicles carrying the heavy equipment. Within a few miles, casualties from turned ankles and sprained muscles began to occur. The advance started to straggle as the men tired, and Colour Sergeant Bill Eades, never lost for words, bellowed out in a parade-ground voice that he didn't know about the assault on Stanley, it "looks to me more bloody like the retreat from Moscow!"

Just before dark, the commanding officer of 45 Commando, Lieutenant-Colonel Andrew Whitehead, called a brief halt for a meal. Gratefully, the Marines broke out their portable stoves and ration packs, but just at that moment an air raid alert came through and all lights had to be extinguished; the next six hours' march in the freezing night therefore took place on largely empty stomachs. When they reached Newhouse, a deserted sheep farm, most men collapsed into their sleeping bags wherever they were, without bothering about tents. Then it rained. The irrepressible Sergeant Eades commented, "You've got to laugh, or you would bloody well cry."

Next day it was still raining, but the Marines reached the comparative comfort of the village of Douglas, where the local inhabitants, who had been locked in the Community Hall by the Argentines, rapidly made them welcome and set peat fires burning. After a good meal and a proper night's rest, 45 Commando was off again, "yomping" to the next objective, Teal Inlet. For this stage of the march, having seen the difficulties encountered on the first two days, Colonel Whitehead lightened the men's packs, piling as much of the heavier support equipment as possible on to the Volvos. Although the weather had turned colder, with heavy snow, the second stage of the march was easier for the Marines since the cold had hardened the boggy ground. By the time they arrived at Teal, however, the Marines were beginning to run out of supplies, and Colonel Whitehead called a halt while he tried to organize a helicopter airlift for the remaining miles to Mount Kent. However, the weather thwarted this and, after a day's delay, 45 Commando was back on the move. The going was again steady and the men were in good spirits when they made camp on the night of 3 June.

On 4 June, the Marines were awakened before dawn and ordered forward without even the benefit of a hot brew because of the risk from showing any lights. They were allowed a breakfast stop two hours later, though, and reached the camp that K Company had established on Mount Kent in the afternoon, in the middle of a blizzard. There they, too, began to make themselves as comfortable as possible in the appalling conditions.

By the end of the first week in June, the Argentines in Port Stanley were surrounded. 42 and 45 Commandos were well dug in, with 3 Para on their flank and 2 Para in reserve, in a line from Bluff Cove Peak to Mount Kent. Meanwhile, the anxiously awaited reinforcements from the second wave of the Task Force had arrived at San Carlos. These comprised 5 Infantry Brigade, 1 Battalion 7th (Duke of Edinburgh's Own) Gurkha Rifles, 2 Battalion Scots Guards and 1 Battalion Welsh Guards. The Argentine positions in and around Stanley were mercilessly bombarded both from the sea with naval gunfire and from the air by RAF Harriers, while the Fleet Air Arm's Sea Harriers provided cover against enemy air attacks.

A constant series of patrols was undertaken at night to scout out and harass the enemy. Typical was the patrol sent out in the early hours of the morning of 10 June. Lieutenant David Stewart of X-Ray Company, 45 Commando, had briefed his men during the previous afternoon, and by midnight they were ready. Heavily armed, with two machine-guns per section plus 66 mm rocket launchers and 2-inch mortars, the Troop moved off stealthily into the moonlit night towards a ridge some 4 km (2½ miles) away where Argentine movement had been observed. Keeping well spaced out because of the good visibility, they moved across the rocky ground using the numerous shell holes for cover, and by 04:00 were set to cross the final stretch of open ground in front of the enemy positions.

Using a shallow stream for cover, they moved up the slope and deployed into position among the rocks in front of the Argentine trenches. With the help of a light-intensifying night scope, they could see sentries moving about. Suddenly, an Argentine machine-gun opened fire and the Marines launched a couple of flares from their 2-inch mortars, firing back with their own machine-guns and rifles. Within seconds three Argentine soldiers and two Marines were dead. Other figures could be seen running on the hill to the left, and four more Argentine soldiers fell to the accuracy of the Marines' fire.

By this time, the Argentine troops further up the slope were wide awake, and a hail of fire forced the Marines to crouch in the shelter of the rocks. The situation was becoming decidedly unhealthy and Lieutenant Stewart decided to retire, with the objective of killing and harassing the enemy well and truly accomplished. However, a machine-gun to the Marines' right was pouring fire over their getaway route, and Stewart sent his veteran Sergeant, Jolly, with a couple of other men to take it out. After a difficult approach with little cover, there was a short burst of fire and the Argentine machine-gun fell silent. Leap-frogging by sections, the Troop retreated to the stream, by which time the Argentine fire was falling short and there were no further casualties. Stewart reported the success of the raid to his company commander, Captain Ian Gardiner, and the weary Marines trekked back to Bluff Cove Peak and a welcome breakfast.

Such raids were invaluable in lowering Argentine morale prior to the main assault, in which the Royal Marines would play a crucial role. As a preliminary to taking Port Stanley itself, the British had first to seize a line of rugged hills in which the Argentines were dug in in strength. 45 Commando was tasked with the capture of Two Sisters and 42 Commando with that of Mount Harriet, while 40 Commando was to remain in reserve with the Welsh Guards, who had been so badly mauled on 8 June when the landing ships *Sir Galahad* and *Sir Tristram* had been bombed at Fitzroy. 3 Para was to assault Mount Longdon. Once these positions had been taken, the plan was that the remainder of the force—5 Infantry Brigade, the Gurkhas, the Guards and 2 Para—would consolidate, and the Marines would then have the honour of the final assault on Stanley itself; an assault which never took place, as it turned out, because of the Argentine surrender.

Captain Ian Gardiner's X-Ray Company spearheaded the attack on Two Sisters. After assembling at their start-line, the Murrell Bridge at the bottom of Mount Kent, on the day after the raid described above, the Marines began moving forward in the cold, menacing darkness. Argentine fire was intense, with 105 mm guns and 0.50 calibre machine-guns pounding the Marines on the exposed hillside. 45 Commando's CO, Lieutenant-Colonel Andrew Whitehead, realized that a single company could not hope to secure Two Sisters, and brought up the battalion's two other companies. Stealthily, while X-Ray Company continued to draw the brunt of the enemy fire, the Marines crept and crawled up the flanking sides of the ridge, with its distinctive twin peaks. Milan anti-tank launchers were brought into play, hammering at the Argentine bunkers, but the defenders held on grimly. Not all the Argentine troops were under-age conscripts, by any means. Sergeant-Major George Meachin, a career veteran with 21 years' experience, was in the attack on Two Sisters. "We came under lots of effective fire from 0.50 calibre machine-guns ... At the same time, mortars were coming down all over us, but the main threat was from those machine-gunners who could see us in the open because of the moonlight. There were three machine-guns and we brought down constant and effective salvoes of our own artillery fire on to them directly, 15 rounds at a time. There would be a pause, and they'd come back at us again. So we had to do it a second time, all over their positions. There'd be a pause, then 'boom, boom, boom,' they'd come back at us again. Conscripts don't do this, babies don't do this, men who are badly led and of low morale don't do this. They were good steadfast troops. I rate them. Not all of them, but some of them."

Despite the stubborn resistance, suddenly the Commandos were inside the Argentine positions and the cold, frightened, but still defiant defenders began throwing down their arms. Two Sisters was secure and the weary Marines began wrapping themselves in captured Argentine sleeping bags and ponchos to snatch some sleep in the drifting snow.

For the attack on Mount Harriet, 42 Commando's Lieutenant-Colonel Nick Vaux decided a frontal assault would be suicidal. Accordingly, he led K Company on a dangerously exposed march around the south of the hill, through an Argentine minefield which an earlier patrol had scouted and in which two Marines lost their legs as a result of detonating anti-personnel mines. Once through the minefield, K Company made a 180° turn to come up on the Argentine positions from the rear, while L Company engaged the Argentines' attention from the front and J Company remained in reserve to secure the position.

The battle for Mount Harriet was hard and furious. While the Marines pounded the Argentine bunkers with 66 mm and 84 mm anti-tank missiles, grenades and machine-gun fire, the Argentines responded vigorously with their lethal 0.50 calibre machine-guns, 7.62 mm assault rifles and a mixture of 7.62 mm and 0.45 calibre sub-machine-guns. The noise was horrific, the crunch of explosions and the hammer of automatic weapons blending with the screams of the wounded and the hoarsely shouted orders of officers and NCOs. But by first light Mount Harriet had fallen. K Company collected nearly 70 prisoners and had suffered no fatal casualties, although two officers and five Marines were wounded. When J Company moved up on the bitterly cold morning of 12 June, the total catch was 300 petrified prisoners, many of whom believed they would be shot out of hand.

While the Marines were assaulting Two Sisters and Mount Harriet, 3 Para were completing a similar assault on Mount Longdon and the stage was set for the penultimate act: the taking of Wireless Ridge by 2 Para and of Mount Tumbledown by 5 Infantry Brigade. This was followed by the Gurkhas' attack on Mount William and the Welsh Guards' assault on Sapper Hill. On 14 June, the Argentines had been forced right back into Port Stanley itself and had no further room to manoeuvre. The Argentine troops in Stanley were mesmerized as the hills in front of them suddenly seemed to come alive with "thousands" of English troops running down the slopes towards them, yelling and screaming like madmen. They knocked the guns out of the Argentine conscripts' hands, and Marines and Paras both exchanged their steel helmets for their proud green and maroon berets.

Major-General Jeremy Moore ordered the troops to halt at the racecourse as the Argentine commander, General Menendez, had sent a message to say that he was prepared to discuss surrender. Back in England, at 22:12 on 14 June, a jubilant Prime Minister Margaret Thatcher rose to her feet in the House of Commons. "After successful attacks last night, General Moore decided to press forward. The Argentines retreated. Our forces reached the outskirts of Port Stanley. Large numbers of Argentine soldiers threw down their weapons. They are reported to be flying white flags over Port Stanley."

To the sounds of cheers from the members of all political parties, Mrs. Thatcher concluded: "Our troops have been ordered not to fire except in self defence. Talks are now in progress between General Menendez and our Deputy Commander, Brigadier Waters, about the surrender of the Argentine forces on East and West Falkland."

The war was over.

THE SPECIAL BOAT SQUADRON AND RAIDING SQUADRONS

Like the Special Air Service Regiment, the Special Boat Squadron and the three Royal Marine Raiding Squadrons owe their origins to the need during World War 2 for men able to land on an enemy coastline and penetrate inshore on clandestine reconnaissance and sabotage missions, to attempt the capture of high-ranking enemy officers and to perform similar tasks. Again like the SAS, the Special Boat Squadron began its life as an almost unofficial unit, and by the time its existence became officially recognized, on 14 April 1942, it had already seen considerable action, notably in the abortive raid on the North African coast to kill Rommel, in November 1941. The raid failed because Rommel was in Rome at the time and many of the commandos were killed, including their leader, Lieutenant-Colonel Geoffrey Keyes.

As constituted in April 1942, the SBS consisted of just 47 officers and men, commanded by Major R. J. Courtney. Its members were drawn from both the Army and the Royal Marines, and for the remainder of the war they played a sterling role in harassing the Germans and Italians by lightning raids in North Africa, the Aegean and the Adriatic. They trained in the techniques of canoe-handling, landing from submarines, cliff-scaling, mine-laying, underwater sabotage and other necessary skills, in the north of Scotland, practising landings on the Isle of Arran and elsewhere. The SBS was also active on D-Day and afterwards, demolishing underwater obstacles on the Normandy beaches to clear paths for the waves of landing craft; but its most famous exploit was in December 1942, when five canoes were launched into the estuary of the Gironde river in France and the SBS blew up a number of German ships. This episode formed the basis for the popular film, *The Cockleshell Heroes*.

Throughout the war, the SBS operated closely alongside the SAS and there was a constant interchange of personnel which continues today, even though the SAS is an Army unit, while the SBS is part of the Royal Marines and therefore under Admiralty command. Later, in the 1950s and '60s, the SBS took part in counter-terrorist operations with the SAS in Borneo, Malaya and Indonesia and, as we shall see, 2 SBS played a very active role in the Falkland Islands.

SBS today

Even more so than the SAS, the SBS has always kept a very low profile and neither its strength nor many details of its organization and equipment are discussed in public. Today's recruits for the SBS come primarily from the Royal Marines. Having completed the already rigorous commando training, volunteers take a further 12-month course alongside the SAS, including psychological indoctrination against interrogation, parachute training at Brize Norton, and ski training with the Mountain and Arctic Warfare Cadre in Norway.

For obvious reasons, special attention is paid to teaching the volunteers all aspects of seamanship and diving, and they become well versed in both underwater sabotage and in the protection of British installations, such as oil rigs, against terrorist attack. An obvious role for the SBS would be the rescue of hostages in the event of a ship being hijacked. In these tasks the squadron shares responsibility with Comacchio Group (see page 61), but it also operates alongside the three Royal Marines Raiding Squadrons.

The men for these units are selected from commando volunteers who have shown special talent in boat handling, and train at Poole, in Dorset. Their special skill is in the use of small boats—both inflatables, such as the Gemini, and small glass-fibre launches known as Rigid Raiders. In time of war, the role of the Raiding Squadrons is to ferry commandos or members of the SAS and SBS ashore, usually secretly and by night.

The Falklands campaign

In the Falklands, however, they came "into the open," operating an invaluable ship-to-shore shuttle service for the Task Force in San Carlos water, even in the middle of Argentine air attacks. However, that the men of these squadrons are not just glorified "taxi drivers" was clearly shown right at the end of the Falklands campaign, when No. 1 Squadron put in a diversionary raid on Port Stanley as 2 Para were taking Wireless Ridge.

Four Rigid Raiders, packed with men from 2 SBS and 22 SAS, sneaked into Port William, the estuary of the

Murrell river, during the night of 13–14 June. Unfortunately, they were spotted by the crew of the Argentine survey ship *Bahia Paradiso,* and searchlights flashed across the dark water. Although all hope of taking the Argentines by surprise had now been lost, the four craft, led by Sergeant Plym Buckley, accelerated in to the beach where they were met by a hail of gunfire. A landing was obviously out of the question and the four boats, leaking from several bullet holes, retreated into the cover of the night, dropping their occupants on an unoccupied stretch of the coast. The men stayed low throughout the night, watching the intense firefight taking place on Wireless Ridge, and later witnessed 2 Para's jubilant entry into Stanley.

The SBS, though, had been active in the South Atlantic from the very beginning. As we have seen (page 52), the attempt to land on South Georgia by Gemini inflatables met with near disaster, but SBS patrols were later landed

Dressed in SCUBA gear, men of the Special Boat Squadron rehearse a clandestine landing on a hostile shore.

successfully on both East and West Falkland and, indeed, the first people the commandos and paras encountered when they landed at San Carlos were a group of tired and bearded SBS men who had been on the islands for several days, reconnoitring Argentine dispositions. As with the SAS, in time of conflict the men of the SBS and Royal Marine Raiding Squadrons will usually be found first in and last out.

III

UNITED STATES

SPECIAL FORCES OPERATIONAL DETACHMENT DELTA • THE "GREEN BERETS" • THE RANGERS • THE AIRBORNE DIVISIONS • THE MARINE CORPS • THE UNDERWATER DEMOLITION AND SEA-AIR-LAND TEAMS

Firing his Colt Commando in short bursts to preserve ammunition, Sergeant Fred Zabitosky helped keep his own men's morale up and the Vietcong attackers' heads down as he waited for the retrieval helicopters to arrive. The weapon, a cut-down version of the famous Armalite assault rifle, was not always popular with American Special Forces personnel because—particularly at night—its vivid muzzle flash was much too noticeable for comfort. In the daytime this was less of a disadvantge, and Zabitosky and the mixed force of nine Green Berets and South Vietnamese irregulars with him used their weapons with deadly effect, as wave after wave of Vietcong troops broke against their perimeter.

Zabitosky's tiny command was one of the Special Operations Group reconnaissance teams which were used in Vietnam by the Central Intelligence Agency to confirm reports of Vietcong troop movements and assembly points. On 19 February 1968 his "A" Team had been dropped by helicopter in the dense jungle and tall elephant grass of the junction between the borders of Vietnam, Laos and Cambodia, west of the Special Forces training camp at Dak To. As usual, Zabitosky's team had landed from one of a group of helicopters, each of which came in to hover briefly above a different clearing in the jungle. This decoy manoeuvre meant that, although any Vietcong troops in the vicinity would be aware that an enemy patrol had been dropped, they would not know at which of the landing zones. Unfortunately, on this particular day, Zabitosky's team had landed practically on top of a battalion of Vietcong and had come under heavy fire moments after the transport helicopter's departure.

Retreating towards a clearing where helicopters could come down to rescue his tiny force, Zabitosky tied a couple of white phosphorus smoke flares to a Claymore antipersonnel mine, which he hurled into the leading ranks of the attacking Vietcong. The two heavily armed Skyraider ground-attack aircraft circling overhead were called in and dropped napalm on the white smoke, wiping out the first wave of the attack. As his men pulled further back, Zabitosky repeated the trick, and on their second run the Skyraiders disrupted the Vietcong with high-explosive bombs.

Reaching the landing zone, Zabitosky went from man to man of his team, encouraging them to stay calm and pick their targets, while the Skyraiders—whose ability to carry enormous loads of bombs, napalm containers and rockets had become legendary—continued to blast and strafe the

Vietcong. Eventually, three helicopters returned to the landing zone where Zabitosky's team was still, miraculously, intact. Keeping four men with him, the Sergeant ordered the remaining five into the first helicopter, which took off for safety. The second machine spiralled in and the rest of the force eagerly leaped aboard. As it ascended, a Vietcong guerrilla, armed with a grenade discharger attachment on his AK47 assault rifle, fired a grenade at the escaping helicopter.

When Zabitosky regained consciousness, he was lying on the ground with broken ribs and injured spine a few metres away from the crashed helicopter, having somehow been thrown clear. Although the helicopter was burning fiercely, the injured man managed to pull out the dazed pilot and then returned for the unconscious co-pilot. As Zabitosky was pulling him out, the helicopter's fuel tanks exploded, hurling blazing liquid and debris in all directions. Zabitosky rolled in the grass to extinguish his own and the co-pilot's burning clothing, then picked the still-unconscious man up in a fireman's lift and ran towards another helicopter which, seeing the fate which had befallen its companion, had returned to pick up any survivors. Although the co-pilot later died of his injuries, Zabitosky was awarded a well-earned Medal of Honor.

The reconnaissance mission might have been a failure in one sense, but Zabitosky's team and the two Skyraiders succeeded in killing well over 100 Vietcong, and the incident—one out of hundreds of similar engagements which took place during the Vietnam War—clearly demonstrates the courage and cool thinking of the men in the various élite formations of the US Army, Navy and Marine Corps.

Evolution

The United States seems to have produced more specialist units and formations from its armed forces than any other country. It has been suggested that this is a result of the size of the American armed forces, rivalries between the services, and competition between their supporters in Congress. But it may also derive from using the division (or its equivalent) as the basic administrative unit, and recruiting for it from all over the country. The British use a much smaller unit—the regiment—which has strong local ties and a long history and tradition. Since many of the tasks done by US élite forces are carried out in the British and Commonwealth armed forces, for example, by normal units, there has been some interest in the US in using the British regimental system, and both the Rangers and "Delta Force" come close to this.

The Japanese naval air attack on Pearl Harbor on 7 December 1941, which brought the USA into World War 2, resulted in the real development of airborne formations, with the 82nd and 101st Divisions as parachute units. This war was also the birthplace of many of the other élite units which survive today with, for example, the Canadian-American Special Service Force later spawning the US Army Special Forces. After the Korean War (June 1950– July 1953) most of these were wound down, but saw a revival in the late 1950s. British and French experiences in the many guerrilla wars they were fighting at the time had some influence on this.

American involvement in Vietnam produced an upsurge in the élite forces, and gave rise to much of the present-day confusion of units, with each service having élite and specialist forces. Since Vietnam, there has been an attempt to rationalize organization and to eliminate overlaps, and, on

Soldiers of the 1st Air Cavalry Division disembark from helicopters near Dak To in November 1967.

1 January 1984, the Pentagon set up the Joint Special Operations Agency to make the management and response of these forces more unified and efficient. This agency replaces the Joint Special Operations Command, which conducted the Grenada operation in October 1983.

Today, the United States élite forces are as follows. The US Navy has its Underwater Demolition Teams (UDTs) and Sea-Air-Land (SEAL) teams. The US Marine Corps is an élite force all of its own, and includes an Air Wing which flies helicopters and broadly similar combat jets to those of the US Navy, but which is also acquiring the V/STOL (Vertical/Short Take Off and Landing) AV-8B version of the Harrier that performed so well in the 1982

Falklands campaign. The US Army has the greatest number of élite and specialist units, such as the 82nd and 101st Airborne Divisions (currently only the 82nd has a parachute role—the 101st being an air-mobile unit); the 1st Cavalry Division ("Air Cavalry") which used helicopters in Vietnam but is now possibly being superseded by the 101st Airborne; the 75th Infantry Regiment (the Rangers); the US Army Special Forces (the "Green Berets"); and the 1st Special Forces Operational Detachment Delta (known as "Delta Force" or just "Delta," for short).

In most of the operations that the USA has mounted since the Korean War—especially in Vietnam, but also afterwards—in which élite forces have been used, elements of many of these have been working together. For example, the Grenada operation in 1983 involved the Marines, Rangers, SEALs and Airborne; and Operation "Eagle Claw" in 1980 used US Army Special Forces, Delta, Rangers, USMC, USAF Aerospace Rescue and Recovery Service (ARRS) and 1st Special Operations Wing (SOW). With so much combined activity, it is expected that the joint planning, training and understanding which ought to come about through the presence of the new Joint Special Operations Agency should hone performance to a finer edge.

The need for such an agency is clearly demonstrated in the following pages, where so much duplication of effort and sheer logistic complication muddies the waters of what should have been clear-cut operational requirements. Instead of one team of men with a close rapport and a single objective, the task forces described have suffered from being muddled together, relying on different chains of command and mission priorities. It is for these reasons that the success rate of American special forces, despite the courage of the individual soldiers concerned, has been lower than that of the British or Israelis, for example. Confused objectives, political considerations—especially in Vietnam—and inter-Service rivalries have also served to inhibit the potential of the US special forces.

Because the disparate units of the American élite forces have been obliged to work together on combined operations, in a way which does not happen in other, smaller, armies, it seems logical, therefore, to consider their origins, organization and status first, before going into details of some of their operations, in order that the reader can understand more fully the difficulties under which they have laboured.

Delta Force

Delta was the brainchild of Colonel Charles Beckwith, and eventually came into being on 19 November 1977. Its official name is Special Forces Operational Detachment Delta, presumably after the other Operational Detachments ("A," "B," and "C" Teams) into which the Special Forces are divided. The prime role of Delta is to deal with terrorist incidents affecting the USA and its interests, as a result of studies conducted after the Olympic Games massacre in Munich in August 1972 and the Mogadishu rescue of October 1977. The inspiration for Colonel Beckwith's force was the British 22nd Special Air Service Regiment with which he served in 1962–3, being one of the few US Special Forces' exchangees to gain selection. He developed a great love for the regiment and, on his return to the US Army, tried for a number of years to persuade it to form a unit with the same organization, purpose and functions as the British regiment.

Once his dream had been made reality, Colonel Beckwith proceeded to organize Delta into squadrons (initially there was only "A" Squadron, but this was split in 1979 to form "B" Squadron as well) which are subdivided into troops of 16 men. The basic group, or "chalk," is the 4-man patrol, but the troops can operate in groups of 2, 4, 8 or 16 men. Selection and training in Colonel Beckwith's time closely followed the SAS pattern, and had a strong element of weeding out "cowboys" and an accent on intelligence and self-reliance. Very high standards of marksmanship are required: snipers must score 100 per cent hits at 600 m (650 yd.) and 90 per cent at 1000 m (1100 yd.). Special Forces personnel volunteering for Delta are often surprised at the degree of competence demanded by SAS criteria.

Little more is known about Delta, as befits a "child" of the SAS, and Colonel Beckwith has now retired from the US Army. His brainchild survives, unaffected by the failure of Operation "Eagle Claw," and will presumably come into the limelight again when some other terrorist activity threatens the lives of US citizens.

The "Green Berets"

The US Army Special Forces (the "Green Berets") became well-known to the world during the Vietnam War. They trace their origin—like the British Special Air Service Regiment, with which they have some affinity—back to World War 2, when the Canadian-American 1st Special Service Force was formed on the authority of General George C. Marshall. This force was made up of three regiments of two battalions each, and fought in North Africa, Italy, southern France and the Aleutian Islands. Their tasks included raids and covert strikes, and their members were trained in demolition work, parachuting, amphibious assault, rock-climbing and skiing.

After World War 2, the force was disbanded, but, on 20 June 1952, the concept was revived with the formation of the 10th Special Forces Group at Fort Bragg, North Carolina. On 25 September 1953, the 77th Special Forces Group was born and, on 24 June 1957, the 1st Special Forces Group was activated in Okinawa. In the same year, 1 SFG sent a team to Nha Trang in South Vietnam to train a small group of men from the Army of the Republic of Vietnam (ARVN). Four years later, on 21 September 1961, the 5th SFG was formed at Fort Bragg: it later moved to Vietnam and became responsible for the activities of all personnel from the Special Forces Groups serving in the country. In that same year, President Kennedy authorized the wearing of the now-famous green beret, and ordered the deployment of the first Special Forces personnel to Vietnam in November 1961.

Although the original concept of the 1950s was that of fighting a guerrilla war against conventional troops, this was modified in the light of the new conditions encountered in Vietnam. The Special Forces' expertise fitted them well for a counter-insurgency role, and the tactic of "setting a thief to catch a thief" was being proved successful at the same time by the British in Malaya, Kenya, Aden and Cyprus. Circumstances and policies were slightly different in Vietnam, however, and the US Army Special Forces acquired the role of helping and instructing the Vietnamese Montagnard tribes to defend themselves against the Vietcong, and later to take a more active part. This was the Civilian Irregular Defense Group (CIDG) programme, and the Special Forces gained considerable expertise in organizing such "armies," although their value in the field varied enormously and was often unpredictable.

With the end of the Vietnam War, the "Green Berets" lost some favour in US Army circles, but it was soon realized that such a force was an essential element of a modern army. While retaining their ability to organize counter-insurgency armies for low-intensity warfare, the Special

Forces have now rediscovered their intelligence-gathering and covert operations role, bringing them back in line with the SAS.

The basic Special Forces sub-unit is the Operational Detachment or "A" Team of 12 men, and there are 12 such teams to a company. The companies themselves are formed into battalions and the battalions into groups, of which there are at present seven, with two more battalions and a group headquarters currently being raised. Of the seven groups, two are Army reserve and two are National Guard formations. The other three are regulars. All Special Forces groups now come under command of the 1st Special Operations Command of the Army, which is part of the Joint Special Operations Agency.

All members of the Special Forces are volunteers, who must be parachute-qualified or willing to become so. A rigorous training programme, lasting between 44 and 62 weeks, weeds out unsuitable candidates, after which the accepted recruits undergo a further period of training. All Special Forces soldiers must have at least two particular trades, such as demolitions, intelligence, special weapons or communications, and often they must become proficient in foreign languages. Each group has a coloured shield-shaped patch which is worn on the beret, and on this is set the officers' badges of rank or, for enlisted men, the SF cap badge.

The Rangers

The US Army's Ranger battalions are, in effect, its Light Infantry: their training, equipment, role and history make them what the British Army's Light Division ought to be. In general war, the Rangers' missions include deep recon-naissance into enemy-held territory, strategic raids, ambush patrols, and in low-intensity warfare their tasks are geared to counter-guerrilla and counter-terrorist operations.

At present, there are two Ranger battalions in the US Army with a third on its way. Known generally as the 1st and 2nd (and, presumably, 3rd) Ranger Battalions after their World War 2 predecessors, they are in fact the 1st and 2nd Battalions of the 75th Infantry Regiment (1/75 and 2/75, with 3/75 to follow). The 1st Battalion has its depot at Hunter Army Airfield, Georgia, and the 2nd Battalion is based at Fort Lewis in Washington State. The 3rd Battalion will be based at Fort Benning, Georgia, along with the Ranger Regimental Headquarters and the Ranger School.

First formed during World War 2, the Rangers were disbanded after Korea, but re-activated as a long-range reconnaissance force in Vietnam. In 1969 they were re-formed as the present two battalions of the 75th Infantry Regiment, whose basic combat unit is the squad of 11 men. Officially, the current Ranger mission is "to conduct special military operations in support of the policies and objectives of the USA." Typical missions would include operations against targets deep behind enemy lines and in conjunction with conventional forces; rescues; safeguarding US lives, property or investments; protecting US citizens abroad during emergencies; and air-mobile or airborne anti-armour operations in support of larger units. To act effectively, the battalions must be ready to deploy anywhere in the world; manoeuvre with speed and surprise in all types of terrain and climatic conditions by day or night; and to use air, land, water and parachute infiltration to carry out raids, ambushes and attacks against key targets in enemy territory. In addition, the Ranger battalion performs all the other traditional Light Infantry tasks.

Becoming a Ranger is a lengthy business, and the wastage rate is high: less than 50 per cent of the candidates win that black beret. All Rangers are volunteers from a parent Army unit, and do a two-year tour with the 75th Infantry Regiment. This may be extended by six months, on the Commanding Officer's recommendation. After this time, the Rangers go back to their units, taking their newly acquired skills and their coveted black berets with them.

Candidates need first to have a high-school graduation diploma, a high General Aptitude score, and to be able to gain a "Secret" security clearance. As most volunteers are infantrymen, they go through basic and advanced training at Fort Benning. After completing the Advanced Individual Training Course, the recruits go on to airborne school, also at Fort Benning. On passing out from this, they begin the four-week Ranger Indoctrination Program, which is designed to perfect their individual battle skills and acquaint them with Ranger standard operating procedures (SOPs).

After about one year in a Ranger battalion, and having proved his leadership qualities, a Ranger is sent to Ranger School. On graduating from this course, he is eligible for certain specialist schools such as Special Forces SCUBA (diving), SF Medical, Sniper, Demolitions, free-fall parachuting, and so on. As the Ranger qualification is a "trade" available to all Army units, many soldiers complete Ranger School, even if they do not subsequently join a Ranger battalion.

The two battalions have an arduous training schedule. Exercises are conducted all over the USA and abroad in order to find as many different climates and environments as possible, and the training year is divided into two gruelling 5½-month periods with just two fortnight block leaves in between.

The Airborne Divisions

"Airborne!" is the traditional chant and greeting of the members of the United States Army's parachute formations but, today, only one of the two World War 2 US Airborne divisions is "in role": the other has been turned into an air assault formation, specializing in helicopter operations using the Sikorsky UH-60A Black Hawk. The 82nd Airborne Division (the "All American"—hence the Double-A formation sign) is currently the US Army's only full-time parachute unit. The other famous Division—the 101st (the "Screaming Eagles" from the eagle's head divisional sign) —is now a 17,900-man-strong air assault formation, but it still keeps "Airborne" on its sign. Both are part of XVIII Airborne Corps, based at Fort Bragg, North Carolina.

The 82nd Airborne Division is made up of a divisional headquarters, a divisional support command, and three Airborne brigades. Each brigade consists of three parachute battalions with the usual headquarters and support arms. The present "rig" is the MC1–1B steerable parachute, which gives almost the same manoeuvrability as a hang glider.

Entry into the Airborne forces can be either by direct application or by volunteering from another unit. All candidates must pass a tough selection procedure, followed by a rigorous training and parachute course, after which they get their "wings" and can wear the maroon beret.

The primary task of any airborne unit is to arrive by air, take control of the ground, and hold it until relieved by main force units. The 82nd Airborne Division is at present the mainstay of the US Rapid Deployment Joint Task Force and as such takes part in the annual "Bright Star" Exercises in Egypt. One parachute battalion is kept on an 18-hour standby, with one of its companies on 2-hour standby. One of the brigades—the Ready Brigade, which, like the standby battalion, rotates around the division—is on 24-hour notice. The airlift capability for the Division is provided by the Lockheed C-141 Starlifters and C-130 Hercules of the USAF. The 82nd Airborne Division is equipped with three days' combat rations of food, ammunition, POL (petrol, oil and lubricants), spares, water, and clothing; after that period, air resupply is necessary.

United States Marine Corps

The largest élite force in the world is the USMC, with some 194,000 personnel of both sexes; making it larger than the total armed forces of many countries. It is organized into three regular and one reserve divisions, each incorporating a Marine Air Wing. The US Marine Corps has a unique all-arms air-land capability with a particular emphasis on amphibious operations, although it has often fought in conventional battles alongside the Army and the two other air forces.

The general role of the USMC has been put into three broad categories: amphibious capabilities for use with USN fleet operations, land operations which are necessary for successful maritime campaigns, and providing security detachments for US Naval bases and principal warships. The Corps may also, of course, carry out any other duties given it by the President.

The Marine division is larger than its Army counterpart with a strength of 18,000 men and some women (of which the Corps has approximately 4000). Each division is made up of a headquarters and three Marine brigades or regiments, plus supporting artillery, tanks and ancillary formations. A Marine battle group, known as an Amphibious Unit, comprises between 1600 and 2500 men. Number 22 MAU was the USMC contingent in the Grenada operation.

Recruits to the USMC enlist directly into the Corps, going to one of two training depots either at San Diego in California or at Parris Island in South Carolina. There they undergo the 11-week "Boot Camp," which is analogous to the Royal Marines' Beret Course, passing out at the end as "leathernecks." Officer selection is rigorous, and potential officers must endure a tough selection process and training course at Quantico, Virginia, before being commissioned.

The USMC does not have its own officers' academy; some officers are accepted from the Naval Academy at Annapolis, but most come from either the Naval Regimental Officers Training College, the Officers Candidate School, or the Platoon Leaders' Class run by the USMC. The Boot Camp and the Quantico course instil in the Marines the Corps' traditional doctrine of aggressive offensive action, which has been the hallmark of their combat engagements.

Underwater Demolition and Sea-Air-Land Teams

The Underwater Demolition Teams and the Sea-Air-Land Teams are the US Navy's principal élite forces. The UDTs were formed during World War 2, mainly to destroy water obstacles laid in the approaches to landing beaches. However, they also perform beach reconnaissance missions, and beach marking. Other activities which they are trained for include the destruction of certain targets near coasts, such as key bridges and crossings over which an enemy would have to move reinforcements to the beach defenders. In general, UDTs and SEALs have a range of tasks equivalent to those of the British Royal Marines' Special Boat Squadrons and the Boat Troops of SAS Squadrons.

SEAL team personnel are recruited from volunteers from the UDTs, and they receive special training to fit them for their role. The UDT members are themselves volunteers from other parts of the Navy. After the selection process, UDT volunteers go through an intensive and physically demanding 24-week course. The first four weeks consist of physical preparation: endurance and speed runs, PT, swimming, and marches. Recruits then embark upon several weeks of classroom work, physical and tactical exercises, open-sea swims, reconnaissance exercises and demolition training. This period is then followed by a week's E-and-E (escape and evasion), survival training and land navigation exercises. Finally, the volunteers go through a three-week parachute course and then to underwater swimming school.

SEAL volunteers go even further: they take foreign language courses and qualifications, study low-intensity warfare, and complete a HALO (high altitude/low-opening) free-fall parachute course. The SEAL teams' role requires them to work in hostile waters with little friendly support, or on land where they may have "contacts" with the enemy. They may be taken into action by submarine—coming out either while it is still submerged or when it is on the surface—to swim or paddle ashore in inflatable boats. They could also parachute towards their objective: their HALO training would allow them to jump from the aircraft some distance from the target and "track" towards it. They might also come ashore by the US equivalents of Geminis, Rigid Raiders or canoes.

Two US Marines check out an abandoned Vietnamese village after fierce fighting in the Quang Tri province.

Both UDTs and SEALs wear standard naval uniform with specialist trade insignia. On exercise or operations, they wear the appropriate gear. SEALs often wear leaf-pattern combat kit, and sometimes also the face-veil *shimag* around the head that has been popularized by the SAS. Jungle hats and camouflaged berets are alternative headgear.

Control over the UDTs and the SEALs and the USN Reserve special forces is under the Naval Special Warfare Groups (NAVSPECWARGRUs) of which there are two. Number 1 (NAVSPECWARGRU 1) commands SEAL Team 1, UDTs 11 and 12, Special Boat Squadron 1 and Swimmer Delivery Vehicle (SDV) Team 1. Its base is the Naval Amphibious Base, Coronado, San Diego, in California, but it also administers Naval Special Warfare Unit 1 at Subic Bay in the Philippines. NAVSPECWARGRU 2 has its depot at Little Creek, Norfolk, Virginia, and has under command SEAL Team 2, UDTs 21 and 22, and a similar spread of units to NAVSPECWARGRU 1.

UDTs consist of 15 officers and 111 ratings ("enlisted men"), while SEAL teams consist of 27 officers and 156 ratings. A SEAL team is divided into five self-contained platoons, each of which is able to operate independently.

There is no doubt that the scope of the United States' élite forces, as detailed above, is mindboggling. The number of men—and women—involved, the range of training, and the multiplicity of equipment and skills, might make these formations seem unwieldy and difficult to coordinate in the field. All three of the actions described in the remainder of this chapter were combined operations and in some part may serve to illustrate the advantages, or disadvantages, of having so many independent units on call in times of emergency.

THE MAYAGUEZ RESCUE

The sun had not long risen when the two helicopters reached their destination—the island of Koh Tang. As the Marines looked out from the first helicopter, all that met their gaze was a peaceful, tropical paradise of warm blue seas lapping a deserted beach. Their hopes high, the men dropped to the ground and spread out along the shore. Suddenly, all hell broke loose—the Khmer Rouge had organized a welcoming party.

No one could have expected this complex operation to run like clockwork, given the number of unknown factors, but at least it achieved its objective: the recovery of the SS *Mayaguez* and the rescue of its crew. The *Mayaguez* rescue was, perhaps, the last major US military operation in the south-east Asian conflict.

Following the hurried evacuation of the US embassy in Saigon at the end of April 1975, American air power was concentrated in Thailand and on ships in the Gulf of Thailand. During the first week of May two merchant vessels bound for Thailand were intercepted by Cambodian gunboats: a Korean ship was shot at, but escaped, and, on 7 May, a Panamanian-registered vessel was seized and held for 35 hours, then released. Then, on 12 May, the American-registered freighter SS *Mayaguez* was stopped and held by Cambodian naval gunboats in the Gulf, some 10 km (6½ miles) off Poulo Wai. Before the Cambodians took control, the radio operator had managed to send a message asking for help, which was picked up and relayed to Washington.

At 06:15, three hours after the seizure, the officer of the watch at the State Department's Intelligence and Research Bureau woke up the Secretary of State, Henry A. Kissinger. Dr. Kissinger passed the news on to the President,

Gerald R. Ford, 1½ hours later. After this briefing, the President called a meeting of the National Security Council for noon. One of the problems of rescue attempts in Vietnam was the delay involved in mounting them: by the time the Council sat down in Washington, the *Mayaguez* had already been in Cambodian hands for 5¾ hours.

The Master of the *Mayaguez*, Captain Charles T. Miller, managed to stall the Cambodians from moving his ship to Sihanoukville (Kompang Som) on the mainland. So, the vessel was still riding at anchor off Poulo Wai, when a US Navy Lockheed P-3C Orion patrol aircraft spotted it just after dawn on 13 May. Later that morning, the headquarters of Pacific Air Force ordered the USAF Aerospace Rescue and Recovery Service units in Thailand to prepare a rescue force for the 39 crewmen being held by the Cambodians. On orders from President Ford, the US Navy Commander-in-Chief Pacific Fleet instructed fighter-bombers and gunships to prevent the ship or its crew from being taken to the mainland. They were to fire warning shots across the bow and, if that failed, they were to strafe the after-deck and stern in an attempt to disable the freighter. If the Cambodians tried to tow the vessel, they would be warned and the tug sunk, if necessary.

The aircrews received these orders late in the afternoon of 13 May. That night, AC-130 Spectre gunships of the USAF special operations units circled over the vessel. A Cambodian gunboat fired at the aircraft, the Spectres attacked and forced the boat aground. During the evening of 13 May, the Joint Chiefs of Staff in Washington ordered eight HH-53 helicopters (callsigns "JG"—"Jolly Green") from 3rd Aerospace Rescue and Recovery Squadron, and eight CH-53s (callsigns "K"—"Knife") from 21st Special Operations Squadron to the Royal Thai Air Force Base at U-Tapao on the Gulf. They were to carry 75 security policemen from Nakhon Phanom as a possible rescue force.

Sadly, a tragic accident happened during the move. One of the "Knife" helicopters crashed into wooded country 60 km (37 miles) west of Nakhon Phanom, killing all on board: five crewmen and 18 policemen.

At 08:17 the next day, two "JG" helicopters took off from U-Tapao to look for survivors of a Cambodian gunboat, earlier sunk by strafing from A-7 Corsair IIs. None was found, and the aircraft returned to U-Tapao. The same flight of A-7s which had sunk the gunboat spotted soon after a wooden fishing boat full of people heading for the mainland. Suspecting that the *Mayaguez* crew was on board, they fired warning shots and dropped tear gas all around it. But the gas actually prevented the crewmen and the Thai fishermen from overpowering their Cambodian captors. They were taken to Sihanoukville and later transferred to Kaoh Rong Samloem—a nearby island. Corsairs, Phantoms and Hercules aircraft resumed watch over the *Mayaguez*. In the mid-morning, Corsairs sank a patrol boat towing a barge east of Koh Tang island and, during that night, a Hercules sank another patrol boat as it approached the ship.

Washington was meanwhile trying diplomatic approaches in an attempt to secure the release of the crew. At the same time it was putting rescue plans in motion—just in case! On 14 May, two companies of Marines were flown from Okinawa to U-Tapao, bringing the total number of available USMC personnel to somewhere around 600. American ships were also steaming as fast as they could to the scene. The nearest vessel was the frigate USS *Harold E. Holt,* which was by chance in the area, and the fleet carrier USS *Coral Sea* and the destroyer USS *Henry B. Wilson* were hurrying down from the north-east.

By nightfall on 14 May, nobody knew for certain where the crew of the *Mayaguez* was. Military preparations continued in Thailand and, when it became clear that diplomatic efforts were getting nowhere, President Ford ordered the Joint Chiefs of Staff to take appropriate measures to reclaim the ship and secure the release of the crew: the military in south-east Asia had been given the "green light"!

The plan was for 60 Marines to be flown out to the *Holt* in three helicopters. These men would board the SS *Mayaguez* and capture the ship. Intelligence estimates indicated that the crew was being held on Koh Tang, guarded by a handful of Cambodian civilians and Khmer Rouge terrorists, but this information proved to be wrong. Up to 600 Marines were to be flown out to the island in helicopters, with an Army interpreter in the first aircraft to tell the Khmer Rouge that the Marines had landed, and that their only hope of safety was to hand over the *Mayaguez* crew unharmed. Eight helicopters would transport an initial wave of Marines for a landing at first light on the two northern beaches of Koh Tang (called West Beach and East Beach) to establish a beach-head. A second wave would then be flown in, and a third was to be held in reserve.

In the early morning of 15 May, eight helicopters (five "Knife" CH-53s and three "Jolly Green" HH-53s) flew towards the two beaches carrying the first two waves of Marines. At 06:45 two CH-53s, "Knife 21" and "22," flew in to West Beach. No resistance was met until most of the Marines off the first chopper—"Knife 21"—had fanned out across the beach. Then the Khmer Rouge opened fire at close range with rifles, missiles and mortars, knocking out one of "Knife 21's" engines as it took off. The helicopter skipped over the waves until it was about a kilometre out, then settled into the water.

"Knife 22" stood by until "Jolly Green 41" and "Knife 32" arrived, then headed in to the beach to unload its Marines. "Knife 32," fully laden, had to dump fuel before its para rescue man could fish the crew of "Knife 21" out of

WEAPONS OF THE AMERICAN ÉLITE FORCES

Designation	Type	Calibre	Magazine	Rate of fire	Range	Remarks
L9A1	Browning automatic pistol	9 mm	13 rounds	Single shot	40 m	Most widely used hand gun in world
M3	Browning sub-machine gun	0.45 in	30 rounds	450 rpm cyclic	100 m	The faithful old 'grease gun'
M16A1	Armalite assault rifle	5.56 mm	20 or 30 rounds	700–950 rpm cyclic	400 m	
M16A2	Armalite assault rifle	5.56 mm	20 or 30 rounds	600–940 rpm cyclic	400 m	With 3-round burst capability
CAR15	Colt Commando carbine	5.56 mm	20 or 30 rounds	700–800 rpm cyclic	200 m	Carbine version of Armalite
M10	Ingram sub-machine-gun	9 mm or 0.45 in	32 rounds (9 mm), 30 rounds (0.45)	1090 rpm, 1145 rpm	100 m+	Has replaced the unsuccessful Stoner
M11	Ingram sub-machine-gun	9 mm short or 0.38 in	16 or 32 rounds	1200 rpm	100 m	
M60	Machine-gun	7.62 mm	100-round belt	550 rpm	1000 m	Dual-purpose light/heavy machine-gun
M224	Mortar	60 mm	Single-shot	18 rpm	Not available	New section light mortar
L16A1	Mortar	81 mm	Single-shot	15 rpm	5650 m	The standard British mortar

the water. He managed to save the pilot, co-pilot and one of the crewmen, but tragically the other, Sergeant Elwood E. Rumbaugh, was lost. Showing great bravery, the Sergeant had saved the co-pilot's life by diving down to help him out of the wreckage, but had then disappeared and was presumed drowned. "Knife 32" managed to land its Marines on the beach, and then returned to U-Tapao with the injured and survivors of "Knife 21."

Approaching the beach through a hail of fire all the way, "Knife 22" took many hits, one of which damaged a fuel line causing a major leak. It was unable to land, and so it struggled back towards Thailand escorted by two "Jolly Greens." Just as the disabled helicopter reached the Thai coast, it ran out of fuel and had to make a forced landing on the beach.

The East Beach landing was experiencing the same sort

Designation	Type	Calibre	Magazine	Rate of fire	Range	Remarks
M79	Grenade launcher	40 mm	Single-shot	6–10 rpm	150 m	
M249	FN Minimi light machine-gun	5.56 mm	30 rounds (box) or 100- or 200-round belts	750–1000 rpm cyclic	600 m	Extremely versatile
G3	Heckler and Koch assault rifle	7.62 mm	20 rounds	500–600 rpm cyclic	400 m	West German design
MP5	Heckler and Koch sub-machine-gun	9 mm	15 or 30 rounds	800 rpm cyclic	200 m	Used by British and Germans
Cobra	Anti-tank missile	100 mm	Single-shot	Not applicable	2000 m	Second-generation weapon
M47 Dragon	Medium anti-tank armour weapon	Not available	Single-shot	Not available	1000 m +	Third-generation weapon
TOW BGM71A	Anti-tank missile	152 mm	Single-shot	Not available	3750 m	
Stinger	Anti-aircraft missile	70 mm	Single-shot	Not applicable	1500 m +	One-shot 'disposable' weapon, also used by British SAS
Redeye	Anti-aircraft missile	70 mm	Single-shot	Not available	Not available	

of problems. As "Knife 23" and "31" headed in, they received a hostile welcome from small-arms, heavy machine-guns, rockets and mortars just as they were about to touch down. "Knife 23" was hit in the rotor system, and was forced to make a controlled crash landing in the surf, its tail boom snapping as it struck. The pilot ordered everyone to abandon the helicopter, and the 20 Marines, together with the air force crew, charged ashore to fight on the beach. "Knife 31" was also badly damaged and, as it was being ditched in the shallows, it burst into flames. Eight people died in the wreckage. Of the 18 survivors, 4 more were killed and 1 other died later of wounds when they were fired on by the Khmer Rouge as they tried to swim out to sea. The 14 survivors were picked up by a launch from a USN destroyer.

An hour after the attack began, there were 14 Americans dead or missing, 3 helicopters had been shot down and 2 more severely damaged, and there were 54 Marines and USAF personnel pinned down on the two beaches. It was not the happiest of situations.

During these actions, the USS *Holt* came alongside the *Mayaguez* and put the Marine boarding party on to the ship. It found that the vessel had been abandoned, so the *Holt* put a line aboard and towed the *Mayaguez* away from Poulo Wai. Thus, an hour and a half after the main assault at least the ship had been recovered.

Elsewhere, but soon afterwards, the missing crew was rescued. It seems that, together with the crew of the Thai fishing boat, the sailors had managed to escape from their guards at Kaoh Rong Samloem, and had put to sea in the boat. The destroyer *Wilson* was sighted, and the *Mayaguez* crewmen stripped off their underwear to make white flags. The *Wilson* was at battle stations before anyone saw the underwear flying from the fishing boat's mast, but, within an hour, the *Mayaguez* crew was safely in American care.

Attention now centred on extricating the embattled Marines from Koh Tang. With the *Mayaguez*'s crew safe, it was now possible to use A-7s, F-4s and AC-130 Spectre gunships to give fire support on the island: previously these had been held back for fear of hitting the captured crew. But while the *Mayaguez* men were approaching the *Wilson,* more Marines had been landed on Koh Tang. "Jolly Green 42" and "43" approached on their first run in, and "Jolly Green 41" headed in, after refuelling, to West Beach. They were all driven off by heavy fire, so "Jolly Green 43" flew down the coast a little way and landed its 29 Marines 800 m (875 yd.) south of the main body. It took them many hours to fight their way back to link up. "Jolly Green 42" managed to land its Marines on West Beach after another try, but put them down on a small patch of sand about 900 m (1000 yd.) from the other group. The helicopter sustained heavy damage, and had to be escorted back to U-Tapao by "Jolly Green 43." The third helicopter tried again, but was driven back and had to refuel once more. At about 08:00, "Jolly Green 13" was seriously damaged while trying to pick up the 20 Marines and 5 USAF crew of "Knife 23" on East Beach, and was left with no option but to return to Thailand.

"Jolly Green 41" did not give up easily: it approached West Beach four times in an attempt to land its troops, but was driven back each time. Finally, it called in a Spectre to shoot at enemy positions with 20 mm, 40 mm and 105 mm rounds. With this support, "Jolly 41" flew in to the beach to drop off its Marines, with its crewmen furiously shooting up the jungle fringe with their miniguns. Nevertheless the aircraft came under mortar fire as it unloaded; one round passed through the rotor disc and exploded near the chopper, causing serious damage. "Jolly 41" had to retire to Thailand, after refuelling, with five Marines still on board.

"Cricket," the airborne command post, marshalled the five remaining helicopters to fly in reinforcements. "Knife 51," "Knife 52" and "Jolly Green 43" flew in the first wave, with "Jolly Green 11" and "12" forming the second wave. "Knife 51" landed 19 Marines and took out 5 wounded at West Beach, while "Jolly Green 43" put another 28 Marines ashore, refuelled, and then circled in case it was needed for aircrew recovery. As "Knife 52" approached the landing zone, it was hit several times in the fuel tank, so the pilot was forced to abort the landing and return to Thailand. The second-wave helicopters managed to put all their Marines ashore, however. "Jolly Green 12" took on casualties and flew them to the mainland, while "Jolly Green 11" refuelled from the Hercules tanker and returned to Koh Tang to join "Jolly Green 43" in orbit. A-7s, F-4s, and OV-10A Broncos strafed, bombed and dropped tear gas on the enemy positions, but the gas was ineffective due to adverse winds.

By midday, there were 222 Americans on the island: 197 on West Beach and 25 on East Beach. The West Beach force managed to fight its way towards East Beach across the "neck," but could get no further than a clearing about half-way across. At 14:30 another pick-up was attempted after the air attacks. "Jolly Green 43" again came under heavy fire on its approach, sustaining damage to fuel lines and one disabled engine, but gamely carried on. It landed and took on a full load of Marines, and then precariously skipped over the waves escorted by "Jolly Green 11" to make a forced landing on the *Coral Sea* 100 km (60 miles) away. "Jolly Green 11" returned yet again to Koh Tang.

"Cricket" and the airborne forward air controllers directed more tactical strikes against the Khmer Rouge positions before the evacuation was resumed. By this time, only three helicopters were operational, and two others were being hurriedly repaired: "Jolly Green 44," previously out of commission at Nakhon Phanom, and 'Jolly Green 43' on board USS *Coral Sea*. By 16:00, "Jolly Green 44" was thankfully back in service and rushing to U-Tapao. It arrived at Koh Tang at 17:30, just as "Jolly Green 43" was returning from *Coral Sea*, and the two helicopters joined up with "Jolly Green 11," "Jolly Green 12" and "Knife 51." Before the five went back into action, a Hercules dropped a 6800 kg (15,000 lb.) bomb on the centre of Koh Tang island, devastating an area the size of an American football pitch and killing everyone inside a 45 m (50 yd.) radius of the explosion.

While the enemy was still reeling, "Jolly Green 11" headed in to East Beach, supported by minigun fire from "Jolly Green 12," "Knife 51" and two machine-guns, mounted in a longboat, from the *Wilson*. It was feared that the 25 men would not survive the night, and rescue was essential. "Jolly Green 11" came under heavy fire from the Khmer Rouge as soon as it neared the beach. The helicopter hovered at the water's edge, while the party on the beach raced for the chopper in pairs, firing blindly into the jungle as they dived inside the aircraft. The flight mechanic manning the rear ramp minigun, Sergeant Harry W. Cash, was giving covering fire for the Marines and USAF men coming in off the beach. As the last pair scampered aboard, he yelled into his headset for the aircraft to take off, but there was no response: one of the first men aboard had ripped out the intercom system in his hurry. Black-clad figures were pouring out of the undergrowth, and Sergeant Cash swung his minigun to cut them down. One of the figures attempted to throw a grenade, but was killed before he could manage it. Nevertheless, the grenade rolled inexorably towards the chopper and exploded. The pilot had had enough of this unfriendly treatment, and decided to go, whether or not everyone was on board—fortunately, they were. "Jolly Green 11" flew the relieved Marines back to the *Coral Sea*.

As darkness approached, there were 202 Marines still to be evacuated off West Beach. "Knife 51" headed in under intense small-arms fire to pick up 41 of them, "Jolly 43" took off 54 more, and both choppers flew them to the *Coral Sea*. "Jolly Green 44" then loaded up with 34 Marines. The pilot decided that he could save the 20-minute round trip to the aircraft carrier by landing the Marines on the *Holt*, as the situation on the beach was becoming increasingly desperate. With one of the crewmen hanging out of the door and giving him directions, the brave pilot managed to get one wheel on the corner of the *Holt*'s helicopter pad with barely any clearance for the rotor blades. The Marines got out as fast as they could, and "Jolly Green 44" hurtled back to the beach.

The remaining 73 men had withdrawn into a 45 m (50 yd.) perimeter only a short sprint from the landing zone. OV-10A Broncos and A-7 Corsair IIs strafed the nearby jungle, but still the Khmer Rouge pressed their fierce attacks. At 19:25, the Marine commander on the beach radioed that it looked as though his position would be overrun within 15 minutes. As a Spectre shot up the tree-line beyond them, the Marines assembled a strobe light to guide the incoming helicopters. "Jolly Green 44" followed the light to the beach and picked up 40 Marines, but due to engine power loss it was forced to fly out to the *Coral Sea;* there was no way that it could repeat the aerobatics at the *Holt.* "Knife 51" spotted the strobe light and made its way to pick up the remaining Marines, while an OV-10A orbited above the spot, occasionally turning on its landing lights to draw fire away from the rescue chopper. "Knife 51" touched down on the landing zone, and 27 of the Marines clambered to safety. The para rescue man had to run up the beach to grab the remaining two, who were still courageously giving covering fire. With all 29 on board, "Knife 51" took off, and America's military involvement in south-east Asia was at an end.

During the action on Koh Tang, around 230 men were landed on the island and then taken out. It had proved a costly operation, both in lives and equipment: 15 men were killed, 49 wounded and 3 were missing; of the 15 helicopters which took part, 4 were destroyed and 9 damaged. But the SS *Mayaguez* and its crew were safe. The operation was a success.

OPERATION "EAGLE CLAW"

Orange flames from a burning petrol tanker cast shadows darker than the night across the primitive desert road as the pilot of the Sea Stallion helicopter peered anxiously through the sand-pitted windscreen. He was already running nearly a hour behind schedule because of the dust storms and mechanical failures which had plagued the eight choppers ever since they had lifted off from the flight deck of the nuclear-powered carrier *Nimitz* at 19:30. Even as the pilot settled in to land, using the blazing vehicle as a beacon, it was obvious that more than just the weather and the vagaries of sophisticated machinery were conspiring to thwart Operation "Eagle Claw"—the attempted rescue of American hostages who were being held in Tehran by the fanatical followers of the Ayatollah Khomeini.

On 4 November 1979, a group of Iranian "students" rushed into the American embassy compound in Tehran and took the 53 occupants hostage; three more Americans were held in the Foreign Ministry. America was outraged. Any prospect of a diplomatic solution was complicated by the nature of the Iranian regime, which appeared to have only a notional control over the captors, and negotiations for the hostages' release proved inconclusive. As time passed, President Carter became increasingly worried for the hostages' safety.

From soon after their capture, one of the options kept under constant review was the possibility of a rescue, and contingency plans were worked out. When the decision was eventually taken to try to bring out the hostages by military means, the plan centred around using Delta Force under Colonel Charles Beckwith, with support from Rangers, Green Berets, the USMC Air Wing, and Special Operations Squadrons of the USAF.

The rescue plan was complicated, to say the least. At its core were eight RH-53D Sea Stallion helicopters. It was agreed from the beginning that an absolute minimum of six Sea Stallions was essential during the later phases of the operation, so, theoretically, there would be two helicopters in reserve.

The mission was to be in three phases, plus some preliminary moves. Delta personnel under Colonel Beckwith were to fly to Masirah airfield (the former RAF base used by the hijackers in the Mogadishu affair) in Oman, via Germany and Egypt, by Lockheed C-141 Starlifter of USAF Military Airlift Command. At Masirah they were to trans-ship to three MC-130E Hercules flown by USAF Special Operations Squadron personnel, which would take them at very low level (to avoid radar detection) across the Gulf of Oman and southern Iran to a remote spot in the Dasht-e Kavir salt desert, some distance north of the town of Yazd and west of the Kuh-e Sorkh mountain. This key site was code-named "Desert One," and was located some 490 km (306 miles) south-east of Tehran.

The eight RH-53D Sea Stallions were scheduled to arrive at "Desert One" some 30 minutes after the main party. These helicopters were minesweeping versions of the HH-53 "Super Jolly Green Giant," and had been chosen because of their payload, range and shipboard capability. It was also felt that minesweeping helicopters would attract less notice from prying Arab eyes than troop-carrying versions. These eight aircraft had been deployed to the British airfield at Diego Garcia, in the Indian Ocean, some weeks earlier, and had been picked up by the USS *Nimitz*, which was at the centre of a Carrier Task Force operating in the Indian Ocean and the Gulf of Oman. The Sea Stallions were to be flown by USMC crews from the *Nimitz* at very low level to "Desert One," where they would refuel from three EC-130E Hercules flown in from Masirah.

Overall command of the operation was in the hands of Major-General James Vaught, the Commander Joint Task Force, who was located at Wadi Kena airfield in Egypt. The commander of "Desert One" was Air Force Colonel James Kyle—a last minute change of plan—while Colonel Beckwith assumed command of the rescue forces on the ground. Vaught had a satellite link back to Washington, so that he could talk to the chairman of the Joint Chiefs of Staff, General David Jones, and to the President. Colonel Beckwith had a similar "satcom" link to General Vaught.

As "Desert One" lay near a road (albeit little used), a road watch team was included in the main party flown to the spot. Four Department of Defense agents were also to be positioned in Tehran before the operation to organize, or act as, guides. They were to arrange for six Mercedes-Benz trucks: one agent would take the 12-man driving team of 6 drivers and 6 assistants-cum-interpreters to collect the trucks. The agents would first guide the assault group from a forward rendezvous nearer to Tehran to hides, where they would lie up during the day.

The main party at "Desert One" was to consist of the 12-man driving team, made up of volunteers; the 12-man road watch team, comprising some Delta men and some Rangers from the 75th Infantry Regiment; the Foreign Ministry assault team, made up of a 12-man Green Beret "A" Team plus one other man; and the main assault group for the embassy. This group consisted of Delta personnel in three "elements": "Red" Element (40 men) was to secure the western end of the embassy compound; "Blue" Element (also 40 men) the eastern sector of the embassy; while "White" Element (13 men) was to secure Roosevelt Avenue during the rescue action, and then cover the withdrawal.

Phase One of the rescue was the occupation of "Desert One." Phase Two consisted of two concurrent actions: the embassy rescue and the Foreign Ministry rescue. Phase Three was the airlift. The first phase called for the six Hercules aircraft (three MC-130Es as troop carriers, and three EC-130E command and control variants to ferry in fuel for the helicopters) to land at "Desert One" and wait there for the RH-53D Sea Stallions, which were due to arrive about 30 minutes later. The road watch team would deploy to intercept and detain any passers-by. The refuelled helicopters would load the assault teams plus the driving team and fly north-west towards Tehran to a forward landing zone, where the agents would be waiting. The men would be dropped off, and the Sea Stallions would go on to a helicopter hide some 24 km (15 miles) to the north. The agents would guide men to their lying-up point, and, at sundown, one agent would take the driving team to collect the trucks.

At 20:30, the assault teams would board the Mercedes trucks and begin the drive to Tehran. The rescue itself was timed to start between 23:00 and 24:00. At the embassy, the Elements were to take care of the guards and release the hostages. If possible, they were also to clear a landing zone in the compound by removing the poles which the "students" had erected, so that the helicopters could come in. If this was not possible, the group with the hostages was to go to a nearby football stadium, where the helicopters would collect them. Simultaneously with this action, the "Green Berets" were to attack the Foreign Ministry and take the three hostages to a nearby park for helicopter pick-up.

While the actions at the US embassy and the Foreign Ministry were taking place, a company of Rangers was to capture Manzarieh airfield, some 55 km (35 miles) south of Tehran. Several C-141s would then fly in to Manzarieh, with General Vaught on board one of them. The Sea Stallions would fly everyone from Tehran to the recently captured airfield, where they would board the Starlifters, and be flown out. The Rangers would leave last and the helicopters would be destroyed at the airfield.

It was a fiendishly complex plan, but the actual execution of Operation "Eagle Claw" began quite promisingly. The preliminary moves worked, and the first MC-130E duly landed at "Desert One" carrying Colonels Beckwith and Kyle, "Blue" Element of the embassy assault group, and the road watch team. This team immediately took up its positions, and then the problems began. As the road watch team scanned the darkening desert landscape, they observed with horror the headlights of an approaching bus.

Stepping into the middle of the dusty desert track, they flagged down the vehicle and put the 45 frightened passengers under guard. A few minutes later, however, two more vehicles drove up from the south. The first was a petrol tanker which was hit by an anti-tank missile and burst into flames; the driver ran off to board the second vehicle, which drove off at high speed.

A dramatic scene thus greeted the remaining C-130s as they turned up to deliver their troops. The third MC-130E and the three EC-130Es remained at "Desert One" while the first two troop carriers returned to Masirah. The men at "Desert One" could do nothing but wait for the helicopters to arrive before any changes of plan could be carried out.

The eight Sea Stallions had taken off from USS *Nimitz* at 19:30 local time, as scheduled, but complications soon reared their ugly heads. At about 21:45, Number 6 had to land with an impending "catastrophic blade failure"; the crew destroyed any sensitive documents, and were picked up by helicopter Number 8. About an hour later, the leading RH-53Ds flew into a dust storm. The gritty particles blinded the pilots of the helicopters, who had to rely on instruments alone, and who breathed sighs of relief as the dust finally cleared and the stars re-emerged. Their relief was short-lived, however, since shortly afterwards they met a second, and worse, storm. The commander of the helicopter force, Major Seiffert, had lost his inertial navigation system earlier and was flying blind. Followed by Number 2 helicopter, he flew back out of the first dust storm and radioed General Vaught, who informed him that the weather over "Desert One" was clear. The two aircraft took off after about 20 minutes and headed for "Desert One" once again. At about the same time, Number 5 had a major electrical failure and lost the use of its instruments. It was forced to return to the *Nimitz*, leaving just six helicopters to carry on with the mission. The operation proper had not yet begun, and already the Americans were down to the bare minimum of helicopters.

The first helicopter to clear the dust storms was Number 3, which used the burning petrol tanker as a beacon to land at "Desert One," about 50 minutes late. The other five helicopters came in from different directions over the following half-hour. They immediately started to refuel, and the assault group began to board their respective aircraft. By this time, the operation was running 90 minutes behind schedule. Then came the final blow: it was discovered that Number 2 helicopter, which had had a hydraulic failure during the flight, could not be repaired with the facilities available and should therefore be counted out.

The rescue force now had less than the minimum number of helicopters for the operation. Nevertheless, Colonel Kyle radioed General Vaught in Egypt and explained the situation. The General suggested that they might try to carry on with the five aircraft they had, but the decision was eventually taken to call off the operation. It is still not known whether this decision came from Washington, as has often been suggested, or was made at "Desert One," by the men on the spot. Anyway, there seemed no major problem in "aborting" the mission.

There was a minor hindrance, however. Helicopter Number 4 needed to top up with fuel for the long flight back to the *Nimitz*, as it had been on the ground longest with its engine running. Only one of the EC-130Es had enough fuel left for it and, to clear a space for refuelling, Number 3 took off and banked to the left, but was unable to keep hovering because of its weight—around 19,500 kg (42,000 lb.)—and the height above sea level—some 1500 m (5000 ft.). At 02:40 it slid back towards the ground, and crashed into the C-130 tanker. Both aircraft exploded, throwing debris in all directions, and ammunition began to detonate. It was a tragic end to an ill-fated mission. Five USAF personnel in the C-130 and three Marines in the Sea

Stallion were killed. Amazingly the 64 Delta men in the Hercules managed to escape from the blazing wreckage, rescuing the Hercules' loadmaster in the process. The decision was then taken to abandon the remaining helicopters and return to Masirah in the three remaining C-130s.

Later, the Iranians staged a tasteless propaganda jamboree. The world was treated to the gruesome sight of Ayatollah Khalkhali gloating over the remains of a dead American serviceman. Khalkhali himself was later killed in a bomb explosion in Tehran. As for the hostages, Algerian intermediaries eventually managed to negotiate their release from Khomeini's Iran.

Although the rescue attempt failed, it was not the fault of the forces on the ground. Some of America's allies have raised questions about the operation, the Israelis saying that, in any helicopter operation of that kind, there should be a 100 per cent reserve of aircraft: double the number necessary should have been tasked to "Desert One"—that is, 16 RH-53D Sea Stallions. Also, the British 22nd Special Air Service Regiment, who had two observers present at some of the planning for the rescue, was unhappy about parts of the plan.

Nevertheless, the very fact that America tried meant something to the luckless captives. It was also a declaration that America will always try to rescue any of its people held unjustly, if diplomacy fails. There is no doubt that Operation "Eagle Claw" could have succeeded, like the Koh Tang raid or the Grenada rescue.

GRENADA

As the 12 Rangers floated down through the Grenadan sky towards Point Salines airfield, they watched helplessly as the aircraft from which they had just jumped flew off into

While smoke rises from burning buildings in the background, men of the 82nd Airborne Division wait at Point Salines.

the distance, carrying with it their comrades from the 1st Battalion, forced to abandon the remainder of the drop by the fierce anti-aircraft fire from below. The 12 said silent prayers as they drifted downwards, easy prey for the enemy below. By some miracle, they all touched down in one piece, but the Rangers' troubles were not over by a long chalk. They were surrounded by hostile forces, with no knowledge of when reinforcements would reach them, and with the clear realization that, until the airfield had been secured, their jeeps and equipment would have to stay put—far above in the clear blue sky!

This incident was, happily, just a hiccup in the relatively smooth rescue by US forces—with a small eastern Caribbean contingent—of some 600 American medical students from the small island state of Grenada: the biggest, and most successful, combined arms operation mounted by the Americans since the Koh Tang SS *Mayaguez* rescue of May 1975. It was the first major campaign under the direction of the Joint Special Operations Command, and is interesting because it involved elements of nearly all the US élite forces.

Political developments on Grenada, a member of the British Commonwealth, had been causing concern to many people, not least the USA and neighbouring eastern Caribbean countries. Finally, on 19 October 1983, martial law was imposed, with an announcement that "all citizens are asked to remain at home . . . anyone who violates this curfew will be shot on sight." The same day, the airport, shops, and news media were closed down, and several government officials—including the Prime Minister, Maurice Bishop—were arrested. These people were then shot by troops of General Austin's New People's Revolutionary Army, an act which prompted the Governor, Sir Paul Scoon, to ask for help from neighbouring Caribbean states and America. Britain was unable to assist materially, although HMS *Antrim* and the Royal Fleet Auxiliary *Pearleaf* joined the US Navy Task Force, which sailed for Grenada from the Colombian port of Cartagena, where they had been paying a goodwill visit. A force of some 300 men, from Jamaica, Barbados, Dominica, St. Kitts-Nevis, Antigua/Barbuda and St. Vincent, joined the US force. Although small in number, this contingent was politically very important. American worries about the expansion of Cuban and Warsaw Pact influence in the Caribbean were exacerbated by the prospect of US citizens being held hostage, as had happened in Iran earlier.

Joint Special Operations Command contingency plans were put into operation on the directive of the President, Ronald Reagan, and various units were put on ready-alert. The 1st and 2nd Ranger Battalions (1/75 and 2/75 Infantry Regiment) were on standby from about 23 October, and were deployed to their staging base at Savannah, Georgia, on 24 October. The 23rd Air Force was similarly alerted for transport and fire support duties.

A week before the invasion of Grenada took place, a US Navy Task Force of nine vessels was steaming to the Lebanon to relieve the American forces there. While still in the western Atlantic, it was diverted—probably immediately following the arrival of news of Mr. Bishop's murder and Sir Paul Scoon's request in Washington DC on or about 20 or 21 October—to rendezvous with another Task Force of six vessels off Grenada.

The nine-vessel force was commanded by Rear Admiral Joseph Metcalf III, flying his flag in USS *Guam*, a special amphibious assault ship equipped as a helicopter landing platform for CH-46 Sea Knight and CH-53 Sea Stallion aircraft, and refitted in 1971 as a sea control ship. He also had with him the USS *Saipan*, a general-purpose amphibious assault ship specially designed and equipped to mount and support a Marine amphibious landing. Among the USMC personnel with the Task Force was the 22nd Marine Amphibious Unit (22 MAU), commanded by Lieutenant-Colonel Ray Smith, some 400 men strong, and trained and equipped to secure a beach-head against strong opposition. Among their equipment were M-60 Patton main battle tanks and LVTP-7 Amtracks (armed with 0.50-calibre machine-guns). The largest vessel in the group was USS *Independence*, a multi-purpose aircraft carrier equipped with Vought A-7 Corsair II and Grumman A-6 Intruder attack aircraft, as well as Grumman F-14 Tomcats.

A build-up of supplies and equipment at Barbados' Grantley Adams International Airport began. The airport was also used as a staging point for the invasion of Grenada, and several support aircraft were based there, particularly the AC-130 Spectre gunships of the 16th Special Operations Squadron of 1st Special Operations Wing (23rd Air Force).

Facing the US forces were 784 Cubans (of whom 44 were women and 636 were construction workers), all of whom had been given weapon training in Cuba and were competent shots. Colonel Pedro Tortoló Comas had arrived from Cuba on the day preceding the invasion, and was on hand to control the Cubans at Point Salines Airfield. There were certainly some 43 military personnel among the Cubans: one of them, Captain Sergio Grandales Nolasco—a 49-year-old transport and armoured vehicle expert—was killed in the subsequent fighting.

In addition to the Cubans, there was the 1000-strong Grenadan Regular Army under General Hudson Austin, and an indeterminate number of militia personnel. Vast stocks of ammunition and weapons were later found, as Austin had intended to increase the size of the Grenadan Army to some 10,000. Soviet-made armoured personnel carriers were also in evidence and the US Rangers later destroyed two such BTR-70s (armed with 14.5 mm machine-guns) at Point Salines airfield. As most of the Cubans were concentrated at Point Salines, much of the resistance met by the US forces was put up by the Grenadan regulars, militia, and other local troops.

The plan was for the invasion to begin with a covert operation, in which a USN SEAL team would secure the

Safely on the ground, soldiers of the 82nd Airborne Division prepare to move out in the direction of Grand Anse.

Governor-General's residence and ensure his safety. Point Salines was to be taken during the hours of darkness by the two battalions of the 75th Infantry Regiment in two waves: an initial parachute drop from MC-130s of the 23rd Air Force, followed by the rest of the regiment and the heavy equipment, which would be landed on the runway. AC-130 Spectre gunships were to give airborne fire support. As the Rangers were dropping in on Point Salines, 22 MAU was to be taken by helicopter to Pearls Airport on the western coast of the island, and launch a vertical assault. Once the airfields were secure, the Rangers were to take the True Blue campus of the St. George's University Medical School. Some 5000 men of the 82nd Airborne would then be flown in to Point Salines.

The Marines would take the militia barracks at Sauters, and would then be moved round to Grand Mal Bay, north of St. George's, while 82nd Airborne would secure the Grand Anse campus of the Medical School, to the south of the capital. The Americans would then have St. George's encircled, and could contemplate moving forward to occupy the town.

In the early hours of Tuesday morning, 25 October, the USN SEALs' detachment came ashore on the west coast of the island, just north of St. George's, and quickly moved surreptitiously across the kilometre or so that separated them from Government House, in the north-east part of the town. They had secured the house and made certain that Sir Paul Scoon was safe, when the furore caused by the Rangers' action at Point Salines alerted the defenders, and the SEALs found themselves pinned down at Government House by Grenadan fire. They were kept there until 07:45 the next day, when the Governor-General was evacuated by helicopter to the tactical headquarters of 22 MAU at Queen's Park stadium, and thence to the USS *Guam* for discussions with the Task Force Commander, Admiral Metcalf.

The Marines of 22 MAU were taken by helicopter to Pearls Airport at 05:00 local time on Tuesday, 25 October. They had a brief firefight with the Grenadan regulars operating some Soviet-made anti-aircraft guns, who were eventually overcome, but not before one of the helicopters had been hit.

The contingents from the 1st and 2nd Ranger Battalions of the 75th Infantry Regiment left the staging airfield at Barbados, in the early hours of Tuesday morning, in MC-130E aircraft of 8 Special Operations Squadron (23rd Air Force). The plan was to attack Point Salines airfield in two waves. The 1st Battalion (with a 12-man team of 317 Tactical Airlift Wing to supervise the drop) would jump from 300 m (1000 ft.) at 05:30 local time. Once the runway was secured, the 2nd Battalion would be landed with the heavy equipment. The men of the 2nd Battalion would drive off the aircraft in their gun-jeeps and occupy the hills surrounding the airfield.

As the first "stick" of 12 men went out over the dropping zone, the aircraft came under heavy anti-aircraft fire and the drop plans were aborted. This left the 12 Rangers floating down on their parachutes. The C-130s went round to come in at a lower altitude and put the Rangers out at only 150 m (500 ft.)—below the AA gunfire. This new situation was radioed to Lieutenant-Colonel Hagler (CO of 2/75th Infantry Regiment). The first 12 Rangers were by this time on the ground and fighting hard. The runway was obstructed by bulldozers and other obstacles, so that the aircraft could not land. Colonel Hagler decided that the 2nd Battalion would re-rig for a low-level jump and recover their jeeps once they had won the airfield.

The 1st Battalion men jumped at 150 m (500 ft.) to rejoin their embattled comrades on the ground. Meanwhile, the aircraft carrying the 2nd Battalion was circling above the airfield at high altitude, while the jeeps were hurriedly unloaded of their equipment. Organized chaos reigned way above the ground as rucksacks crammed with ammunition, mortar rounds, Claymore mines, light anti-armour weapons, water and food were repacked for a combat jump. Parachutes (no reserve—150 m is too low to do anything about a malfunction of the main parachute, other than pray) were put on, with all the problems of water wings, weapons storage, straps, helmets and so on, in the cramped conditions of the Hercules.

As the Rangers dropped over the runway, there was a possibility that they would under- or over-jump at either end, or even drift to the ocean side of the field, and land in the water. With their 50 kg (110 lb.) packs, this would be extremely hazardous. In fact, one Ranger did hit the water but, keeping his head, he allowed himself to sink to the bottom, where he released his gear. Calmly picking up his rifle and pack, he swam to the beach and waded ashore, none the worse for his experience!

AC-130H Spectre aircraft had been called in to deal with the searchlights and the anti-aircraft artillery. The Rangers took on two BTR-70 armoured personnel carriers, which were equipped with 14.5 mm machine-guns. Using 90 mm recoilless rifles, the Rangers managed to immobilize them, and then called up the Spectres to finish them off.

Ranger snipers killed several Cubans and, in another firefight, a Ranger medical orderly, Pfc Underdonk, killed a couple of Cubans and wounded some others. He then administered combat first aid to his victims, and was subsequently recommended for the Silver Star.

By 07:00 the Rangers were in complete control of the airfield. The Cuban military personnel who had been captured were separated from the other combatants. However, Colonel Tortoló and a few others managed to escape and spent some time looking for refuge in St. George's, eventually taking sanctuary in the Soviet embassy. The runway was speedily cleared, and at 07:15 the first C-130 landed, and several Sikorsky UH-60A Black Hawk helicopters were brought in. A rapid build-up of men and equipment from the 82nd Airborne Division began. Eventually, a total of some 5000 personnel from the 82nd was on the island.

The next objective was to bring out the medical students from the True Blue campus, which was at the eastern end of the Point Salines runway. At the time of the landing, there were only a few dozen students on the campus, and the majority of those who had not left the island on one of the charter flights the day before were being accommodated in a dormitory block, a couple of kilometres northeast on the St. George's road. In an air assault from Black Hawks, 2nd Battalion Rangers came down behind resisting forces and gave covering fire, while the students were emplaned and evacuated, and were then taken out themselves. The operation had begun at 08:30 and was over within 26 minutes.

During the day, AC-130H Spectres and Vought A-7 Corsair II aircraft from USS *Independence*, flown by US Navy and USMC Air Wing pilots, attacked targets and keypoints on the island. Some Spectre strikes were within only a few metres of US troops! One Ranger fire team was engaged in a firefight at night with a superior force across the road from their position. Their officer called in direct to a Spectre for an air strike and gave the coordinates. When told that the enemy was too close, he replied, "either you shoot them or else they will shoot us!" The Spectre aircraft fired its Gatling guns into the jungle right next to the fire team's position, killing the enemy.

The Navy and Marine A-7s attacked the barracks at Calvigny, on the east side of the island, and certain targets in and around St. George's. Just before midday, they attacked Fort Rupert, overlooking the entrance to St. George's harbour, destroying the anti-aircraft guns there and scattering their crews with rockets. Butler House, the Prime Minister's office, was hit a number of times and set on fire. As the continuing air strikes drove the fire brigade away, the building was allowed to burn itself out. There was one tragic case of a mistaken target: Fort Matthew (a mental hospital) was attacked in error, instead of the nearby Fort Frederick, and demolished. At least 30 patients were killed, and many inmates wandered dazedly around St. George's until rounded up and handed over to the General Hospital.

Whenever an aircraft flew overhead, the Grenadans would fire at it with any weapon to hand. In the middle of Tuesday afternoon, for example, an American helicopter was shot down on the Tanteen field on the other side of the harbour entrance from Fort Rupert, and the pilot was killed. That day, aircraft also attacked the Sauteurs Militia Base at the northern tip of the island, and 22 MAU later captured the base.

The paratroops of 82nd Airborne moved north from Point Salines to close in on the Grand Anse campus of the university in order to free the students staying there. Just before last light on Wednesday, 26 October, men of 82nd Airborne took the campus in an action preceded by attacks from helicopter gunships and Spectres. The 82nd men guarded the students while resistance at Radio Free Grenada was overcome, then loaded the students on to helicopters bound for Point Salines.

In the early hours of the same morning, 26 October, the Marines had been flown around the island to land at Grand Mal Bay, north of St. George's, at 04:00. Their disembarkation point was only a few hundred metres north of the city limits, and Colonel Smith, in charge of 22 MAU, established his tactical headquarters at Queen's Park Stadium. Heavy equipment, including M60 Patton main battle tanks, was brought ashore, and three of these tanks were stationed on the St. George's road. At 07:45, 22 MAU received the Governor-General and took over his security from the USN SEALs. The aerial bombardment and the numbers of troops surrounding the capital seemed to convince the resisters within St. George's to give up, and the city was secured with little more trouble.

That afternoon, 22 MAU Marines climbed up Morne Jaloux ridge to capture Fort Frederick and the Richmond Hill Prison. At about the same time, 60 Rangers of the 2/75th Infantry Regiment were taken around to the east of the island in a trio of Sikorsky UH-60A Black Hawk helicopters to mop up at Calvigny Barracks.

As the Black Hawks finished the 8 km (5 mile) flight they came under fire from a heavy-calibre machine-gun. The first helicopter had just landed and the Rangers were getting out; the pilot of the second helicopter was killed by the gunfire; his chopper crashed into the first one, and Rangers were spilled out of the wreckage. One man was hit by the spinning rotor blades and died instantly. The opposition's fire was concentrated on the landing zone, and the last Black Hawk made a bad touchdown.

The uninjured Rangers attacked the defenders and provided covering fire for the wounded. Sergeant Stephen Trujillo, who had Special Forces medical training, stayed to treat the injured. Using the SF's advanced paramedical techniques, he treated Lieutenant William Eskridge, who was bleeding heavily from a leg wound, and, although the officer eventually lost a leg, Sergeant Trujillo had saved his life. Trujillo was awarded the Silver Star for his actions in aiding the injured. Eventually the defenders were subdued and rounded up, and the Calvigny Barracks were secure.

Although there was much criticism of the American action in Grenada, the Grenadans themselves were mostly delighted to have been saved from a deteriorating situation. The invasion also gave a boost to flagging American morale following recent events in the Middle East. On the Sunday before the invasion was launched, at 02:27, Washington had received news of the bombing of the US Marines' headquarters in Beirut, with many dead and injured. The Grenadan operation restored confidence after the failure of Operation "Eagle Claw," and seemed to show that the freeing of the crew of the SS *Mayaguez* was not just a flash in the pan. It was also an operation in which nearly all the US élite forces from the Army, Navy, Marines and Air Force were involved, under the control of the Joint Special Operations Command, and they cooperated well together. This success seems to have been the spark which led to the formation of the Joint Special Operations Agency at the Pentagon on 1 January 1984.

IV

THE COMMONWEALTH & SOUTH AFRICA

THE AUSTRALIAN SPECIAL AIR SERVICE REGIMENT • THE CANADIAN MOBILE COMMAND • THE RHODESIAN SPECIAL AIR SERVICE, SELOUS SCOUTS AND GREY'S SCOUTS • SOUTH AFRICAN SPECIAL SERVICES • THE NEW ZEALAND SPECIAL AIR SERVICE

Although it may be old-fashioned to talk about the British Commonwealth, it seemed appropriate to group together the special forces of those countries which have always maintained a special relationship with the "old country," no matter how far politics and politicians may have strained this relationship in recent years.

In the international sphere, Australia and New Zealand have been far more active than the other three countries considered, their Special Air Service troops being modelled on British lines and being largely British trained following joint experiences in Korea and Malaya. Both countries also contributed forces to the futile war in Vietnam, adding to the knowledge and expertise which their SAS veterans have been able to share with others. Canada has retreated into isolationism under the American umbrella ever since Korea, and her special forces have none of the Australian, British or New Zealand experience of counter-insurgency warfare, apart from the brief affray with Québécois separatists in 1970. Rhodesia, now Zimbabwe, in contrast, has the greatest experience in this type of campaigning, while South Africa is readying itself—while pretending not to—for the inevitable conflict to come.

The Australian Special Air Service Regiment

By the time the Australians began pulling out of their involvement in Vietnam in 1970, the 3rd Special Air Service Squadron had killed more than 500 Vietcong guerrillas for the loss of only one man. Introduced into Vietnam as part of the Australian Task Force reinforcement in 1966, for nearly five years this special jungle-trained unit helped first to secure and then to protect, the whole of the Phuoc Tuy province east of Saigon. In fact, they were so successful that General Westmoreland, overall commander of the Allied forces in Vietnam, requested the assistance of the Australian SAS in setting up special training camps for American soldiers with the aim of providing each American brigade or division with at least one long-range patrol company versed in these effective Australian tactics. What makes this surprising is the fact that the Australian Special Air Service Regiment had only recently been formed, fol-

A Centurion tank and M113 armoured personnel carrier of the Australian Regiment during operations in Vietnam.

lowing Australian observation of the triumphs of British SAS and SBS units, alongside whom they fought in Malaya and Indonesia.

Since Gallipoli in 1915, the Australian Army has always had a reputation for toughness and endurance in adversity which is second to none. During World War 2, particularly in the Western Desert and in Italy, the Germans had come to respect the Australian infantryman above all others for his doggedness and tenacity, and these same qualities were ably demonstrated in Korea.

In Malaya, the Australians contributed 3000 men in support of the 50,000 British, Gurkha and Malayan regulars who were fighting the communists. (It is ironic that these same communist guerrillas had originally been armed and trained by the British during World War 2 to fight against the Japanese invaders.) In Malaya, the three reinforced battalions of The Australian Regiment learned a great deal from the tactics of the British special forces. In particular, they learned a lesson which neither the French nor the Americans in Vietnam ever seemed to understand: that in a campaign of this type it is necessary not merely to defeat a guerrilla army in the field, but that in some ways it is even more important to win over the hearts and minds of the local civilian populace so that they will refuse to hide or support the terrorists.

This knowledge proved vital in Indonesia when President Soekarno tried to "liberate" the Dutch East Indies and what had been British North Borneo. Indonesian troops would frequently disguise themselves as innocent farmers or fishermen in their attempts to infiltrate behind the Australian and British lines, and the Allies' persistence in feeding, clothing and educating the local population, in providing them with medical centres, schools, roads and bridges, meant that the inhabitants of the threatened provinces would usually deny the Indonesians shelter at the least, and give them away to Australian or British patrols at the best. Even had Soekarno not been overthrown by a Muslim junta which called off the campaign, it is likely that Allied tactics would, in any case, have provided the same ultimate end to the conflict as in Malaya.

The Australians entered Vietnam reluctantly, and to begin with provided just 30 advisers to help train the Army of the Republic of Vietnam (ARVN) but, by the time they withdrew, the strength of the Australian contingent had grown to over 8000 infantrymen, aircrew and warship crewmen. The original 30 advisers gradually increased in number to 100, and their training activities were stepped up to a point where Australian officers and NCOs would lead South Vietnamese offensive patrols in search-and-destroy operations against the Vietcong.

Four Victoria Crosses

Warrant Officer K. A. Wheatley was just one of four members of the Australian Army Training Team to win the

Victoria Cross in Vietnam. Like the rest of the soldiers in the team, which included several other SAS men, Wheatley had been selected from the toughest and most experienced veterans of Korea, Malaya and Indonesia, and was a professional soldier through and through. On 13 November 1965 he was part of a company-sized patrol of Vietnamese Civil Irregulars commanded by Captain F. Fazekas, another Australian adviser. Wheatley was in the right-hand platoon, together with Warrant Officer Swanton, as the patrol marched from the Tra Bong Special Forces camp down the Tra Bong valley. They had not gone far, and were walking across open rice paddies, when Wheatley's platoon came under heavy fire from concealed Vietcong positions. He sent a radio message to Captain Fazekas, whose own platoon in the centre of the company was still forcing its way through the jungle towards the rice fields.

The heavily outnumbered Australians and Vietnamese Irregulars continued to fire back at the unseen enemy in the jungle on the other side of the paddy fields, but then Warrant Officer Swanton was hit and the Irregulars fled. Left on his own, apart from the dying Swanton and one Vietnamese soldier, Dinh Do, Wheatley asked Fazekas to call an air strike on the Vietcong positions; then, abandoning the radio, he picked up Swanton's inert body and began to struggle back towards the safety of the jungle from which the platoon had emerged. Dinh Do urged him to leave Swanton but Wheatley refused, so the Vietnamese Private took to his heels. By this time the Vietcong had emerged from the jungle on the other side of the clearing and were running to encircle Wheatley. Laying Swanton's body on the ground, he primed two hand grenades and stood over his friend, calmly awaiting the enemy. Moments later, Captain Fazekas heard the sound of two explosions. In staying with his dying comrade, Wheatley had deliberately sacrificed himself, and the citation to his Victoria Cross stated: "His acts of heroism, determination and unflinching

WEAPONS OF THE COMMONWEALTH ELITE FORCES

Designation	Type	Calibre	Magazine	Rate of fire	Range	Remarks
L9A1	Browning automatic pistol	9 mm	13 rounds	Single-shot	40 m	
L1A1	Self-loading rifle	7.62 mm	20 or 30 rounds	40 rpm	600 m	The Belgian FN FAL
Parker Hale	Sniper rifle	7.62 mm	Single-shot	Single-shot	1000 m+	Australia only
F1	Sub-machine-gun	9 mm	34 rounds	640 rpm cyclic	100 m	
M3	Browning sub-machine-gun	0.45 in	30 rounds	450 rpm cyclic	100 m	
Uzi	Sub-machine-gun	9 mm	25 or 32 rounds	600 rpm cyclic	100 m	Israeli-made; Australia and South Africa
BXP	Sub-machine-gun	9 mm	22 or 32 rounds	800 rpm cyclic	100 m	South Africa
Galil RAM	Assault rifle	5.56 mm	35 or 50 rounds	650 rpm cyclic	400 m	South Africa only
M16A1	Armalite assault rifle	5.56 mm	20 or 30 rounds	700–950 rpm cyclic	400 m	
L2A3	Sterling sub-machine-gun	9 mm	34 rounds	550 rpm cyclic	200 m	Particularly favoured in Canada
L4A4	Light machine-gun	7.62 mm	30 rounds	500–575 rpm cyclic	800 m	New Zealand and Zimbabwe

courage in the face of the enemy will always stand as examples of the true meaning of valour."

The Australians' use of small patrols in Vietnam, living off the land for up to a fortnight at a time, paid dividends when compared with the more conventional American tactics. Dropped by helicopter deep behind Vietcong lines, the men of the 3rd Special Air Service Squadron, in particular, created havoc. Although good soldiers when they controlled the situation, the Vietcong were basically lazy, and their discipline became slack when they felt themselves safe from observation. SAS patrols often caught them unawares in their base camps, where they carelessly lit cooking fires and became drunk and rowdy on rice wine and native beer. Sentries were rarely posted, and the Australians were often able to creep silently through the dark

Designation	Type	Calibre	Magazine	Rate of fire	Range	Remarks
M1919A4	Machine-gun	7.62 mm	250-round belt	400–500 rpm cyclic	1000 m	Canada only
FN MAG	Machine-gun	7.62 mm	100-round belt	600–1000 rpm cyclic	1200 m	New Zealand, Zimbabwe
M60	Machine-gun	7.62 mm	100-round belt	550 rpm cyclic	1000 m	Australia
M2HB	Machine-gun	0.5 in	50-round belt	450–600 rpm cyclic	1500 m	South Africa
2 in mortar	Light mortar	2 in	Single-shot	15 rpm	800 m	New Zealand, Zimbabwe
L16A1	Mortar	81 mm	Single-shot	15 rpm	5800 m	
ENTAC	Anti-tank missile	60 mm	Single-shot	Not applicable	800 m	Australia only; obsolescent
L1A1	Anti-tank missile	66 mm	Single-shot	Not applicable	300 m	Canada only
Carl Gustav	Anti-tank missile	84 mm	Single-shot	4–6 rpm	1100 m	Canada only
Redeye	Anti-aircraft missile	70 mm	Single-shot	Not available	Not available	Australia only
Blowpipe	Anti-aircraft missile	76.2 mm	Single-shot	Not available	3000 m+	Canada only

(Most Commonwealth nations use much the same weapons, but where an entry is applicable only to one country this is indicated in the remarks column.)

jungle to encircle an encampment without being observed. Then they would open up with their Bren guns to send the Vietcong into a state of pandemonium. In the face of such an attack, most of the guerrillas would attempt to flee into the jungle, where many were caught by the patiently waiting SAS men standing motionless behind rubber trees. Then, when the guerrillas had either all been killed or had fled, the SAS could move in to destroy the camp, being careful to watch out for booby traps and the cunningly concealed pits which the Vietcong had dug, their bottoms lined with sharpened stakes smeared with human excrement to cause wounds to fester and septicaemia to set in.

It was a lonely, dangerous and demanding war—both mentally and physically—for the SAS patrols, particularly during the monsoon season, when it was impossible to keep anything dry, when the humidity sapped strength and willpower, and when skin diseases and leeches were prevalent. However, the SAS had a demoralizing effect on the enemy, who were frequently astonished to see a squadron of Phantom or Skyhawk fighter-bombers materializing out of nowhere to blast with rockets and napalm a concealed encampment which the Vietcong troops had thought hidden and inviolate.

The SAS patrols also brought back much vital information on Vietcong dispositions and strengths to assist in the planning of major American offensives, many of which failed even then because, by the time the Americans, with their large numbers of men and noisy tanks and other vehicles, reached their objective, the Vietcong could easily have slipped away into the jungle.

The Australian SAS today

Organized and trained in exactly the same way as is the British SAS, in four squadrons, the Australian Special Air Service Regiment is an élite unit which, with Aussie nonchalance, does not regard itself as an élite. Its men are all volunteers from other regiments in the Australian Army, particularly from The Australian Regiment which, although composed of one-third national-service conscripts, maintained the nation's reputation for producing tough soldiers in many operations in Vietnam.

Amphibious and jungle operations obviously form a much greater part of the Australian SAS's training than they do for its British counterparts, because in time of global war it would be committed to ANZUS, the mutual defence pact between Australia, New Zealand and the United States, and the theatre of operations would be the islands of Australasia and the mainland of Malaysia, Indo-China, Korea and China. The men are well experienced and equipped for this role, but they also have other duties in the counter-terrorist task. The Philippines, Japan and Korea are also members of ANZUS, and Australian SAS advisers are on call to all three countries to help cope with hijackings and other terrorist threats.

In fact, the main role of the whole Australian Army today can largely be seen as one of counter-insurgency. Since 1972, when its strength was reduced from 32,000 men in three divisions, each of five battle groups plus a support group, to the present single division of six infantry battalions, one armoured and two mechanized infantry regiments, four artillery regiments, two signals regiments and other supporting services, the Australian Army has only a minor role to play in a global context.

The Army is organized along British lines, and volunteers, who train at Duntroon or Portsea, Victoria, serve for an initial period of six years. However, as in World Wars 1 and 2, one can be assured that Australian recruiting stations would be full if any major international emergency arose.

The Canadian Mobile Command

Canadian armed forces have not seen action since Korea, when a brigade was committed to help staunch the communist offensive and, particularly since the country opted for unilateral nuclear disarmament, there has been a steady run-down of Canadian military power until, today, the entire Army consists of only 18,000 regulars and 15,000 reservists. This force is extremely stretched, both physically and financially, and is devoted solely to internal defence, with the exception of the 3000 men of the Mechanized Brigade Group Europe based at Baden-Söllingen in Germany. Canada is also committed to the United Nations peace-keeping role, and one air-mobile battalion of the Airborne Regiment, based at Edmonton, Alberta, is on permanent 12-hour standby.

Mobile Command comprises three brigade groups, of

which one is airborne, each consisting of two or three infantry battalions plus light armoured and artillery regiments, and support services.

As with all the Canadian forces, the Airborne Regiment is composed of both English- and French-speaking soldiers, and consists of the *1er Commando Aéroporté*, the 2nd Airborne Commando, and the 1st Airborne Battery of 105 mm air-portable guns. Each of the Commandos is of approximately battalion size (600–700 men) and would be taken into action by transport and attack helicopters.

Canadian troops are extremely well trained in mountain and arctic warfare techniques as well as mountain search and rescue operations, and they have acted on several occasions as peace-keeping forces under United Nations auspices in Egypt, the Congo, Kashmir, Cyprus and Lebanon, wearing the UN's blue beret.

The Rhodesian Special Air Service, Selous Scouts and Grey's Scouts

From the time that Ian Smith made his unilateral declaration of independence (UDI) in 1965 and took Rhodesia out of the British Commonwealth, until the creation of the modern state of Zimbabwe in 1979–80, the country suffered from one of the worst internal struggles in history. Black nationalism had been particularly prevalent in southern Africa ever since 1959, when Northern Rhodesia was granted independence as Zambia, and from 1960 black insurgents mounted an escalating campaign of terror against Rhodesian whites which eventually resulted in the country being carved up into a string of armed fortresses. In the early days, the terrorist attacks and incidents were relatively mild, ranging from communist-incited riots in African townships to petrol-bomb attacks on government offices. Although there were also several murders, of both blacks and whites, the Rhodesian police succeeded in containing the incidents until 1965 and UDI.

By this time, the Russian- and Chinese-trained African nationalist guerrillas, armed with Eastern Bloc weapons, were becoming more organized, and Ian Smith's declaration lit the fuse to a powder keg of violence. Terrorists slipped across Rhodesia's borders by night and infiltrated into the black townships on sabotage and murder missions, but their attempts at achieving really spectacular successes, such as blowing up the Kariba power lines or the oil pipeline from Mozambique, were foiled, largely due to the efforts of the Rhodesian Special Air Service Regiment.

Comprising three squadrons, each of 60 white men, and organized and trained along British lines, the Rhodesian SAS played much the same role as does the British SAS in Northern Ireland, particularly in information-gathering, surveillance and the laying of ambushes. In these duties, the SAS was ably helped by the élite Selous Scouts, a mixed force of more than 1000 blacks and whites, and by the smaller force of horsemen in Grey's Scouts. Like so many other military formations in southern Africa, the origins of these two units date back to the Zulu and Boer Wars, and the Selous Scouts in particular were adept at tracking and "hot pursuit" tactics, chasing and running down terrorists even across the borders into neighbouring African countries. While the Rhodesian SAS was recruited exclusively from white Rhodesian Army units—the élite Rhodesian Light Infantry, for example—the Selous Scouts employed a mixture of blacks and whites from all walks of life, including numerous mercenaries from Europe and North America. They were commanded by Lieutenant-Colonel Ron Reid-Daly who had fought earlier with the British SAS in Malaya. Grey's Scouts never amounted to more than a quarter the strength of the Selous Scouts, some

250–300 men, but they were all first-class horsemen and were mainly employed on border patrol work, riding up and down the barbed wire fences protecting Rhodesia's borders and looking for signs of terrorist intruders.

As the terrorist campaign mounted in intensity, the need for men trained in counter-insurgency work increased, and the Rhodesian Army eventually became the most skilled in the world in this field, with the possible exception of the British Army in Northern Ireland. South Africa sent military assistance in 1968, and for a few months it seemed as though the terrorists had been beaten back outside Rhodesia's borders (a lull which happened to coincide with Ian Smith's referendum on UDI, and which may have contributed to its result). In 1970, however, the intrusions resumed, many whites being killed during an attack on Chisuma police camp, although an attempt to sabotage the main railway line from Salisbury to South Africa was foiled.

By 1973, the terrorists were stepping up their campaign even further, and were now organized in commandos of up to 100 men armed with modern Soviet automatic weapons, rocket launchers, mortars and grenades. Their favourite tactics were hit-and-run assaults on isolated farmhouses and rural police stations, after which they would disappear back into the bush. The Selous Scouts, on permanent alert, could usually be at the scene of an incident within half an hour and, using helicopters as well as skilled native trackers, proved very successful at bringing such groups to ground. Even so, there were casualties.

A typical hit-and-run incident

Robin "Brown" was a relative newcomer to the Scouts and was out on his first bush training exercise when the terrorists struck. The patrol, under the command of a veteran

Sergeant-Major, had been dropped by truck deep in the
bush and the men had been marching for seven hours.
There had already been one mock attack from two Bren
guns which suddenly opened fire, sending the recruits
sprawling to the ground before they realized that the Sergeant-Major was still standing, and the men had practised
their own marksmanship on targets concealed in the scrub
which suddenly sprang up when activated by the Sergeant.
By 17:00 the six trainees in the patrol were hot, tired, foot-
sore, thirsty, and barely aware of their surroundings as they
stumbled along under the Sergeant's baleful eye. As they
sank gratefully to the ground for a brief rest, the men did
not realize that they were under observation from a nearby
kopje by two blacks, both armed with Kalashnikov AK-47
assault rifles, who had been attracted by the earlier firing.
The terrorists could not resist a sitting target and opened
fire from a distance of less than 50 m (55 yd.). To begin
with, Robin did not react, thinking that it was another exercise like the one which had scared him in the morning.
Then he noticed that the Sergeant-Major had crumpled to
the ground, a red stain spreading across his thin bush shirt.
Another man screamed, tried to run, was hit, stumbled,
was hit again, and also fell. Robin and the remaining four
Scouts fell prone and began firing their 7.62 mm FN rifles
at the rocky outcrop. Being untrained, the men soon exhausted the four magazines of ammunition each carried,
and would have been easy targets for the terrorists had the
two blacks not already slipped away. Too late, a Gazelle
helicopter, which had been sent to pick up the patrol, arrived on the scene. However, it raced off after the terrorists
and succeeded in catching and mowing one down with the
pintle-mounted machine-gun in the open helicopter door.

In 1975, South Africa withdrew military support from
Rhodesia, and the terrorist attacks intensified still further.
Black nationalist sympathizers also began infiltrating Rho-

desia from Mozambique and Botswana for the first time, and the Smith government set up four regional military commands to try to contain the situation—"Tangent" on the Botswana front, "Repulse" with responsibility for the Port Victoria area and the vital rail link to South Africa, "Thrasher" in the eastern highlands, and "Hurricane" at Bindura in the north. However, despite these efforts, the rapidly combining groups of freedom fighters were becoming so strong that the border areas of Rhodesia began to resemble World War 1 battlefields, with fortified block-houses and farms protected by barbed wire fences, minefields, searchlights, electronic warning devices and machine-guns, while civilians wishing to travel more than a few miles did so in convoys under the protection of heavily armed armoured cars and personnel carriers.

The regime could not last, nor did it, despite all the efforts of the élite forces (among which one should really include the paramilitary Police Anti-Terrorist Units, or PATU, formed from volunteers in the British South Africa Police, which operated for weeks at a time in the border areas on intelligence-gathering and infiltration missions), and ultimately the Smith regime had to fall, to be replaced by a black democracy which is still finding its feet.

South African Special Services

Little is said in public about the crack quick-reaction and counter-insurgency forces of South Africa, which today has one of the largest armies in the Western world, comprising some 18,000 regulars and 60,000 national servicemen, plus 130,000 members of the Citizen Force and 110,000 men in the Commandos. (The latter, although today basically a "home guard," maintain their original Boer names and traditions. There are ten Commandos in all, most bearing famous names such as Wynberg or Tugela, and their role is much the same as that of the UDR in Northern Ireland.)

Because of the country's schizophrenic politics, all white males are subject to conscription, but all blacks and Indians in the armed forces have to be volunteers. Moreover, the units themselves are segregated by the controversial policy of apartheid, blacks and Indians serving in the separately administered Cape Corps. Needless to say, there are not many volunteers for the latter.

The mainstay of South Africa's counter-insurgency forces, many of whose members have direct experience of fighting against terrorists in Rhodesia, are the 1st Parachute Battalion and Tank Squadron, and 1st Special Service Brigade, which are based at Bloemfontein and fall under the Orange Free State Command, plus the Parachute Commando based at Kroonstat. Since the Sharpeville crisis in 1960, which made the Republican National Party realize

A Grey's Scout checks his weapons before moving off on patrol.

for the first time the very real threat from black African nationalism, the South African special forces have been fighting a rearguard action against the inevitable.

Although the government has always claimed to have a vital role to play in the defence of the West by providing a second Gibraltar between the Atlantic and Indian Oceans, thereby keeping open the sea lanes from Europe to Australia and New Zealand, the argument rings hollow when one considers that over two-thirds of South Africa's army is dedicated to preserving internal order rather than to any possible external obligations. Moreover, since 1963 South Africa has been subject to a United Nations arms embargo (made mandatory in 1977 but still flouted by France and other countries). This has restricted progress in the Army's acquisition of modern battlefield weapons, although, since it was established in 1969, the Armaments Development and Production Corporation of South Africa (ARMSCOR) has made great strides in the design and development of armoured vehicles intended for counter-insurgency operations and manufactures under licence many small-arms of European origin.

The New Zealand Special Air Service

Although isolated geographically, New Zealand's tiny standing army of 5500 regulars (supported by 6000 territorials and 1500 reservists) is one of the best-trained, most experienced and most capable of rapid deployment in the world. Like the Australians, New Zealand troops have long been known for their fighting quality, a reputation which was upheld during World War 2 at the battles of El Alamein and Monte Cassino, to name just two of the most significant. Since World War 2, the New Zealand Army has taken an active part in the counter-insurgency campaigns in Malaya, fought bravely in Korea, and even contributed a token force of 550 men to the support of the Australians in Vietnam. Here, the two squadrons of the NZ Special Air Service Battalion proved as adept as their Australian counterparts in dealing with the enemy on his own terms—and small wonder, for New Zealand does not maintain a military academy of her own, so all her officers are trained either at Sandhurst or at Duntroon.

New Zealand abolished conscription in 1973 and since then has severely curtailed her military commitments, although she has maintained a battalion-strength garrison in Singapore under the terms of the 1971 Five Power Defence Arrangement which has been abandoned by both Australia and Britain, and continues to adhere to other defence agreements with Indonesia, New Guinea, Fiji and Tonga. Other than this, New Zealand is still a signatory of SEATO, the South-East Asia Treaty Organization, and contributes troops to United Nations' peace-keeping missions, but is otherwise primarily concerned with the defence of her own long and rugged coastline from infiltration or attack, and with protecting the sealanes which are so vital to her economy.

V

WESTERN EUROPE

FRANCE: THE 2ND PARACHUTE REGIMENT OF THE FOREIGN LEGION • HOLLAND: THE ROYAL NETHERLANDS MARINE COMMANDOS • WEST GERMANY: GSG 9

As the forces of international terrorism flexed their muscles during the 1970s, the governments of France, Holland and West Germany began training military and paramilitary units to counteract this new menace. The Olympic Games murders in Munich in 1972 shocked the world, while the Israelis' success at Entebbe gave inspiration.

The French Foreign Legion has, of course, always been one of the toughest of all fighting forces, and the establishment of parachute units which trained alongside the fledgling British airborne forces during World War 2 produced a new élite within an élite. From Indo-China to Algeria, the men of the *2ᵉ Régiment Etranger Parachutiste* acquired a reputation for courage and skill in adversity second to none, and their training and experience proved invaluable in May 1978, when they parachuted into the little mining town of Kolwezi, in Zaïre, to rescue technicians and their families from a bloodthirsty group of Katangese rebels.

Earlier, in 1975, Dutch Marines had rescued hostages from a train which had been hijacked by South Moluccan extremists, while in 1977 the élite West German commandos of GSG 9 had successfully emulated the Israeli action at Entebbe, freeing the passengers of a hijacked Boeing 737 from Red Army fanatics who were demanding the release of prisoners in a German jail.

What all three countries—as well as Britain—have clearly demonstrated is a determination, which must be maintained, not to give in to terrorism in any way, shape or form. If terrorists know that their demands will not be met, and that the best they can hope for is their own deaths, then they will have to pause for thought.

THE FRENCH FOREIGN LEGION

At about 15:15 on 19 May 1978, in a sweltering bungalow where he had been hiding with his family for the past six days, an Italian mineworker named Rafaello Rubeis thought he heard the sound of heavy aircraft engines. He crept to the window and peered at the western sky, taking care not to show himself to the wandering gunmen who had subjected this little mining town of Kolwezi, in Zaïre's Shaba Province, to a reign of terror ever since they had burst from the bush at dawn on the 13th. The whistling roar in the sky grew louder and, as Rafaello peered at the strip of sky visible at the top of his window, the silhouette of a C-130 Hercules transport aircraft floated slowly into

view, only about 200 m (600 ft.) above the shanty roofs of
the native Old Town. The transport's doors were open, and
a long line of green parachutes was blossoming across the
sky behind the aircraft. Rafaello snatched up a camera and
took a hasty photograph: he wanted to remember this moment, when his life had been handed back to him after he
had despaired of ever leaving the town alive.

The gift came by courtesy of the legionnaires of the *2e
Régiment Etranger Parachutiste* (REP)—France's 2nd Foreign Parachute Regiment: one of the crack "fast-reaction"
units of the French Army, and one of the most formidable
fighting regiments in the world.

The Legion takes to the air

The French Foreign Legion, swollen by a flood of recruits
from a ravaged Europe in the years immediately after
World War 2, played a major part in France's war against
the Communist Viet Minh in Indo-China between 1946 and
1954. As the conflict grew in intensity, and guerrilla attacks flared all over France's colonies in Vietnam, the
150,000-man Expeditionary Force of French, Arab, and
Foreign Legion troops was spread dangerously thin. Most
of them were tied down in small garrisons, scattered up
and down the network of roads and towns, which inade-
quately controlled a vast, wild land of jungle, mountain
and swamp. In such wars the advantage always lies with
the elusive guerrilla bands, who can pick their time and
place to fight, and melt away into the bush before the security forces can bring their superior firepower to the
threatened sector along the few, easily ambushed roads.

In this kind of fighting mobility is everything; and
France, desperately short of troops capable of forming a
mobile reserve to take the war into enemy-held country,
soon began to pin her hopes on the possibility of "vertical

envelopment"—the paratrooper's unique ability to drop right into a battle without first slogging through swamps, scrambling up mountain ridges or fighting his way along mined and ambushed roads. Although always short of transport aircraft to drop and re-supply the paratroopers, the French command began to build up a precious reserve of airborne troops, to use both as a "fire brigade" for stamping out sudden Viet Minh initiatives, and as a weapon of sudden attack when enemy refuges in the mountain jungles were identified. In April 1948, the 3rd Foreign Infantry Regiment of the Legion, rich in wartime veterans including a number of former German paras, formed an experimental "integral parachute company." Operating with a battalion of French paras, the company proved itself a success. Shortly afterwards, a parachute school was established near the Legion's Algerian head-quarters at Sidi-bel-Abbès, and in November 1948 the 1st Foreign Parachute Battalion—*1er Bataillon Etranger Parachutiste* (BEP)—arrived in the Far East. It was soon followed by the 2e BEP. The para company of the *3e Régiment Etranger d'Infanterie* (REI) was absorbed by the 1er BEP, and a third battalion was formed and retained in Algeria, acting as a pool for training the replacements for the two units in Vietnam.

For the next five years, both of the Legion para units were heavily committed to the increasingly savage war in Vietnam. Thanks to Chinese support, the Viet Minh's General Giap was able to build up his forces from scattered guerrilla bands into large and well-equipped units able to face the French in pitched battle. The fighting grew in scope and intensity. Given their special capability and role, it was inevitable that the paras would often be dropped in an attempt to save already disastrous situations: their casualties were commensurately high. Jumping over appallingly rough drop zones in thick forest or on to the tops of precipitous cliffs, against an enemy of unknown but usually far greater strength, with little hope of serious support unless they could fight their way through to a major road, the paras fought like tigers—but paid a heavy price.

In September and October 1950 the French suffered a disastrous defeat on the Cao Bang ridge, which runs along the northern edge of Tonkin immediately south of the Chinese border. The French garrisons were pulled out, and began a retreat along the single road through the jungled cliffs. They were ambushed by the Viet Minh in massive strength—as were their would-be rescuers, pushing up Route Coloniale 4 to meet them. Both columns were virtually annihilated; among several battalions wiped out were the 1er BEP, and Giap captured enough weapons to equip a division.

With the Communist Chinese border now open to them, the Viet Minh enjoyed safe refuge, training camps, and a steady flow of weapons. Soon Giap had a force of some half-a-dozen conventional divisions of about 10,000 men each, with modern small-arms, plentiful machine-guns, mortars, and heavy artillery support. The war moved towards its climax. Some of Giap's early attempts to fight pitched battles were premature, and he suffered costly reverses at the hands of paras, legionnaires, tanks, artillery and French air power; but he learned from his mistakes.

Encouraged by their success at Na San, a fortified camp reinforced, supplied and supported entirely from the air, the French command planted a much more ambitious "airhead" in the valley of Dien Bien Phu in late 1953. Far behind Viet lines, and surrounded by hills, 11,000 French Union infantry, paras, artillery and tank men in inadequate entrenchments were soon surrounded by 50,000 Viet Minh, backed up by some 200 well-camouflaged artillery pieces and strong anti-aircraft batteries. The trap closed on 13 March 1954, with a shattering artillery barrage. For two months the French garrison clung on, in one of the epic defences of modern warfare. Among the original garrison were the legionnaires of the 1er BEP, and their sister battalion was parachuted into the shrinking perimeter to reinforce them during the battle. By the end of the siege, in early May, the few survivors of the 1er and 2^e BEP were fighting in a small, composite battalion. They resisted like heroes, but the cause was hopeless. On 8 May 1954 Dien Bien Phu fell; three months later France had signed a cease-fire, and was pulling out of her Asian colonies.

The agony of Algeria

The mauled survivors returned to the Legion's adopted homeland of Algeria in time to be pitch-forked straight into another bloody guerrilla war. Retitled the 1st and 2nd Foreign Parachute Regiments (*Régiment Etranger Parachutiste*), and brought up to strength with new recruits and transfers from other units, the two green-beret regiments saw almost continuous active operations between 1955 and 1961. They became famous as two of the most effective units of the French mobile reserve—but the 1er REP also became tainted with a reputation for brutal interrogation of suspects, which clung to the whole 10th Parachute Division, after its ruthless crushing of the Algerian liberation ALN terrorist network in Algiers city in 1957.

Parachute drops played no major part in the Algerian War. The airborne units would be inserted into the harsh mountains of the interior, by helicopter or simply by truck, after an ALN unit had been spotted. Then they would take off after the enemy on foot, setting a killing pace despite the scorching heat of summer or the freezing snows of winter, while the French command used air reconnaissance and radio to weave a net around the guerrillas. The Legion paras usually ran their quarry to earth: by the end of the war in 1962 the 2ᵉ REP had recorded 4000 enemy killed, for a loss of 598 legionnaires. This impressive combat record made all the more inevitable and tragic the traumatic episode which accompanied the end of the war.

Humiliated in 1940, and defeated despite heroic sacrifices in Vietnam, the French Army had been determined not to lose again in Algeria. And they had not: Algeria was a military victory. The ALN never achieved the formation of large, conventional units in the Viet Minh tradition. The soldiers they trained in camps in Morocco and Tunisia never managed to penetrate the effective French frontier defences in any numbers. The guerrillas were limited, by 1960, to the same furtive raids and dispersed hide-outs in the mountains that had characterized the outbreak of rebellion in 1954. Nevertheless, President de Gaulle knew that France had to go with the tide of history. The time for colonies was past, and the military successes, won with such effort, merely gave him strong bargaining counters in the negotiations over Algerian independence. The pride of the army, the future of the large white settler community, and the lives of the Algerians who had stayed loyal to the mother country, must all be sacrificed to extricate France from a position she could not maintain in the long term.

When it became clear, in 1960, that France was going to abandon her colony, the men of the Foreign Legion were faced with an agonizing choice. The corps had been raised in 1831 specifically to fight in Algeria, and had played a major role in the colony's history ever since. Without Algeria where would they go? What would be the justification for their existence? Cheated of what they felt to be their just rewards, some of the finest units in the French Army collapsed in mutiny. The 1st Foreign Parachute Regiment, wiped out twice in four years in the service of the Republic, now spearheaded the coup led by four generals in April 1961. It was an almost bloodless episode. The re-

WEAPONS OF THE PRINCIPAL EUROPEAN ÉLITE FORCES

Designation	Type	Calibre	Magazine	Rate of fire	Range	Remarks
Automatic pistol	Browning	9 mm	13 rounds	Single-shot	40 m	
Automatic pistol	Walther PP	7.65 mm	8 rounds	Single-shot	40 m	
M3	Browning sub-machine-gun	0.45 in	30 rounds	450 rpm cyclic	100 m	Holland only
Uzi	Sub-machine-gun	9 mm	25 or 32 rounds	600 rpm cyclic	100 m	West Germany and Holland
FAMAS	Individual weapon	5.56 mm	25 rounds	950 rpm cyclic	400 m	France only
MP5	Heckler and Koch sub-machine-gun	9 mm	15 or 30 rounds	800 rpm cyclic	200 m	
G3	Heckler and Koch assault rifle	7.62 mm	20 rounds	500–600 rpm cyclic	400 m	
FR-F1	Sniper rifle	7.5 mm	10 rounds	Single-shot	1000 m+	France only
FN FAL	Self-loading rifle	7.62 mm	20 or 30 rounds	40 rpm	600 m+	
FN MAG	Machine-gun	7.62 mm	250-round belt	600–1000 rpm cyclic	1200 m	
MG3	Machine-gun	7.62 mm	50- or 100-round belt	700–1300 rpm cyclic	1000 m+	Modern equivalent of the wartime MG42 'Spandau'
AA-52	Light machine-gun	7.5 mm	250-round belt	800 rpm cyclic	1000 m	France only
L7A2	Machine-gun	7.62 mm	100-round belt	750–1000 rpm cyclic	1800 m	
L16A1	Mortar	81 mm	Single-shot	15 rpm	5800 m	British-made
Soltan	Mortar	120 mm	Single-shot	10 rpm	6500 m	Israeli-made; France and West Germany
Cobra	Anti-tank missile	100 mm	Single-shot	Not available	Not available	
SS-11	Anti-tank missile	164 mm	Single-shot	Single-shot	3000 m	French-made
Milan	Anti-tank missile	90 mm	Single-shot	3–4 rpm	2000 m	
LRAC-89	Anti-tank missile	89 mm	Single-shot	Not available	400 m	France only
Carl Gustav	Anti-tank missile	120 mm	Single-shot	4–6 rpm	500 m	
TOW	Anti-tank missile	152 mm	Single-shot	Not available	3750 m	

mainder of the army, and the nation, remained loyal to de
Gaulle, and on 30 April the 1er REP was disbanded for the
last time. A number of former members of this and other
Legion units went underground to pursue, in the ranks of
the Secret Army Organization, what quickly became a futile career as gangsters.

The Legion reborn

The early 1960s were years of low morale throughout the
Legion. Some critics called for its disbandment: they
claimed that in the post-colonial world there was no need
or place for "foreign mercenaries" of uncertain loyalty.
Gradually, however, a more far-sighted attitude prevailed.
France still had colonies, which needed rather more hard-
bitten garrisons than conscript national servicemen could
provide. She still had a network of defence agreements
with former possessions in troubled parts of Africa. The
Legion, reduced in size, was posted to new bases in
France, Corsica, French Guiana, the Horn of Africa and
Polynesia. It was at Camp Raffali, at Calvi in Corsica, that
the 2^e REP worked tirelessly to fit itself for its new role.
France still needed units of full-time professional, long-ser-
vice soldiers who would accept the toughest training and
conditions in preparation for rapid intervention in overseas
emergencies. The 2^e REP was determined to become
trusted and respected once more, as the finest "fast-reaction" unit in the army.

The regiment transformed itself from a tough but basically conventional parachute infantry unit into an extraordi-
narily flexible air-commando regiment. Apart from its
conventional mission—for which it recruited more selec-
tively, and trained more mercilessly, than any other unit in
the army—the 2^e REP equipped itself with a wide range of
special skills: mountain and arctic warfare, amphibious and

In the stricken city of Algiers, a Moslem civilian submits to a search by two grim French soldiers.

"scuba" operations, night fighting, demolition and sniping, and deep penetration and intelligence-gathering. Using the network of Legion garrisons scattered from South America to the Persian Gulf, the 2ᵉ REP honed its techniques in environments ranging from snow-clad peaks to steaming jungle and arid desert. As part of France's 11th Parachute Division, the regiment was given several opportunities to show off its new skills under combat conditions.

In the 1960s and '70s the 2e REP, in detachments and in full strength, served in the harsh deserts of Chad in support of the government of this ex-colony against various rebel elements. Companies rotated regularly through Djibouti, supporting the permanent garrison provided by the Legion's 13th Half-Brigade in this strategic corner of Africa. In 1982, the unit was sent into Beirut as part of the multinational force supervising the withdrawal of the PLO guerrillas. But the most famous operation of the past few years was undoubtedly the rescue of the European community trapped in the rebel-held mining town of Kolwezi, Zaïre, in May 1978.

Operation "Leopard"

There were about 2300 Belgian, French, Italian, Portuguese and other white technicians and their families living in the New Town of Kolwezi in May 1978. During the previous year, an attempt to invade Shaba Province from camps in Angola had been made by the Katangese rebels of the Congolese National Liberation Front—FNLC—who were armed and trained by Cuban instructors. It had been repelled by General Mobutu's Zaïrean army, stiffened by Moroccan and French advisers. Now the FNLC were back, and this time they drove the small garrison out of the town without difficulty.

They seemed to have no strategic plan for advancing further towards the provincial capital, Lubumbashi, and they made no very serious attempts to fortify the town against counter-attack. Their precise strength is unknown, but there were between 1500 and 4000 men armed with modern Soviet and Belgian small-arms, machine-guns, mortars and rocket launchers, and supported by a few captured Zaïrean army AML armoured cars. The FNLC seemed content to settle down to a leisurely, medieval sack of the town. They smashed in the doors of shops and houses, helping themselves to what they wanted. At first under some kind of discipline, they later degenerated into drunken savages. The European quarter was searched repeatedly, though in a random fashion. The first unfortunates to fall prey to the FNLC's impromptu "courts" and firing parties were those who they decided were "Moroccan and French mercenaries": anyone who had an Arab appearance, or a French passport. Later, the violence became an end in itself. Men, women and children, black and white alike, were tortured, raped, murdered and mutilated. The stench of death and the sound of swarming flies haunted the wrecked, empty streets. For days on end, terrified families hid in their barricaded bungalows, helpless to intervene as their neighbours suffered.

The situation in Kolwezi was known: a radio operator at the Gécamines offices had stayed on the air long enough to inform his head office at Kinshasa, the national capital. The Zaïrean Army was obviously incapable of mounting a serious operation. The Belgian government—the logical choice for a rescue mission, since they had intervened before in their former colony to rescue hostages, and since the largest group of whites at Kolwezi were Belgians—was indecisive. It was willing to supply transport, and an escort to bring out refugees—but not to fight. At last, after four days, an appeal from President Mobutu reached Paris, through the offices of the French ambassador and military advisors in Kinshasa. The appeal was accepted, and, early on the morning of 17 May, a warning order reached Lieutenant-Colonel Erulin of the 2ᵉ REP at Calvi. His regiment was placed on six hours' notice of immediate movement.

The sheer speed of the operation was dazzling. There was no time to construct the perfect plan; there was reason to fear that hints of a rescue operation were already reaching the FNLC "Tigers" over transistor radios, and that they might begin a wholesale massacre (this fear was well founded). The legionnaires would have a rich opportunity to show their skill in obeying the Foreign Legion's unofficial motto: *"Démerdez-vous!"* ("Make do!").

By 20:00 on the night of the 17th, Erulin had somehow managed to gather together the personnel and sub-units of his regiment, which had been dispersed in the normal routine of exercises and courses. All through the night they frantically prepared to fly out; and at 01:30 on the 18th the movement order arrived. By 08:00 that morning, the bulk of the regiment was assembled at Corsica's Solenzara airfield.

During the day, the first echelon—650 men of the four rifle companies, regimental tactical headquarters, and reconnaissance and mortar platoons—would fly the 6000 km (3750 miles) to Kinshasa in five French DC-8 airliners: an eight-hour flight. The second echelon, with the unit vehicles, had to wait to be flown direct to Lubumbashi on USAF C-141 and C-5 transports. By 23:30 on that stifling night, Erulin and the first of his men were on the ground at Kinshasa, facing their second sleepless night as they struggled to improvise a battalion combat drop with inadequate and unfamiliar facilities in a few hasty hours. The rest of the paras arrived during the night, joining the grim, purposeful chaos on the overcrowded airfield. Kit was hastily off-loaded and repacked, weapons were checked, ammunition was issued, and a minimal briefing was handed round on duplicated slips of paper.

To hot, exhausted, jet-lagged NCOs like Sergent-Chef Paul Fanshawe of the 3rd Company, the preparations heralded a paratrooper's nightmare. A six-year veteran of the US Army and Marine Corps, and eight years a legionnaire, Fanshawe was grimly amused as each new surprise was revealed. Jumping out of an aircraft under tactical condi-

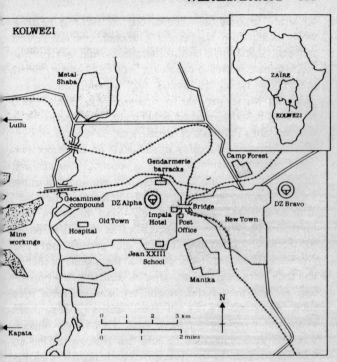

KOLWEZI

Metal Shaba

Luilu

ZAÏRE

KOLWEZI

Camp Forest

Gendarmerie barracks

Gécamines compound

DZ Alpha

Bridge

DZ Bravo

Old Town

Impala Hotel

Post Office

New Town

Hospital

Mine workings

Jean XXIII School

Manika

N

Kapata

0   1   2   3 km

0   1   2 miles

tions is a complex and dangerous business, and familiarity with the aircraft and the equipment is essential. Fanshawe's paras were to be crammed into a C-130 Hercules—a fine machine, but completely strange to all but the few Americans in the ranks. It transpired that only four serviceable C-130s and one C-160 were available; so 80 men had to ride in an aircraft built for 66. To save time, space and weight, the 2^e REP had left their own parachutes in Corsica, and were issued at Kinshasa with American T-10 rigs —again, fine pieces of equipment, but incompatible with the jump-bags in which the legionnaires carried their gear on the drop. They would have to hitch rucksacks to their leg-straps as best they could, and tie the rest of their weapons and kit to the harness with cord, tape and fervent prayers. Squad light-machine-gunners could not use the quick-release valises to dangle the 9 kg (20 lb.) guns below them before hitting the ground. As Fanshawe watched Legionnaire Misse struggle to strap the AA-52 and 2000 rounds of belted ammo across his chest, he reflected, "The poor bastard's in for a real experience!"

The paras would carry minimal kit on the drop: two water canteens, two ration packs, a poncho, a sweater, and ammunition. Even this last was in short supply. Most of the legionnaires would jump over an unprepared and "hot" drop zone armed with—incredibly—just 40 rounds each for their FSA-49/56 self-loading rifles, or about 200 rounds for the MAT-49 sub-machine-gun, plus perhaps four hand grenades. Their mission briefing told them little more than that they were to get on the ground, deal with any opposition as best they could, rescue civilians wherever they found them, and hold on till further orders . . . They could expect no re-supply for three days. Fanshawe's platoon was less than amused to be told that there would be no medical back-up in the first wave: each man was on his own, with the contents of his small personal first aid pouch.

The emplaning process the following morning nearly drove Fanshawe crazy with frustration. Zaïrean and French jumpmasters got in each other's way; awkwardly loaded, red-eyed paras shuffled aboard the strange aircraft with no idea of the correct loading procedure; and "sticks" (sections of paras) became muddled. At last, at about 11:30 on 19 May, the five aircraft lumbered into the sky. They carried, crowded in their bellies in intense discomfort, Lieutenant-Colonel Erulin and just 405 of his 1st, 2nd and 3rd Companies, and a reduced HQ. After four hours of hot, miserable flight, Sergent-Chef Fanshawe was shouting and shoving his muddled sticks of paras into some sort of order as they shuffled towards the door. The green light came on and, to a welcome of machine-gun fire, the 2e REP tumbled awkwardly into thin air in the regiment's first full combat drop since Dien Bien Phu. It was just a day and a half since the unit had received its movement order thousands of miles away in Corsica.

"DZ Alpha" was an expanse of scrub, huge termite-hills and patches of tall grass at the eastern end of the Old Town. The 1st Company was tasked with moving south to the Jean XXIII School; the 2nd with marching west through the town towards the hospital (where it was thought civilians might be held hostage) and the Gécamines compound (from whose motor pool the paras hoped to acquire transport). The 3rd Company was to take the Impala Hotel and Post Office, and set up a blocking position on the bridge leading across the railway towards the New Town.

Not surprisingly, the drop was badly scattered: ten paras were so thoroughly lost that they did not rejoin their comrades until the next day. Sergent-Chef Fanshawe hit the ground a kilometre off course, only 100 m (110 yd.) from his objective—the railway overpass. Quickly releasing his harness, he dashed for the bridge. He could see many parachutes hung up in the tall bush, but, thanks to the 90 sq. m (108 sq. yd.) area of the big American canopies, there turned out to be surprisingly few injuries—even Misse and his AA-52, who hit the ground particularly hard, was only shaken. Even more surprising was the lack of organized opposition. Apart from those first bursts of firing, the drop zone was almost eerily quiet.

It was later discovered that the FNLC had indeed got wind of the forthcoming rescue, and many of them had fled for the Angolan border. Plenty remained, however, scattered all over the Old and New Towns in hidden positions, waiting to fight it out. The companies assembled as fast as possible, heading off towards their objectives without waiting for stragglers, as they were terribly aware of the need for speed if a massacre of hostages was to be prevented.

Just south of the railway overpass to the New Town, Fanshawe managed to assemble all but six of his 2nd Platoon, and established a blocking position. He was agonizingly short of support weapons, and faced the possibility of a major attack with only two light machine-guns, nine rifle grenades, and one LRAC anti-tank launcher with just two rounds. He had not been in position long when three captured AML armoured cars charged out of the New Town on to the approach to the overpass. At the last minute, the leading AML was knocked out cleanly, only 50 m (55 yd.) from the 2nd Platoon positions, with one of the precious rockets. After firing several rounds of 90 mm and 60 mm shells from their cannon, the other two armoured cars retreated in a hail of small-arms fire. The bridge was not attacked again before nightfall, but heavy firing could be heard all around.

The 1st and 2nd Companies were advancing through a maze of alleys, shanties and patches of scrub in a hectic, confused running fight. They came under constant harassing fire, and dealt with each position as they met it, fast and hard; but they could build up no picture of the overall situation against such a dispersed enemy. As they pushed on they saw dreadful sights in the streets and the wrecked buildings. The "Tigers" had been as brutal in their treatment of the native inhabitants as of the whites. The first of the Europeans were now showing themselves, often running dazedly into the middle of firefights in their confused delight at seeing white soldiers. Erulin's HQ team tried to keep a tally of them by radio, and assembled several hundred of them in the Jean XXIII School when it was secured that evening.

Shortly before nightfall, the transport aircraft reappeared overhead with the second wave of the 2e REP. Erulin "waved them off" to Lubumbashi, however, with orders to return at first light. His three companies had secured all the main objectives for the day, and he did not want disoriented troopers falling all over the drop zone in the dark, and shooting at each other in their confusion.

The temperature fell quickly. Huddled in their ponchos in hastily dug rifle pits, the paras sat out the night of 19/20 May—their third without sleep—wherever darkness found them. Swallowing dexedrine tablets from their first aid pouches, they tried to keep alert. There was heavy gunfire all over Kolwezi throughout the night, as prowling units of the FNLC ran into Legion positions without warning. At about 22:00 one group made another attempt on Fanshawe's bridge-block, led—rather strangely—by an FNLC Major in a Volkswagen "Beetle"! After a brisk exchange of automatic and rifle fire, and some rocket-propelled grenades from the FNLC, the attack was beaten off. (The VW was shot to pieces by the two AA-52s, enabling Fanshawe to examine the Major's papers.) Later, Fanshawe heard that a larger enemy unit and an AML armoured car had been prowling his area, but they did not attack.

At first light on the 20th the second wave dropped: the mortars, reconnaissance platoon and remaining HQ element on "DZ Alpha," and the 4th Company on "DZ Bravo," east of the New Town. In not much more than an hour they had combed right through the New Town, silencing all resistance and releasing the European inhabitants from their long ordeal. Meanwhile, the 1st Company finally cleaned up the southern area of the Old Town, and the 2nd mopped up the western area. The reconnaissance platoon moved north, clearing Camp Forest and the old Gendarmerie barracks, and part of the 3rd Company pushed south into the labyrinth of the Manika housing estate. The HQ was established at the Impala Hotel. From here, Erulin was able to begin organizing the evacuation of the Europeans from the airstrip some way outside the town, where Belgian troops and various medical teams had now landed.

Some of the clashes on the 20th had been heavy. Sergent-Chef Daniel of the 4th Company was killed during the clearing of the Metal-Shaba estate that afternoon, and other paras were wounded. The 4th was quickly supported by the 2nd, the mortars and the reconnaissance platoon, and some 80 rebels were killed. Here, as all over Kolwezi, large numbers of weapons and explosives were found, including two recoilless rifles, heavy bazooka-type cannon. Many legionnaires, short of ammunition for their FSA-49/56 rifles, helped themselves to FN/FALs, Russian AK-47 assault rifles, and American M-16 Armalites from the rebel booty.

The night of the 20th was disturbed only by sporadic sniping, and some paras at last managed to have a few hours' sleep. Ambush positions secured all routes into the cleared area, and the men lying awake on guard had plenty to think about. Hideous sights encountered in the New Town had filled them all with a grim rage. In a single charnel-house room in block P2, no less than 38 men, women and children had been found heaped in a pile. Nevertheless, a large number of Europeans had been saved, some after miraculous escapes. The Pansalfin family had emerged from a tiny hiding place in the cavity between their house's double walls. One woman had been found in the hospital, with her limbs riddled with bullets, having lain for nearly 12 hours, holding her dead baby, under the bodies of her neighbours.

The operation was by no means over. For another week, using requisitioned civilian lorries, and their own jeeps and trucks which arrived after driving from Lubumbashi on the 21st, the 2ᵉ REP spread out on wide-ranging patrols, covering more than a 300 km (190 mile) radius. On the 21st there was fighting during the clearing of Kapata to the south-west, and casualties were taken during a fierce clash near Luilu, where several searches were carried out during the period 24–28 May. On that day most of the regiment finally pulled out and drove to Lubumbashi, some of them having received no rations since the first drop.

By 4 June the 2ᵉ REP was back in Corsica. They had saved more than 2000 lives; killed more than 250 rebels, and captured 163; and accounted for two armoured cars, four recoilless cannon, 15 mortars, 21 rocket launchers, 10 machine-guns, 38 sub-machine-guns, and 216 rifles. They had lost 5 legionnaires, and 25 had been wounded.

The 2ᵉ REP today

The Legion, in these days of high unemployment, can turn away all but the best would-be recruits. And of those who survive the extremely punishing basic training, and who apply for transfer to the élite parachute regiment, an even more testing ordeal awaits. There is fierce competition to serve in the 2ᵉ REP, the most famous of the Legion's nine regiments, and the paras can afford to be highly selective.

Today, the regiment has about 1300 officers and men divided into six companies: Command and Services; Reconnaissance and Support; and four numbered rifle companies. Each company is trained to fight as a conventional parachute infantry company within the battalion combat mission. In addition, each has a particular specialist role for which it is highly trained, and maintains a cadre of experts. There is considerable cross-training between these specialities. The 1st Company concentrates on anti-tank, night-fighting and urban fighting techniques. The 2nd specializes in mountain and arctic warfare, and general obstacle-crossing. The 3rd is the amphibious warfare company, and the 4th specializes in sniping, demolition and sabotage.

The Command and Services Company provides HQ,

signals, repair, medical, and other general facilities. The Recce and Support Company—237 men, with 77 vehicles —has a reconnaissance platoon, two platoons of Milan anti-tank missiles with eight launchers each, a platoon of 20 mm electrically operated anti-aircraft cannon, a mortar platoon with eight 81 mm and four 120 mm tubes, and the "pathfinder" platoon. The last named is intensively trained in a wide range of skills: high-altitude jumps with steerable "ram-air" canopies which allow a long horizontal approach to a target; concealment and intelligence-gathering behind enemy lines; and such special tasks as hostage rescue.

The recruit who gains the coveted grenade-and-dragon badge of the 2e REP has a better chance than any other legionnaire of seeing action during his five-year enlistment. He is certain of travelling widely, and of carrying out exercises under tactical conditions in jungle, mountains and desert, often with foreign armies. He will earn at least a third more than his earth-bound comrades. And he will have the satisfaction, ever afterwards, of having proved himself in the company of some of the most skilled and dangerous soldiers on earth.

THE ROYAL NETHERLANDS MARINE COMMANDOS

Holland very nearly had a "first," which would have gone down in history alongside the Entebbe and Mogadishu rescues, when South Moluccan extremists hijacked an express train at Beilen, near Assen, on the main line from Groningen to Zwolle, on Tuesday, 2 December 1975. The South Moluccan cause is one which few people in the outside world had heard of prior to this date, and goes back to the granting of Indonesian independence in 1950. The Moluccan inhabitants of the region, who had fought fiercely for the Dutch against the Japanese invaders during World War 2, had also resisted the independence movement, and feared reprisals under the new regime. As a result, some 15,000 of them emigrated to Holland after being given a guarantee that the Dutch government would negotiate, on their behalf, with the new Indonesian rulers for the establishment of a separate and independent republic of South Molucca. Many of these *émigrés* were given temporary accommodation in former Nazi concentration camps, which cannot have inspired confidence, and, by 1975, a quarter of a century after the Dutch government had first made its promise to them, the younger members of the community had run out of patience.

From 1970 onwards, South Moluccan extremists had been causing the Dutch government concern through such activities as raids with petrol bombs on the Indonesian embassy in the Hague, but, in 1975, members of the youth movement within the Moluccan government-in-exile decided upon even more drastic measures. Six men boarded the express train at Groningen at 09:33 on 2 December, with a sub-machine-gun and automatic pistols wrapped up as a Christmas parcel. They stopped the train at Beilen, shooting the 30-year-old driver, Hans Braam, and herded the passengers into one carriage. Another man who tried to escape was also shot.

Dutch marines, a 25-strong squad trained in counter-terrorist techniques alongside the SAS, were flown in by helicopter to assess the situation and take advantage of any opportunity which arose, but the wide train windows offered the terrorists an excellent view of events outside, while they themselves were concealed from the marines by the crush of 80 passengers.

The flat countryside provided little cover for the marines, although there was one waterlogged ditch which would have given an approach up to 45 m (50 yd.) from

Front-page headlines as the South Moluccan hijackers open fire on their hostages.

the train, but the terrorists appeared alert and a frontal approach was ruled out. Instead, the bright-yellow train, standing in the middle of the bleak farmland, was eventually surrounded by an "overkill" force of some 1000 Dutch policemen, soldiers and marines, including 60 highly skilled snipers.

Over the next 13 days the Moluccans continued to reiterate their demands for the Dutch government to give them a fair hearing on international radio and television, and released a large number of hostages in small groups as a goodwill gesture in return for the food and warm clothing with which they were supplied. During this period, older and saner members of the Moluccan government-in-exile continued to try to act as mediators, even though they had been fired upon at their first attempt. For once, psychological tactics worked. The increasingly cold weather, coupled with the Dutch government's refusal to cooperate in any way with the terrorists' demands and the constant threat of the marines and snipers only metres away from the ma-

rooned train, finally broke the hijackers' will, and they
released the remaining 25 hostages, surrendering themselves to police custody, on Sunday, 14 December.

Holland and NATO

The Netherlands, having been overrun by the Nazis in
1940, is one of the most active member nations of NATO,
since it has no wish to repeat such an experience under the
Russian jackboot. Despite the small size of the country,
and the extreme anti-militaristic and anti-authoritarian attitude of Dutch youth which made the country such a haven
for American deserters and draft-evaders during the Vietnam conflict, its army is one of the best trained, equipped
and motivated in Europe, with no fewer than three divisions committed to the northern flank of NATO (i.e., Norway). The Dutch Army consists nominally of 28,500 men,
of whom 60 per cent are regulars and the balance conscripts called up for the mandatory 12 months' service.
Dutch marines—*Korps Commandetroepen*—are as fit and
well trained as the British commandos (despite their beards
and long hair), and share in joint mountain and arctic warfare exercises in Norway every spring. Armed with a mixture of American, British, German and Israeli equipment,
they are a formidable fighting force.

Norway

Although a founder-member of NATO, Norway has an
even smaller army than that of Holland, with only some
2500–3000 regulars. The balance of the 20,000-strong
force comprises conscripts between the ages of 20 and 45,
who serve for a year before becoming part of the reserve.
However, the reserve is 120,000-strong and, like the
Dutch, the Norwegian people remember the Nazis too well

to welcome being overrun by the Soviet Union. As a result they have a very firm defence policy and welcome the British, Dutch and others who come to practise mountain and arctic warfare techniques in Norway, but they have no élite troops of their own committed to offensive operations.

WEST GERMANY'S GSG 9

The atmosphere was euphoric on the modern, brightly lit concourse of Frankfurt Airport on the afternoon of Tuesday, 18 October 1977. Sipping a drink in the cocktail lounge above the departure area, while waiting for my own flight to Heathrow to be called, I watched with other outward-bound passengers as the Lufthansa Boeing 737 taxied slowly up to the terminal, surrounded by a bevy of official cars and airport vehicles. Landing steps were brought up to the exit hatches, and moments later people began to emerge. One little boy was carried down the steps by an airline official. All around me, people were smiling, laughing and talking animatedly. It certainly made a great contrast to the previous days of tension.

Five days earlier, on Thursday, 13 October, the Boeing 737 had lifted off from the holiday resort of Palma, Majorca, with 86 passengers and a crew of 5, headed for Frankfurt. Unknown to anyone at the time, two men and two women aboard the aircraft were carrying small-arms and plastic explosive. Shortly after take-off, the terrorists broke into the flight deck and threatened the pilot, Captain Jürgen Schumann, and co-pilot Jürgen Vietor, with a Colt revolver and a 9 mm automatic pistol. The two men were ordered to fly the Boeing to Rome, while the hijackers made their demands to the West German government for the release of 11 members of the notorious Baader-Meinhof gang, including Andreas Baader himself, from the top-security Stammheim prison. The hijackers, later identified as members of the notorious Red Army faction, which has activists in practically every country in the world, also demanded a ransom of £9 million.

Aftermath of Munich

The West German government's attitude towards terrorists had hardened considerably since the murder of Israeli athletes by Palestinian gunmen in Munich in 1972, and it had established a special commando unit of 60 men, under the command of Ulrich Wegener, to deal with any similar outrages. Known as Grenzschutzgruppe 9, it was drawn from volunteers in the German police, army and frontier guards, and was trained in counter-hijacking and other tactics by advisors from both Britain's Special Air Service Regiment and the Israeli secret service. However, Chancellor Helmut Schmidt's government was in political difficulties, and to begin with it seemed likely that Germany would take the "soft" rather than the "hard" option by acceding to the hijackers' demands. In particular, left-wing movements in West Germany were incensed at the government's proposals to limit the rights of lawyers defending terrorists and to reintroduce the death penalty, so that many observers thought that Chancellor Schmidt would follow the same course as he had in 1975, when five members of the Baader-Meinhof gang had been released from prison following the kidnapping of Berlin's Mayor-elect, Peter Lorenz.

However, Schmidt was well aware what that had led to: the released terrorists took over the German Embassy in Stockholm in April 1976, capturing 12 hostages and demanding the release of all convicted Baader-Meinhof personnel in German jails. When Chancellor Schmidt refused to give in, the terrorists exploded a bomb inside the embassy, which caught fire. Armed Swedish police stormed the building, killing two of the terrorists and capturing the others, but not before the West German military attaché, Andreas von Mirbach, had been killed.

As the hijacked Boeing refuelled at Rome, Chancellor Schmidt was in urgent consultation not only with his own cabinet but also with other Western European government leaders, including Prime Minister James Callaghan in Britain and President Giscard d'Estaing in France. It had been known for some time that one of the headquarters of international terrorism was in Algiers, where members of the Japanese Red Army had hijacked a Japan Airlines aircraft at the beginning of October 1977 and had blackmailed the Tokyo government into freeing terrorist prisoners in Japanese prisons. Chancellor Schmidt was therefore calling for united pressure on Algeria's dictator, Colonel Boumédienne, in order to persuade him to deny a home to the terrorists.

Meanwhile, the hijacked Lufthansa jet was eastward-bound across the Mediterranean towards its next refuelling stop in Cyprus. From there it flew to Bahrain where it remained overnight, surrounded by police and military vehicles carefully concealed from the hijackers' vision. As the pressure mounted, newspapers around the world were questioning whether anyone had the right to gamble with 86 lives, and left-wing groups began agitating for the Bonn government to give in to the terrorists' demands. Behind the scenes, however, GSG 9 was preparing its equipment —Heckler and Koch sub-machine-guns, 9 mm automatic pistols and plastic explosive—in case it became necessary to blow open the doors of the airliner. A seating plan of the Boeing 737 was obtained from Lufthansa, and various methods of assaulting the aircraft were discussed. Two British SAS officers from Hereford flew out to West Germany to give the benefit of their own expertise and to issue

the German commandos with a quantity of their special
concussion grenades, which shock and immobilize without
killing. However, no final plans could be laid until it was
known where the airliner would finally come to rest.

On to Dubai

From Bahrain it flew on Friday to Dubai, where the Defence Minister of the United Arab Emirates, Sheik Mohamed bin Raschid, installed himself in the control tower
to handle negotiations. He was joined by the West German
ambassador, Dr. Hans Neumann, and for hours they tried
to talk the terrorists into surrender, promising safe conduct
if they would only give up their impossible demands. Peri-
odically during the day, one or other of the hijackers would
come to the forward door of the aircraft to throw out rubbish or collect food, while the white-shirted leader, Harda
Mahmoud, a Palestinian, could frequently be seen in the
aircraft's cockpit by the troops, armed with light machine-
guns, who ringed the Boeing.

At 14:15 Mahmoud called the control tower and
shouted, "We gave the German government 60 hours of
ultimatum to release our prisoners. Nothing has happened.
There is no response. We hold the German government
responsible for what happens to the passengers. We hold
Helmut Schmidt responsible. Our deadline is 12 GMT [1
hour 20 minutes later]. It will not be a second more."

The German ambassador tried to placate the terrorists by
telling them that a Minister of State was on his way from
Bonn, but this only enraged Mahmoud even more. "There
is no more time. We are going to our second destination.
We are not going to wait a second after our deadline."

Sheik Mohamed asked Mahmoud what the hijackers'
next destination was to be and was told Masirah, a former
RAF base on an island off the coast of Oman. Meanwhile,

the aircraft's captain, Jürgen Schumann, had been talking to the air traffic controller in the tower at Dubai and had managed to pass over information on the number of hijackers and how they were armed by means of code phrases inserted into the technical conversation about the aircraft's status. Now he asked, "Headings for Masirah, please," and at 15:19—41 minutes before the expiry of the terrorists' deadline—the fully refuelled Boeing took off into the heat haze. However, instead of proceeding to Masirah, it turned west towards Sallala, the provincial capital of Dhofar in Oman, and circled for a while before being refused permission to land. Thwarted, the hijackers directed Captain Schumann to fly on to South Yemen (formerly Aden), where the aircraft landed again at 18:15 local time. The landing was not a good one and the aircraft touched down very violently, damaging its undercarriage. It is possible that Captain Schumann did this deliberately, in an attempt to "ground" the plane, but this will never be known for certain.

Now the drama began to move into its final phase. Captain Schumann was allowed to leave the aircraft to inspect the undercarriage, and made a run for freedom. He actually reached the control tower, where he had obviously hoped to give Yemeni officials further information about the disposition of the terrorists and, in particular, to tell them how the plastic explosives had been placed. Mahmoud screamed over the radio, saying that he would blow the aircraft up immediately if the pilot was not returned.

Back aboard the aircraft, Captain Schumann was ordered to take off again. To begin with he objected, saying that the undercarriage was unsafe, but Mahmoud insisted. Then, as the plane rose into the sky, Mahmoud told copilot Jürgen Vietor to take the controls and Captain Schumann was man-handled back into the passenger cabin. He was forced to his knees in the aisle while the terrorist leader screamed at him to admit his guilt. A moment later he was shot in the back of the head in front of the shocked and terrified passengers, who included seven children.

The end of the road

The aircraft flew on towards its next destination, Mogadishu, in Somalia. On the ground, nobody knew what had happened in the aircraft, but the West German commando team was already on a Boeing 707, having flown from Frankfurt to Crete while the hijacked 737 was at Dubai. They had wanted to storm the aircraft there, but were thwarted by Sheik Mohamed's insistence that Dubai troops should participate in the assault. This would have proved fatal, for they were completely untrained in the tactics and techniques needed for carrying out such an operation with minimal risk to the hostages.

As the Boeing landed at Mogadishu, the terrorists opened one of its doors and Captain Schumann's body was thrown callously on to the runway. Chancellor Schmidt, and the GSG 9 commandos, knew that time was running out. If the terrorists were prepared to kill one hostage, they were obviously prepared to kill more. Thus, as the hijacked aircraft rested on the runway at Mogadishu in the short tropical dusk, the commandos' 707 began winging its way eastwards from Crete. Inside the aircraft, the commandos checked their weapons and applied black grease-paint to their faces, while Chancellor Schmidt conferred over the hot line with President Barre of Somalia. The Somali government was fully in agreement with the rescue attempt and made no objection as the commando 707 landed in the darkness at Mogadishu, its engines throttled back to reduce noise and all its lights extinguished.

The commandos jumped from the plane and, following their carefully rehearsed schedule, approached the hijacked

Boeing from the rear, where there was least chance of their being spotted by the terrorists in the cockpit. Moving silently with rubber-soled boots, grenades primed and their sub-machine-gun safety catches off, the commandos assembled underneath the aircraft beside the emergency release points which would jettison the aircraft's doors, even if they had been locked from the inside. Two men beside each door held light aluminium scaling ladders ready.

At a pre-arranged moment, all the doors were blown, the ladders were slapped into place and the first commandos stormed into the plane. It all happened so quickly that the passengers barely had time to react. One woman said later: "I didn't hear a thing. Then somebody fell on top of us, covering us with his body—and all we heard was 'Heads down, don't be scared.'"

Another man said, "We really did not know what was going on. Suddenly there were explosions [as the commandos threw their grenades] and men came pouring into the plane shouting 'Hinlegen! Hinlegen!' ['Lie down!'] as the shooting began."

It was all over in a matter of seconds. Blood from the hijackers' bullet-riddled bodies seeped into the airliner's carpet as the commandos gently led the relieved passengers to the waiting ladders. First out of the aircraft was one of the three air hostesses, who had received a minor wound in the leg during the shooting. None of the other passengers was hurt, but they were all suffering from the tension and deprivations of the past few days, and another Boeing carrying a special team of doctors and nurses was already *en route* to Mogadishu to care for them. Chancellor Schmidt's brave gamble had paid off.

In a bizarre postscript to the Mogadishu rescue, the three leaders of the Baader-Meinhof gang—Andreas Baader, his mistress, Gudrun Ensslin, and Jan Carl Raspe —committed suicide. The two men shot themselves, which caused the West German police to tighten security in Stammheim prison, and Ensslin hanged herself from the barred window of her cell. A fourth terrorist, Irmgard Moller, tried to stab herself to death with a breadknife but later recovered in hospital to face the charge of bombing the American embassy in Heidelberg, five years earlier.

For Ulrich Wegener and his commandos there was the sense of satisfaction in a job well done, and for other terrorists around the world there was a clear warning that the élite GSG 9—successors to Otto Skorzeny's famous wartime SS commandos who had rescued Mussolini from his mountain-top prison at Gran Sasso in Italy—is fit and ready to tackle any similar situation in the future.

Training and recruitment

Although recruited from a variety of different sources, GSG 9 is basically a product of the *Bundesgrenzschutz* (BGS, or Federal Border Guard), which was formed in 1950. Equipped with armoured cars and personnel carriers, it is a paramilitary force whose principal role is that of safeguarding a 30 km (19 mile) border against intrusion from the east, and it is well trained in surveillance and detection techniques. The whole BGS comprises some 20,000 men organized in five commands, each of which controls *Gruppen* (Groups) of regimental size organized in two or three battalions.

When the Federal Republic of Germany became a member of NATO, a large number of BGS personnel transferred to form the nucleus of today's 9th *Luftlandedivision* (air-landing division), based in Bruchsal, and the 8th *Gebirgsdivision* (mountain division), based in Garmisch-Partenkirchen; subsequent volunteers for GSG 9 are thus well-versed in either (or both) airborne or mountain and arctic warfare techniques where the training parallels that of British and Dutch paras and commandos. GSG 9 volunteers also undergo specialist indoctrination and courses in military technology at Darmstadt, languages and psychological warfare at Euskirchen, and intelligence at Bad Ems. Their training thus follows the British SAS pattern which inspired it.

VI

ISRAEL

TANK, AIRBORNE AND MOUNTAIN FORCES

Born in war, the state of Israel has fought a major war once every decade since it came into existence, and has been continuously involved in counter-insurgency operations against the Palestinian guerrillas who also claim the country as their own. This has meant that every member of the population, male and female, has had to serve as a soldier, with the result that the Israeli Army, *Zahal*, has become the most finely honed and efficient fighting machine in the world.

Israel is surrounded by potential enemies, with the exception of Egypt—which finally recognized the country's existence under the inspired leadership of the late President Anwar Sadat—and, since 1983, Lebanon. Nor are Israel's enemies insignificant: Saudi Arabia, Iraq, Syria, Jordan and Libya all possess excellent armies with modern equipment and vastly outnumber *Zahal*. The reason Israel has not been crushed so far is mainly the superior quality of the men and women who are prepared to lay down their lives to preserve a dream which finally came true in 1948, after centuries of Jewish wandering and persecution, although rivalries between the Arab states opposed to them, and super-power intervention, have also played a part.

However, before examining Israel's achievements in conventional warfare in more detail, there is one accomplishment which, in the eyes of many people, exemplifies the spirit, determination, military expertise and imagination of *Zahal*.

The most daring raid of all

It was one minute past midnight, local time, at Entebbe Airport, a 50-minute drive from Kampala, the capital of Uganda. Inside the new airport control tower, traffic controllers Badrew Muhindi, Tobias Rwengeme and Lawrence Mawenda were feeling increasingly confused. Only moments earlier an African Airways Boeing 707 *en route* from Nairobi, Kenya, had mysteriously disappeared from the operators' radar screens. Now, suddenly, they were being called up by Israeli Flight 166, which was only three minutes from touchdown. The flight was not unexpected, merely unannounced and far earlier than anyone had predicted. However, as they peered through the green-tinted glass of the control tower windows, the three men were astonished to see not one, but *two* Lockheed C-130 Hercules transports, both in military camouflage, drop on to the main runway of the airport. Moreover, the telephones seemed to be out of order and the controllers could obtain no advice from Kampala.

Out of their sight, behind a rise in the ground, Ugandan soldiers were equally surprised to see a third Hercules touch down. Rapidly reversing propeller pitch to slow down, the huge aircraft taxied towards the old control tower where 104 men, women and children had been incarcerated for the past few days. As the aircraft came to a halt, its rear loading ramp dropped and a Land Rover emerged, closely followed by a black Mercedes-Benz 220 with curtains drawn around the passenger compartment, and a second Land Rover. Although this was totally unexpected, the Ugandan soldiers were used to the unpredictable behaviour of their President, Idi Amin, and in recent days had become accustomed to his visits to the old control tower.

Once off the aircraft's ramp, the small convoy drove at a smart pace towards the front of the control tower and old terminal building, watched by men armed with machine-guns on the roof as well as by two startled Germans, Wilfred Boese and Gabrielle Tiedemann. As the soldiers on the brightly lit tarmac snapped to attention, thinking that their President had returned unannounced from the Organization for African Unity conference in Mauritius, Boese darted back into the building.

The cars slowed as they approached the terminal, and suddenly one of the watching soldiers shouted in alarm. The men in the leading Land Rover were not armed with the usual Russian-designed Kalashnikov AK-47 assault rifles, but with stubby Israeli Uzi sub-machine-guns. At the Ugandan's shout, the windows of all three vehicles suddenly spurted flame, the stutter of the Uzis blending with the harder "crack" of Galil assault rifles wielded by the concealed Israeli commandos in the rear seats of the Mercedes. The Ugandan soldier who had raised the alarm was the first to fall.

The Entebbe raid was on!

The hijack

One week previously, in the early hours of 27 June 1976, sleepy passengers had begun boarding the scheduled flight from Kuwait which was due to arrive in Athens at 07:00. No one took any notice of the 28-year-old German lawyer and his girlfriend who had first-class tickets through to Paris, while even less attention was paid to a pair of anonymous young Arabs travelling in tourist class. Within hours, however, their names were to be on everyone's lips around the world.

At Athens, the attractive German couple and the two Arabs went straight through to the transfer lounge without having to go through any form of security check. The German lawyer, Wilfred Boese, excused himself to his girlfriend and entered the men's toilets. He was joined by one of the Arabs, who was carrying two tins of dates. Inside the toilet, the tins were rapidly opened and the Arab handed Boese two Czech 7.65 mm automatic pistols and a pair of hand grenades; then the two men separated. The girl donned a blonde wig and the four sauntered to join the queue of people waiting to board Air France Flight 139 for Paris; the girl carried two grenades and a pistol in her handbag while her companion had the other pistol in his pocket. Her name was Gabrielle Tiedemann, and both she and Boese were members of the dreaded Baader-Meinhof gang.

In the cockpit of the Air France Airbus, Captain Michel Barcos completed his routine pre-flight checks and the aircraft taxied out to the runway. In the cabin, an air hostess was serving drinks to the first-class passengers. The Airbus lifted off into the cloudless sky and banked on to its course across the Aegean towards Paris. As it did so, the elegant but hard-faced German girl rose to her feet. To the horror

WEAPONS OF THE ISRAELI ÉLITE FORCES

Designation	Type	Calibre	Magazine	Rate of fire	Range	Remarks
Uzi	Sub-machine-gun	9 mm	25 or 32 rounds	600 rpm cyclic	100 m	
Galil ARM	Assault rifle	5.56 mm	35 or 50 rounds	650 rpm cyclic	400 m	
Galil SAR	Assault carbine	5.56 mm	35 rounds	750 rpm cyclic	300–400 m	Paras and tank crews
FN FAL	Self-loading rifle	7.62 mm	20 or 30 rounds	40 rpm	600 m +	
FN MAG	Machine-gun	7.62 mm	100-round belt	600–1000 rpm cyclic	1200 m	
M65	Mortar	120 mm	Single-shot	10 rpm	6500 m	
Cobra	Anti-tank missile	100 mm	Single-shot	Not applicable	2000 m	
SS11	Anti-tank missile	164 mm	Single-shot	Not applicable	3000 m	
LAW	Light Armour Weapon	94 mm	Single-shot	Not applicable	500 m	
TOW	Anti-tank missile	152 mm	Single-shot	Not applicable	3750 m	
Redeye	Anti-aircraft missile	70 mm	Single-shot	Not available	Not available	

of the air hostess and the other first-class passengers, Tiedemann raised a grenade aloft in each hand. "Sit down!" she commanded. "Everyone must sit down." Her companion stood up, holding the automatic pistol, and walked forward to the flight deck. Back in the tourist section of the Airbus, the two Arabs, one wearing a bright-red shirt, the other a yellow one, had also arisen, and there were shrieks of fear from several passengers as they spotted the guns in the Arabs' hands.

From the flight deck, Boese spoke over the cabin intercom, while the two Arabs—who throughout the operation were only referred to by the code numbers 39 and 55—began tying what appeared to be innocent boxes of chocolates to two of the aircraft's emergency exit doors. The boxes, Boese informed the stunned passengers, contained plastic explosive. As the aircraft was flying at over 10,000 m (30,000 ft.), their detonation would produce explosive decompression which would cause the airliner to disintegrate in mid air. However, Boese said that all the passengers would be safe if they did as they were told by his colleagues. They were being taken to a safe destination, he continued, where they would be held hostage against the release of Palestine Liberation Organization "freedom fighters" in Israel, and Baader-Meinhof gangsters in West Germany.

After the Airbus had crossed the Mediterranean, Boese ordered Captain Barcos to contact the control tower at Benghazi, in Libya, where arrangements had already been made for the airliner to land and refuel before departing for its final, and as yet undisclosed, destination. Then the aircraft took off again on the longest leg of its flight, across the barren Bayuda Desert where Lord Wolseley's Camel Corps had battled so valiantly a century before in their attempt to rescue General Charles Gordon, besieged in Khartoum. Eventually the aircraft crossed the border between Sudan and Uganda and began descending towards Lake Victoria and Kampala's main airport at Entebbe. The Airbus landed in the still, pre-dawn air on Monday, 28 June, but few of the passengers realized where they were until Boese announced over the intercom that they had landed in Uganda. There were smiles and the occasional hand-clap among the 257 passengers as the aircraft doors were opened to let out the stale air, and a Ugandan truck delivered hundreds of cartons of cool, soft drinks. Many of the hostages had fallen under the spell of the eloquent and persuasive German lawyer, and had begun to believe that their ordeal might really be over. The next five days were to show how ill-founded these hopes were.

After several hours' acute discomfort in the cramped confines of the aircraft, the passengers were told that it was time to disembark. Blinking in the hot African sunlight, they emerged unsteadily to face a cordon of armed Ugandan soldiers, and the full horror of the situation came home to them. The troops' automatic rifles were directed not at the hijackers, but at the passengers!

The hostages were herded between two lines of soldiers towards the old control tower and terminal complex. Although the buildings were falling into disrepair, the rooms and toilets inside had been freshly cleaned, and the hostages' spirits lifted again as airport personnel began to bring round more cold drinks together with hot food. However, the staple Ugandan diet of rice, bananas and badly cooked meat would soon pall, and the toilets were soon to become blocked. Sickness and diarrhoea would be added to the hostages' misery. To begin with, though, their situation did not seem too frightening, and many people applauded when Idi Amin, the paranoid Ugandan dictator and former British Army NCO, paid his first visit to them. Amin, wearing, of all things, Israeli paratrooper's wings on his camouflage uniform, made a long speech in which he defended the right of the Palestinian people to their homeland. However, he said, "You must not worry. I will take care of you like a father. I will see that you are released." He was to say much the same on every visit.

On Tuesday, 29 June, the Jews among the hostages were terrified when Boese entered the main hall of the terminal building and announced that he had an answer to the overcrowding, which was becoming more and more of a problem. The wooden slats which had barred entry to the adjoining lounge were torn away by Palestinian guerrillas —their numbers now swollen to ten with new arrivals— and Boese began reading names from a list. It rapidly became apparent that all the names were Jewish: the terrorists were segregating their prisoners. A few of the older Israelis remembered the Holocaust—some had actually survived the Nazi concentration camps—and it seemed to them that history was repeating itself.

The terrorist leader did not appear to understand the

Jews' consternation. Confronted with the problem, he frowned and assured the hostages that there was nothing sinister in his actions. "It is simply," he said, "that we have to put about a hundred of you in the other room and, as there are about that many Jews, it is better that you be together." However, several of the hostages later reported that Boese looked worried at the situation, almost as if he resented any implication that his group might be capable of behaving like the SS. Whether this had anything to do with subsequent events is impossible to decide; certainly the discussion was resumed later in the week. Whatever the case, on the following day, Wednesday, 30 June, the hijackers released 47 of their prisoners, while Ugandan soldiers brought blankets for the remainder since, although the days were hot, the nights were very cold. However, no one missed the fact that none of those released was Jewish.

On Thursday, the Israeli cabinet submitted—as far as the outside world was concerned—to the hijackers' demands. The terrorists held in Israeli jails whose release Boese was demanding would be set free as soon as the hijackers could give satisfactory assurances about the safety of the hostages. Boese reacted swiftly and within hours had released a further 101 hostages, who were flown back to Paris.

The remaining 104 prisoners, with the exception of the Air France Airbus crew, who bravely refused to leave, were all Jews. If it had not been clear before, it was now obvious that Boese's target was Israel.

On the Friday morning, Idi Amin paid his third visit to Entebbe, this time accompanied by both his wife and young son. They were on their way to Mauritius for the conference of the Organization for African Unity. He repeated his earlier words of reassurance.

He then appealed to the remaining hostages to help him, urging them all to sign a letter, which would be read over the radio, begging the Israeli government to capitulate completely. As he departed for Mauritius, the prisoners began arguing hotly amongst themselves, some being in favour of writing such a letter and others being totally opposed. Eventually a form of agreement was reached and a letter drafted; a letter which carefully concealed in its syntax a plea to the Israeli government to act positively rather than negatively. Unknown to those who penned the letter, the Israeli government *was* acting positively.

Operation "Thunderbolt"

On Monday, 28 June 1976, the Knesset, Israel's parliament, was in emergency session. Prime Minister Yitzhak Rabin and opposition leader Menachem Begin had spent the previous day at Ben Gurion airport, tracing the course of the hijacked Airbus as it proceeded first to Libya and then on to Uganda. While the politicians talked, Israel's military leaders began planning. Defence Minister Shimon Peres, Chief-of-Staff General Mordecai Gur, his second in command, Major-General Yekuti Adam, and air force commander General Beni Peled, discussed the information which was so far available to them. By any standards, the prospects for a successful military solution to the problem looked gloomy. The hijacked Airbus was 2000 miles away in a country whose dictator was openly hostile to Israel. As well as the Palestinian and Baader-Meinhof terrorists themselves, numerous regular Ugandan troops were guarding the hostages. There were two squadrons of Russian-built MiG-17s and -19s at Entebbe, and the air routes to Uganda from Israel all passed over Arab countries. In contrast to a rescue attempt on an airliner grounded in a friendly or neutral country, therefore, any military operation would have to be aimed at seizing the entire airport and neutralizing the jet fighters as well as rescuing the hostages themselves.

At 17:30, Peres and Gur went to Jerusalem to meet with

the crisis cabinet summoned by Prime Minister Rabin. At this stage, barely 30 hours after the hijack, they had to confess that they could not see a viable military option. The cabinet therefore decided against making any immediate decision on the hijackers' demands. While the government would continue to negotiate with the terrorists in the hope of bringing a bloodless end to the crisis, the military was instructed to carry on pursuing ideas for a feasible rescue operation.

Several plans were considered and discarded over the next hours, including a parachute assault and the possibility of dispatching an airliner, ostensibly carrying the prisoners from Israeli jails whose release the terrorists were demanding, but in fact packed with commandos. None of the ideas were viable because they would all alert the hijackers and so their chances of success seemed remote. Speed, secrecy and surprise were the essentials. The Israelis had to get a strong force on to the ground undetected. They then had to free the hostages from wherever they were being held prisoner; they had to neutralize the hijackers and the Ugandan troops at Entebbe; they had to destroy the MiGs; and they had to be clear of the airfield in less than an hour, or strong Ugandan reinforcements from Kampala would be on top of them. It seemed an impossible task, but Peres and Gur appointed various sub-committees to work out plans for each phase of the operation—the undetected approach, the rescue of the hostages in the middle of a firefight to secure the airfield, and the escape. The large number of hostages—257—was in itself a problem, because it meant that at least three aircraft would have to be used in the operation. But gradually ideas began to gel, and ultimately a number of separate but concurrent operations emerged as the best possible answer.

While the military planners continued to polish the basic concepts for the rescue operation, the Knesset was meeting again and, on Thursday, 1 July, it finally agreed to discuss with the hijackers the release of some of the prisoners in Israeli jails. The hijackers responded by releasing a second batch of hostages, who were questioned closely by Israeli secret service agents in order to ascertain from them as many details as possible relating to the condition of the remaining hostages, where they were being kept, and the disposition of their guards.

Although there was natural concern in Israel about the fact that all the remaining hostages, with the exception of the Air France crew, were Jews, the fact that there were now only just over 100 of them in Entebbe made the military option much more feasible. The plan had several parts. First, three Lockheed C-130 transports would be used for the main assault. They would fly from Israel's southernmost air base, Sharm el-Sheik, at an extremely low level to avoid radar detection from Egypt, Libya, Saudi Arabia and the Sudan, at the same time flying in very close wingtip-to-wingtip formation so that, if they were spotted, they would register on a radar screen only as a single aircraft. This way, if they were detected, they could claim that they were a special flight laid on to ferry the terrorist prisoners to Entebbe. Meanwhile, 10,000 m (30,000 ft.) above them, a specially equipped Boeing 707 aerial command post would fly in close company with a scheduled airline flight from Tel Aviv to Nairobi, in Kenya. Reaching the vicinity of Kampala, the scheduled aircraft—which in fact was being hastily refitted as a mobile hospital—would bank over Lake Victoria towards Nairobi, while the aerial command post would accelerate to its maximum speed of nearly 300 knots and enter the blind zone of the Entebbe radar: this was a cone which, at 10,000 m (30,000 ft.) was 25 km (16 miles) in diameter; since the Boeing's turn radius was only 8 km (5 miles), the command post could circle undetected in this zone for as long as needed to complete the operation.

Further activity was taking place on the ground. Israeli

agents had been filtering into Uganda from Kenya during the middle of the week, their prime task being to gain access to the airfield in the guise of airport workers and airline crew, and to sabotage all the telephone lines out of the airport in order to make it more difficult for the Ugandans to summon help from outside. Meanwhile, in Israel itself, the crack troops who were going to carry out the main assault were rehearsing.

The man chosen to lead the operation on the ground was an exceptional soldier with a remarkable record. Although only aged 39, Dan Shomron was already a brigadier. He had joined the paras in 1955, taking part in the 1956 Suez operation and the later Six-Day War, and had afterwards specialized in counter-terrorist raids against Palestinian camps in the Jordan valley. During the Yom Kippur war he commanded a tank brigade, and he was highly regarded as an intelligent and incisive officer.

The term "hand-picked volunteer" is something of a contradiction in terms, but that is exactly what the force which Shomron assembled at Sharm el-Sheik consisted of. Israel is an egalitarian state, and its predominantly civilian army does not encourage élitism. Nevertheless, many units in the Israeli Defence Forces had made themselves into an élite through sheer performance, drive, determination and skill rather than through any special training. And within the armed forces there were few men who would not have wanted to be part of such a rescue operation, despite the fact that casualty estimates for the strike force ran as high as 40 per cent. In other words, it was anticipated that, of the 200 soldiers taking part in the operation, at least 30 would be killed and another 50 seriously wounded.

So, they assembled at Sharm el-Sheik, 200 bronzed, highly fit young men from the paras, the armoured forces and the Golani mountain troops. First, Brigadier Shomron briefed them on the situation and the obstacles to be overcome, then the men turned the airfield into a full-size replica of Entebbe, marking out the positions of the key buildings, the parked MiGs and other features. The three Hercules aircraft they would be using were taxied into the positions they would occupy on Entebbe airfield and the troops embarked, together with their vehicles. Other soldiers acted the part of the hostages. Again and again the men ran through the exercise: the disembarkation from the aircraft, the dash to the old terminal building, taking out the control towers, sabotaging the MiGs—all these phases were rehearsed extensively. Other Israelis played the part of Ugandan soldiers and terrorists, and a grim mock battle using blank ammunition ensued. Officers watched it all with stop-watches in hand. Instructors pointed to casualties, who had to lie down and be carried back to the aircraft. Eventually the timing improved and, by late on the afternoon of Friday, 2 July, Brigadier Shomron knew that his men could be out of their aircraft and fully deployed within 45 seconds of the loading ramps dropping.

A key figure in the attack was Lieutenant-Colonel Yonatan ("Yoni") Netanyahu, who was leading the strike force in the Hercules with the trickiest task of all—storming the old terminal building without, hopefully, causing any casualties among the hostages. Netanyahu, aged 30, had been born in New York, but his parents had emigrated to the new state of Israel in 1948. He had led a distinguished life in the army, being wounded during the storming of the Golan Heights during the Six-Day War and later defending the same position against Syrian attacks in the Yom Kippur War. Now he was drilling his commandos mercilessly, and, by 16:00 on the Friday afternoon, he was able to report that his men were as ready as possible.

While the assault force was training on the ground, the pilots who would fly the three Hercules were also rehearsing, flying at low level while vigilant Israeli radar operators on the ground tried to spot them, and practising pin-point navigation exercises over the empty wastes of the Sinai Desert. They flew wingtip-to-wingtip in complete radio silence until the pilots also pronounced themselves ready. As darkness fell, Generals Gur and Peled were confident that everything that could be done to make the mission a success had been done. The Chief-of-Staff and air force commander flew back to Jerusalem to report on the day's exercises to the crisis cabinet. Their description of how they intended to carry out the operation brought a burst of applause from the assembled politicians, who had become increasingly concerned at the hijackers' refusal to allow a United Nations force to supervise the exchange of prisoners, even though the West German government had finally capitulated, under protest, and had said that it was prepared to release the Baader-Meinhof prisoners in German jails. Prime Minister Rabin sat quietly for a timeless moment, then looked up at his assembled colleagues. "I am in favour," he announced. The news was received with acclaim at Sharm el-Sheik.

The rescue

On that crucial Sabbath morning, 3 July, Brigadier Shomron carried out a final briefing of all his unit commanders in the presence of Generals Gur and Peled. All the men understood the critical importance of timing, and here the Boeing aerial command post, flying in the radar blind spot above Entebbe, became a vital link in the chain. It could receive line-of-sight transmissions from the small portable radios carried by the troops on the ground and coordinate their activities, as well as being able to monitor radio traffic from Kampala and warn the strike force of any Ugandan troop movements towards the airfield.

After a final dress rehearsal, Brigadier Shomron ordered

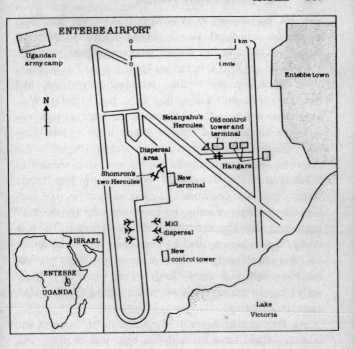

his men to rest. "We go at 16:00 hours," he said. It was a difficult decision to take, for the Israeli meteorological service had reported a severe storm developing, which would be at its worst while the Hercules were flying towards Uganda. It was a further complication to add to the already difficult task of precision flying at low level at night, but it had become apparent that the hijackers' patience was running out and that a delay of even 24 hours could prove fatal.

There was a party in Tel Aviv that night in aid of the United Jewish Appeal, and many of the hundred or so guests remarked on the absence of Generals Gur and Peled. Little did they know that the three Hercules were at that moment thundering 60 m (200 ft.) above the Red Sea, while the scheduled Boeing Flight LY167 to Nairobi, closely accompanied by the aerial command post, was sailing 10,000 m (30,000 ft.) above them.

In the old terminal building at Entebbe, conditions had become unbearable during that long, hot Sabbath. With inadequate water and toilet facilities, the hostages were existing in unadulterated squalor. Many were by now seriously ill, weak and feverish, and constantly haunted by the prowling figure of Gabrielle Tiedemann, who seemed to relish their plight. By contrast, Wilfred Boese was clearly disturbed at their condition and spent most of his time outside the building. Finally, he requested help for the hostages and two Ugandan Army doctors arrived. To their credit, they were appalled by conditions inside the terminal, and immediately set about organizing soldiers to clean out the toilets and supply fresh water, while they themselves moved among the Jews, administering drugs to alleviate the suffering.

As they settled down to sleep that night, none of the hostages could have realized that help was at hand, and that Israeli secret agents were already in action on the airfield, laying plastic explosive charges to demolish all the telephone and telex links with the outside world. When the Hercules suddenly appeared on the flight path at midnight, the Ugandan air-traffic controllers tried frantically to get in touch with Kampala, and could not understand why all the 'phones appeared to be dead.

Although severely buffeted by the storm through which they had flown, the three Hercules had succeeded in keeping station and in avoiding radar detection, assisted by a fortuitous strike among Sudanese air-traffic controllers. Now, as the three gigantic aircraft swept majestically in to land, the commandos inside gripped their weapons even more tightly. Many of them had suffered from airsickness during the rough journey, and for the last hour they had been sitting in total darkness so that their eyes would not have to adjust when the cargo ramps dropped.

As Yoni Netanyahu's aircraft drew up outside the old control tower and the ramp dropped, he shouted "Go!" The two Land Rovers and the black Mercedes wheeled down the ramp and headed for the buildings. As the Ugandan guard shouted the alarm and fire broke out from the three vehicles, the remainder of the commandos concealed inside the dark maw of the Hercules charged out. Ugandan soldiers were already falling in grotesque heaps on to the brilliantly lit tarmac as Gabrielle Tiedemann raised her pistol. She had time for just one shot before she was cut down by a burst of sub-machine-gun fire.

Boese, who had re-entered the control tower to pick up his own sub-machine-gun as the unannounced Hercules landed, ran into the terminal lounge where the hostages were lying, startled into wakefulness by the sudden shooting. He raised his gun to fire. Ilan Hartuv, one of the prisoners who had earlier discomfited Boese by comparing his actions with those of the Nazis, raised his head and looked calmly into the terrorist leader's eyes. Boese visibly hesitated, then turned and ran out of the door. As he emerged from the building he, too, was smashed, dying, to the ground.

As the commandos, led by Yoni Netanyahu, reached the building, a loud hailer was already calling to the hostages "Tishkavu! Tishkavu!" ("Lie down!"). As Yoni pounded down the corridor towards the stairs leading to the roof and control tower, a burst of firing sounded from the terrace. He flattened himself against a wall while the two men with him detached hand grenades from their harness webbing and primed them. Bursting through the door at the top of the stairs, the trio was met by a hail of fire and ducked back hastily, throwing two grenades into the room. The three Palestinian terrorists inside screamed in fear, but were caught in the blast of shrapnel as the grenades exploded. The Israeli commandos swept the room with sub-machine-gun fire in case any of the terrorists had escaped, but they were all dead. A signaller radioed to the circling command post overhead: "We are in the terminal. Yoni is going for the roof."

The roof was soon cleared of terrified Ugandan soldiers, and Yoni and his men descended. He was moving towards the Land Rovers when a Ugandan soldier fired a burst in his direction, and Yoni Netanyahu fell dead with a bullet in his back.

Inside the terminal lounge there was consternation and panic. Most people obeyed the commandos' injunction to lie down, parents shielding their children's bodies with their own, wives clinging to husbands. As soldiers appeared at the terminal windows, one young student leapt to his feet in terror. The commandos were spraying the room with automatic fire at waist to chest height and he fell instantly. An old lady also forced her way to her feet, despite the efforts of those around her to pull her down, and she too fell. Another man was mortally wounded and one woman was hit in the leg by a ricochet. It was a scene of utmost terror and confusion, but gradually order emerged from the chaos. The disbelieving hostages could still hear a fierce firefight going on outside, but the dazed realization that a rescue operation was actually in progress was beginning to sink in.

The firing continued for about a quarter of an hour, then gradually died away as those Ugandan troops who had not been killed, fled. Now Israeli soldiers entered the lounge, moving among the hostages, urging them to their feet and outside to the waiting Land Rovers. Many of the people were so weak that they had to be helped or carried and several of them were in their nightwear. Other commandos encircled the buildings and the dispersal area in a ring of steel, watchful eyes scanning the darkness outside the brilliance of the terminal lights. On the roof of the buildings, snipers with Galil rifles fitted with night sights sought further targets. More Israelis scoured the buildings to ensure that nobody had been left behind.

The people filed into the waiting Hercules, which had been refuelled by a special squad while the fighting was still going on, and, Allison engines roaring, it lifted into the night sky.

Across the airfield at the new terminal and dispersal area, Brigadier Dan Shomron's two Hercules had landed at the same time as Yoni Netanyahu's, and their cargo ramps were being lowered even as the aircraft taxied to a standstill. Jeeps, a command car and an armoured personnel carrier mounting a heavy machine-gun accelerated out, splitting to left and right to encircle the new terminal. Within the 45 seconds achieved during the dress rehearsal, commandos were racing through the building, shooting at anything which moved. However, they could not gain access to the roof, which was held by a strong force of Ugandans armed with light machine-guns whose fire was sweeping the open ground. Dan Shomron ordered the armoured personnel carrier to lay down a withering hail of covering fire to keep the Ugandans' heads down while other commandos stormed the stairs. One Israeli was killed but others hurled hand grenades into the tower and on to the roof, and the Ugandan resistance suddenly ceased.

Meanwhile, another squad was racing towards the parked MiGs, which were heavily guarded. A brief firefight took place before a hand grenade exploded the fuel tanks of one of the fighters, which blew up dramatically, showering the area with debris and burning fuel, and setting light to other aircraft.

Strangely, the Israelis who had been detached to join the

waiting secret agents on the approaches to the Ugandan army camp on the airfield perimeter, found themselves without a job to do. The paranoid dictator, Amin, fearing treachery while he was away in Mauritius, had stripped the troops of their weapons, which were locked in the armoury. The incarcerated Ugandan soldiers, 2000 strong, spent the hour of the raid getting drunk!

With the terminal secured and the MiGs a blazing pile of wreckage, the Israeli commandos scoured the area in order to divert any possible counter-attack by Ugandan troops who might have regrouped, while tanker trucks pumped fuel into the thirsty tanks of the two Hercules. It seemed that time was running out. The circling command post overhead had reported troop movements from the direction of Kampala. Then, with a sigh of relief, Brigadier Shomron watched as the third Hercules with its still disbelieving cargo of passengers lifted off from the old runway. The tanker trucks were quickly disconnected, whistles urgently sounded the recall, and the commandos ran for the ramps of the waiting aircraft. The aerial command post proudly radioed the message "Mission successful" back to the Israeli government, and an astonished world awoke the following morning to the story of one of the most daring and remarkable feats of arms in history. It was a superb achievement.

THE WAR OF INDEPENDENCE

During World War 2, Jews living in the British Protectorate of Palestine suffered divided loyalties because, although they wanted to expel the British military government from "their" country, they were obviously anti-Nazi. As a result, while many Jews served alongside the Allies in the Jewish Brigade, others began preparing for the hiatus which was bound to follow the end of the war in Europe, and formed the *Haganah*, a terrorist organization dedicated to the expulsion of the British Army. Their activities reached a peak just after the war with the bombing of the King David hotel in Jerusalem, but tension was maintained during 1947, since Britain had agreed to grant independence to Egypt in 1949 and began moving military forces from Egypt into Palestine. In this confused situation, the opposing Jewish and Arab groups, both determined to win control of the country after the British finally withdrew, were in constant armed conflict, and atrocities were committed by both sides, including the Jewish massacre of 250 men, women and children in one village and the Arab slaughter of 77 Jewish doctors and nurses in retaliation. The increasing violence and obvious Jewish determination to gain control of Palestine after the British withdrawal, caused hundreds of thousands of Arabs to flee from the affected areas, and by May 1948 it was estimated that the Arab population of Palestine had dropped from 700,000 to a mere 170,000. Herein lay the genesis of the Palestinian problem.

The War of Independence proper lasted from March 1948 to January 1949, with two truces during that period, and resulted in a military defeat for the Arab Legion by the indigenous Palestinian Jews, whose ranks were swollen by refugees from the Holocaust in Europe. Thus, although Israel had declared its independence on 14 May 1948, and *Zahal* had been formally created 12 days later, the country effectively came into existence at the beginning of 1949.

Israeli armour and paras in action

"Shamir and Zebra. This is Tirah. Sunrays to the mike. Over!"

"Tirah, this is Shamir. Sunray speaking. Over."

"Tirah, this is Zebra. Sunray speaking. Over."

"Shamir and Zebra. This is Tirah. Move now and good luck. Over."

The time was 08:15 on 5 June 1967. General Israel Tal, alias Tirah, had just given the order to advance to his two subordinates, Colonels Shmuel and Raphoul. The Israeli "blitzkrieg" was about to break upon unsuspecting Egyptian heads, and its armoured spearhead was General Tal's division in the north. Tal, the founder of modern Israeli tank forces, was then 43 years old. He had fought with the Jewish Brigade in North Africa during World War 2 and had risen rapidly through *Zahal's* ranks after independence, becoming General Officer Commanding Armoured Corps (GOCAC) in 1964. His formation was now charged with the task of creating an initial Israeli breakthrough, its objective the strategically important rail centre of El Arish with its accompanying airfield. At his disposal were three brigades equipped with approximately 150 to 300 Centu-

Israeli tank commanders suffered heavy casualties in exchange for better visibility and therefore faster reactions.

rion and Patton tanks, facing the Egyptian 7th Infantry Division reinforced by an artillery brigade and accompanied by an estimated 100 tanks, holding strong defensive positions protected by deep minefields.

Tal's force was the strongest of the three Israeli spearheads in 1967, the others being the divisions under Generals Abraham Yoffe and Arik Sharon (the founder of the Israeli parachute force, known popularly as "The Guys"), which were operating in the centre and south respectively on a front stretching from Rafa to Kuntilla. Its component forces were "S" armoured brigade, under Colonel Shmuel, "Z" parachute brigade under Colonel Raphoul, and "M" reserve brigade under Colonel Men.

Ever since the conclusion of the 1956 Sinai campaign —when the Israelis had cooperated with British and French forces in seizing the Suez Canal, which had been nationalized by Gamal Nasser—border intrusions and terrorist raids on Israeli *kibbutzim* (communal farms) had been mounting. Under United Nations censure, the British and French forces had been obliged to withdraw from Egypt with great loss of national prestige, while Israel was also forced to withdraw from the territory which *Zahal* had captured in the Sinai. This meant abandoning the airfield at Sharm el-Sheik but, in return, passage of Israeli shipping through the Straits of Tiran was guaranteed by a UN peace-keeping force. As the border incidents continued to increase, in November 1966 Israel launched a massive reprisal raid against *El Fatah* camps in Jordan, and in April 1967 her air force bombed Syrian artillery batteries which had been bombarding *kibbutzim* workers. President Gamal Nasser, who had signed a secret defence agreement with Syria, now demanded the withdrawal of the UN peace-keeping force from the Canal Zone, and closed the Straits of Tiran to Israeli shipping. In May, King Hussein of Jordan flew to Cairo and also signed a defence agreement with

Nasser, while Iraq agreed to provide military support in the event of a war between Jordan and Israel. The noose was tightening around the neck of Israel and, in utmost secrecy, a lightning campaign was planned.

The remarkable efficiency of Israel's "citizen army" was to be proved time and again over the next few days, but in many ways its most dramatic expression came in the speed of the call-up. Brigade commanders summoned battalion commanders, who telephoned or raced around to see company commanders, who organized their Sergeants to notify their men—and women. Shopkeepers, accountants, typists, journalists, schoolteachers, mechanics, salesmen—they all responded to the call and went home to change into their uniforms. After presenting themselves at their respective assembly points, they were issued with arms and ammunition and proceeded to wait. Gradually the tension mounted.

The battle commences

The Israeli cabinet finally took the decision to attack during the long night of 3/4 June 1967, and the time of waiting was over. The preliminary air strike went in at 07:45 on 5 June, and half an hour later the tanks and armoured personnel carriers began to roll.

The Sinai Desert is a harsh and barren wasteland, broken only by the occasional clump of scrub grass, scoured clean by a constant burning wind and inhabited solely, under normal circumstances, by the odd nomadic bedouin. Like all desert landscapes, it appears virtually flat to the uneducated eye, but the successful tank commander is the one who can spot the shallow depressions and low ridges which will enable him to enter into a hull-down position with just his turret showing to the enemy, and who can recognize from afar the deceptively smooth areas of soft

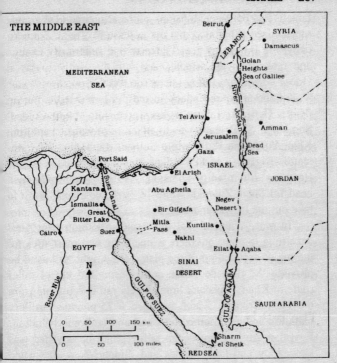

THE MIDDLE EAST

On 5 June, the normally uninhabited Sinai was crowded. By this time the Egyptians had concentrated no fewer than seven divisions in the arena: 4th Armoured, 2nd, 3rd, 6th and 7th Infantry, 20th PLA (Palestine Liberation Army), and a special armoured battle group of divisional strength without a number. Against this might the

sand which will hinder his vehicle's advance. Israeli tank commanders, like their earlier counterparts in the Afrika Korps and 8th Army (and unlike Arab tank commanders, who go into action with all their hatches battened down), have the slow-moving, distant gaze of men accustomed to "the blue."

Israelis had but three divisions—one armoured (Tal's), one mechanized (Sharon's) and one reserve (Yoffe's). Numerically, the Egyptians had a three-to-one superiority in men and tanks over the Israelis. As with the British paras at Goose Green, this did not deter the Israeli troops.

For the armoured attack in the north or Mediterranean flank, General Tal split his force into two: Colonel Shmuel's "S" Brigade was to attack northwards, capturing Khan Yunis and Rafa, while Colonel Raphoul's "Z" Parachute Brigade was to outflank the southern edge of the Egyptian 7th Infantry Division. "S" Brigade would then head for Sheik Zuweid, while "Z" Brigade swung north to take out the Egyptian artillery.

"In war," General Tal once said, "nothing ever goes according to plan, but there is one thing you must stick to: the major designation of the plan." How right he was to be proved. "S" Brigade struck north on the 6.5 km (4 mile) route to Khan Yunis and immediately ran into trouble from the PLA Brigade, which included a 25-pounder artillery battalion and a combined tank and anti-tank gun battalion. Egyptian artillery fire began falling, and the advance was slowed by anti-tank ditches and minefields while, when they reached the town itself, the tank crews became confused in the narrow streets. S/14 Battalion was entrapped and had to summon the help of S/10 which was to have bypassed the town to the south. The two battalions met at the railway station, by which time the PLA defenders were beating a hasty retreat, and together they pushed on towards Rafa. However, six tanks had already been incapacitated and no fewer than 35 tank commanders killed or wounded, largely through machine-gun fire as a result of going into action with their heads and shoulders exposed in their tanks' turrets. Four more tanks were damaged by mines *en route* to Rafa.

S/10 entered the town, meeting minimal opposition, but

again S/14 ran into trouble against a heavily defended
strongpoint with cunningly dug-in and camouflaged anti-
tank guns. The Egyptian gunners put up a stubborn resistance and once again S/10 had to come to S/14's
assistance, racing down on the Egyptian position from the
rear. The gunners began fleeing, with the exception of one
brave man, who attempted to knock out the nearest tank
with an old American bazooka.

In the meantime, Tal's southern pincer, comprising "Z"
Parachute Brigade with "M" Brigade in reserve, had also
encountered stiff resistance, including an Egyptian battalion of Joseph Stalin III heavy tanks, which forced Raphoul's tanks to fight, so leaving the paras in their
armoured half-tracks dangerously exposed. Fierce hand-to-
hand fighting took place during the afternoon, but eventually the paras won through and, by late afternoon on the
first day of the war, General Tal's northern force had
reached El Arish, while the Egyptian positions south of the
Rafa junction were in Raphoul's hands. However, there
was an unpleasant surprise in store for, although they did
not know it at the time, the Israelis had completely missed
the southernmost of the Egyptian brigades. The first in-
kling of this came when helicopters, brought in to evacuate
Israeli wounded, came under intense fire from the ground.
The paras launched an immediate attack, and fighting for
this position continued until well after dark.

Further south still, General Yoffe's mechanized division
had had a much easier day. Advancing through an area of
deep sand dunes which the Egyptians had thought impass-
able, his troops covered close on 96 km (60 miles), reaching the vicinity of Bir Lahfan at around 18:00 without a
single casualty. Here, however, the Israelis encountered
Egyptian reinforcements being sent north towards El Arish.
Fighting continued through the night of 5/6 June, during
which several Egyptian tanks were destroyed, and in the

morning an Israeli air raid sent the remainder packing, hotly pursued by a group of Yoffe's own tanks.

On the Israeli left, or southern flank, General Sharon had split his force into two, one advancing parallel to Yoffe's towards Abu Agheila in the centre, the other even further south towards Kuntilla. Abu Agheila was a vital communications centre which had to be captured before the Israeli advance could continue any further, and naturally it was heavily defended by the incumbent Egyptian 2nd Infantry Division reinforced with 80 to 90 tanks and 6 artillery regiments. General Sharon's plan of attack involved a complex interleaving of all arms: artillery to pin the enemy frontally, followed by four assault columns alternating armour and infantry, with Israeli paras lastly being dropped by helicopter on the Egyptian artillery positions in their rear.

By 15:00 on 5 June, Sharon's forces were in position about 8 km (5 miles) from the Abu Agheila defences. The northernmost of the four assault columns ran into Egyptian tanks which forced Sharon's men to retire, but by dint of renewed effort they pushed through, and, by later in the afternoon, they had reached the Abu Agheila-El Arish road. After dark they pushed further forward, ready to strike southwards in support of the other assault columns. Similarly, the southernmost of the four columns had reached the Kusseima-Abu Agheila road so that, by nightfall, all the Egyptians' lines of communication had been cut. At dusk, helicopters landed a battalion of paras behind the enemy lines while their attention was diverted by the approach of the two central Israeli columns and an intense artillery barrage. Shortly before 23:00 the final attack took place—tanks from the front and north, mechanized infantry from the south and the paras from the rear. Flares and tracer lit the desert sky as the Israelis pressed in on the Egyptian positions with fixed bayonets. There was fierce hand-to-hand fighting in the trenches, but within five hours most of the Egyptian positions were in Israeli hands. As dawn broke, the tanks—which had been largely useless in the dark—moved forward to complete the rout and, by 06:00 on 6 June, Sharon was able to order a further advance towards Kusseima.

Returning to Tal's forces in the north, S/14 had again run into trouble in the Jiradi area. While part of the battalion broke through the strong defences, it soon found itself cut off and another fierce battle took place during which the battalion commander, Major Elad, was killed. The remainder of the battalion broke through in the wake of S/14, but also found itself cut off as the Egyptians regrouped behind, and the reserve "M" Brigade was unable to help because Colonel Men's tanks were practically out of fuel. General Tal therefore ordered the mechanized infantry part of "S" Brigade, which had been mopping up in the Rafa area, to press forward to relieve Shmuel. This task was made doubly difficult by the dozens of wrecked and burned-out vehicles which littered the road, and by heavy traffic jams. Arriving at midnight on the 5th, the infantrymen moved straight into the attack and, after four hours of heavy fighting, the position was taken for the third time.

With their rear secure, S/10 and S/14 pressed on from Jiradi and by 04:00 were not only in El Arish, but had even taken the vital airfield. At daybreak, General Tal split his force again, half being diverted southwards to link up with Yoffe at Bir Lahfan, while the remainder pressed onward to Qantara and the Suez Canal.

Deep sand dunes aided the defenders at Bir Lahfan, and Tal's troops had a hard fight of it before they managed to win through and join forces with Yoffe's columns around midday on the 6th. From here, they planned to move jointly westward as far as Jebel Libni, after which they would split again, Tal's men striking further west towards

Ismailia, via Bir Gifgafa, while Yoffe went south, heading ultimately for the Mitla Pass and Suez. Simultaneously, Sharon would first strike down from Abu Agheila towards Nakhl in order to link up with his other troops pressing west from Kuntilla; then, combined, they would also head for the Mitla Pass, strategically the most important feature in the Sinai.

Wednesday, 7 June, was the third and most decisive day of the campaign. After a short, sharp tank engagement at Jebel Libni, General Tal's northern division sped west towards Bir Gifgafa. Yoffe pressed on rapidly through Bir Hassneh towards Bir Thamada to cut off Egyptian troops retreating west in the southern sector of the front, and reached the vital entrance to the Mitla Pass at about 18:00. Half of his tanks had run out of fuel and had to be towed by those which were still mobile, but they could still fire their guns. Tal established a blocking position at Bir Gifgafa; there would be no escape for the Egyptian tanks whose retreat was being hurried along by Sharon—they would have to fight.

After a pause during the Wednesday night in order to allow his troops—most of whom had been constantly on the move since early Monday morning—to sleep, Sharon continued his long southward trek towards Nakhl. *En route* he came across an amazing sight: an entire brigade of Joseph Stalin III tanks abandoned in the middle of the desert. Their Egyptian commander had heard of the Israeli successes and, deciding that discretion was the better part of valour, had fled with his men in the brigade's half-tracks!

At Nakhl, Sharon laid a trap for the Egyptian forces still retreating from Kuntilla. Leaving the bulk of his tanks deployed on the southern outskirts of the town, he took the remainder in a long loop to the north-east. The Egyptians ran into the blocking force at Nakhl and were then taken in the rear by the rest of Sharon's force. It was slaughter.

At Bir Gifgafa, Tal's similar blocking force of two battalions had a more difficult task against an Egyptian armoured brigade, whose assault was actually accompanied by ground-attack aircraft—one of the few occasions during the war when the Egyptian MiGs saw action, since most of them had been destroyed on the ground during the preliminary Israeli air strike on the Monday morning. The situation at Bir Gifgafa became critical during the Wednesday night, when a new force of Russian-built T-54 main battle tanks blundered unwittingly into the Israeli positions. The Israelis had only the light, French-built, AMX-13 tanks on the spot, and these were no match for the heavier, better-armed and better-armoured T-54s. After a couple of hours, during which the Israelis tried to use their superior speed and mobility to counteract the Egyptians' advantages, Tal withdrew his battalions until heavier armour could be brought forward to reinforce them. The arrival of a company of Centurions redressed the balance, allowing the Israelis to re-occupy their original positions, and Tal then sent a further armoured brigade southwards to come round and attack the Egyptians from the rear. Outnumbered, and having already lost several tanks, the Egyptian brigade was soon overwhelmed.

Yoffe's force at the Mitla Pass, a solitary brigade under Colonel Iska, also found itself in difficulties as thousands of Egyptian troops tried to pour through the 23 km (15 mile) gap towards Suez and, by 22:00 on Wednesday night, he was surrounded and in grave danger of being overrun, despite the courage with which his paras were fighting. A second brigade was ordered to make a night march to relieve Colonel Iska. Advancing through the darkness, it suddenly found itself, like a comedy scene in a bad film, moving alongside a large column of Egyptian tanks headed in the same direction. The Egyptians took the Israeli tanks for friends in the darkness, but the Israelis, knowing that there were none of their own troops in the vicinity, began shooting up the thoroughly confused Egyptians with rare abandon!

Leaving their disorganized foe behind trying to work out what had happened, the fresh brigade pressed on and came as a godsend to Iska's men, who had been fighting continuously now for 72 hours and who were running very short of ammunition. Relieving them in the middle of a pitched battle was not easy, but was finally accomplished on Thursday morning, the fourth day of the war. Unable to break through the stubborn Israelis, and unable to retreat because of General Sharon's approach, several Egyptian tanks actually tried to climb the steep walls of the pass, where they became "stuck like flies," in General Yoffe's words.

During the Thursday afternoon, Yoffe's new brigade battled its way to the western end of the Mitla Pass, where it encountered strongly defended Egyptian positions blocking any further advance towards the Suez Canal. Yoffe ordered a daring night attack, his tanks charging forward with headlights blazing, and the petrified Egyptians abandoned their positions and fled. By 02:00 on Friday, 9 June, Yoffe's forces had reached the canal. One armoured brigade was sent north towards Ismailia, but ran into heavy opposition from Egyptian tanks occupying hull-down positions behind the crests of dunes. The Israelis countered by splitting their force, two companies moving through the dunes while the remainder advanced along the road to draw the Egyptians' fire and make them reveal their positions. By this method the relatively small Israeli force succeeded in destroying some 70 Egyptian tanks for the loss of only 10 of their own.

While this was happening, on Thursday night Nasser asked for a cease-fire. In one of the fastest and most decisive military operations of all time, Israeli forces had succeeded in breaking the hitherto proud Egyptian Army, in capturing over 700 tanks and 5000 officers (Egyptian other ranks, after being given food, water and medical attention, were allowed to swim home across the canal, where a large number of them were inadvertently machine-gunned by their own troops on the western bank).

The battle for Jerusalem

It must be remembered that, at the beginning of the June 1967 campaign, which has ever afterwards been known as the Six-Day War, Jerusalem was still, like Berlin, a divided city: half Jewish and half Arab. As soon as King Hussein of Jordan received news of the Israeli advance into the Sinai, Jordanian forces in Jerusalem and on the West Bank of the River Jordan began opening fire and moved forward to occupy Mount Scopus, which was taken by midday on 5 June, followed by Government House in the early afternoon. Israeli tanks and paratroopers began moving forward and, by 16:00, had retaken the latter strongpoint. The heavily defended Police School was another story. Occupied by about 200 fanatical members of the Arab Legion, it took 500 Israeli paras several hours to capture, and did not finally succumb until 04:00 on Tuesday, after the courageous defenders had lost more than half their men.

By 10:00, most of the fighting in the former demilitarized zone was over, and the Israelis turned their attention to the Old City. This proved a more difficult task, since neither side wished to use heavy weapons which could damage the many historic and religious sites, and in the ensuing firefight the Israelis were at a disadvantage, having to move through the open while the Arabs were well dug-in. To the north-east of the city, however, Mount Scopus finally fell to the Israelis after the collapse of the defence in the Police School.

On Wednesday morning, the Israelis attacked once more, the regiment on Mount Scopus advancing uphill to Augusta Victoria, while infantry attacked the Old City again. This time heavy weapons *were* employed, although great care was taken to avoid the Holy Places, and, by 10:00, the Temple Mount and Wailing Wall were Israeli territory.

With Jerusalem firmly in Israeli hands, *Zahal* was ready to complete operations on the West Bank. There had been only minor activity here on the 5th, when Israeli forces moved down from the north in the direction of Jenin. On the 6th, a further attack in the north from Sandala had reached Jenin and Qabatiya, a third force had advanced eastwards from Kalkilya, and a fourth had reached Ramallah, just north of Jerusalem, and had taken it in a night attack. In the north, around Jenin, the Jordanians had a strong force of M-47 Patton tanks, but they were left in a difficult situation because the Israeli air force made repeated attacks on their supply columns. In the end, nearly half the tanks had to be abandoned for want of supplies.

Now, on the Wednesday, the road seemed clear for the projected Israeli pincer movement—General Elazar's forces moving down from the north, and Colonel Uri Ben-Ali's moving east and north from Ramallah. Ben-Ali pressed on to Jericho, which fell without need of trumpets, while south of Jerusalem Colonel Amitai broke through the Jordanian positions and advanced on Bethlehem and Hebron. By dusk on 7 June, therefore, this phase of operations was complete. Jerusalem, the West Bank, and the Sinai as far west as the Suez Canal were all in Israeli hands. Next came the turn of the Syrians, who had remained ominously quiet so far.

Assault on the Golan Heights

The Golan Heights were the key to the Syrian positions. High, bleak and rugged, they were defended by complex fortifications some 16 km (10 miles) in depth, with dug-in tank, artillery and rocket launcher batteries. For two solid days the Israeli air force plastered these defences with everything in their arsenal, but the Syrian fortifications were deep and strong. However, the Arabs' morale began cracking under the merciless bombardment, with a new air raid every ten minutes. They were still strongly in evidence on the Friday morning, though, as Israeli bulldozers began advancing up the slopes to clear a path for the following tanks and armoured personnel carriers. The Israeli engineers suffered heavy casualties from well dug-in Syrian tanks, which eventually had to be destroyed by infantry with hand grenades.

Two more attacks further south, in the Gonen and Ashmura vicinities, were also successful, and by nightfall the Israelis had two footholds on the Heights. On the following morning both forces struck towards Qnaitra through the difficult, rocky terrain, reaching it by 13:00 and capturing it after an hour's fighting. Meanwhile, in the south, a further attack by infantry and tanks up the Yarmouk Valley succeeded in pinning down the Syrians while a paratroop force was dropped by helicopter in their rear. By the Saturday evening, therefore, the Heights were firmly in Israeli hands, and both sides accepted the cease-fire for which the United Nations Security Council had been calling since Friday morning.

The Six-Day War left Israel in a stronger position than at any time since her temporary occupation of the Sinai in 1956–7. She had possession of the crucial Golan Heights; Jerusalem was a united city once more; the West Bank had been cleared of hostile troops; and Israeli soldiers sat on the banks of the Suez Canal. Sharm el-Sheik had fallen, with its vital airfield defending access to the Red Sea, and, for the first time, Israel had territory to trade in exchange for time if ever counter-attacked.

For the next few years, an uneasy peace settled over the

Middle East, a peace interrupted only by Israeli engineers building fortified defence posts along the east bank of the Suez Canal, while desultory Egyptian artillery barrages bombarded them, and during which the strong Syrian defences on the Golan Heights were turned to the Israelis' advantage. Known as the "War of Attrition," this period lasted until 1970, when President Nasser died. His successor, Anwar Sadat, was determined to restore Egyptian prestige and redress the humiliating military defeat of 1967. After first expelling all the Soviet advisers in Egypt, Sadat shortly afterwards relented, and a new flood of Soviet arms and equipment began to enter the country. By April 1973 a new war seemed imminent. A partial mobilization of Israeli forces took place the following month in response to a strong build-up of Egyptian forces on the west bank of the Suez Canal, but nothing happened and *Zahal* reverted to its normal alert status. However, the mobilization had cost several million Israeli pounds and would be remembered when a similar situation arose later in October of the same year.

This time, the Arab leaders were determined that the "boot" should be on the other foot, and were planning to take Israel by surprise. There were secret talks between Egypt, Syria and Jordan, and further discussions with the Gulf States—particularly Saudi Arabia—aimed at producing an oil embargo to prevent super-power intervention.

THE YOM KIPPUR WAR

Despite the vast strides in training, morale and equipment which had been made in the Egyptian Army since 1967, its task in 1973 was not an easy one, thanks to the high ramparts on the Israeli side of the Suez Canal which made a tank crossing impossible. The initial assault thus had to be made by infantry, equipped with scaling ladders and sufficient supplies and ammunition to hold their own for at least 24 hours. Breaches were to be blown in the Israeli ramparts not by explosives, but by high-pressure water hoses, no fewer than 80 special units being created and trained for this specific task. After consolidating their bridgeheads, Egyptian forces were supposed to head for the Mitla and other passes into the Sinai, but in fact this second phase never materialized, due to the speed of the Israeli response.

The Egyptian assault was planned for 6 October for both military and psychological reasons. It was not only a moonlit night, but also the tide in the canal was just right for crossing. Moreover, October is the Muslim fast month of *Ramadan,* during which *Zahal* was unlikely to expect an attack, and the 6th itself is the Jewish fast day of *Yom Kippur,* when defences were confidently expected to be at a low ebb. Secrecy was total. Right up until the last moment, Egyptian soldiers thought that they were merely going on yet another exercise. Indeed, they were not informed until the morning of the attack that this time it was "for real," and only 5 out of 18 officers of Colonel and Lieutenant-Colonel rank were let in on the plan before the day itself.

To a large extent, the Israeli Defence Force (IDF) had been lulled into a sense of complacency, partly as a result of its success in the Six-Day War, and partly because of the non-event of the alert earlier in the year. Besides, it was a national holiday and the reserves were on stand-down when the attack materialized. The Egyptians had 3 armies mobilized along the canal, consisting of 4 infantry divisions, 3 mechanized divisions, 2 armoured divisions and 2 independent armoured brigades, and 16 artillery brigades. Against this, Israel had five under-strength "divisions." However, the Suez Canal constituted only half the picture. Five Syrian divisions, two of which were armoured, were also in place and ready to go on the eastern front, while Israeli defences on the Golan Heights were slim.

At dawn on 6 October, General Eli Zeira, the Director of *Mossad*—the Israeli secret service—received a telephone call from an agent which confirmed that an attack was imminent. He immediately notified Defence Minister Moshe Dayan and General Elazar, who contacted General Beni Peled, commander of the air force, as well as General Tal, and an urgent meeting was held at 05:50. Unfortunately, Israeli intelligence had got the time of the attack wrong—18:00 instead of 14:00. The traditional times for an attack are dawn and dusk, whichever puts the sun in the defender's eyes, and 18:00 would have been ideal for an Egyptian attack. However, this would have acted in the Israelis' favour on the Syrian front, so the two Arab allies had selected the completely unlikely hour of 14:00 as a compromise.

While the Israeli high command uncharacteristically dithered, calling up only part of the reserves and refusing suggestions for a pre-emptive air strike, the Arabs completed their preparations and, at 13:45, a Syrian artillery bombardment erupted upon Mount Hermon. Helicopter-borne commandos followed and rapidly overran the Israeli positions as the massed tank and infantry formations began rolling forward. Unfortunately for the Syrians, their sheer weight of numbers ensured that the comparatively small force of Israeli tanks and guns could hardly miss, and the leading wave of Syrian troops fell in droves. However, numerical superiority did begin to tell, and in the south the Israeli 137th Armoured Brigade was cut to pieces and overrun. In the north, however, the crack 7th Armoured Brigade held on manfully, despite being completely surrounded on several occasions. The arrival of a fresh armoured brigade helped to stabilize the situation for the Israelis on Sunday, 7 October, although their forces on the Golan Heights were still heavily outnumbered. By midnight on that day, though, the Syrians had advanced as far as the Israelis were going to let them. Their casualties were often in the ratio of five or even ten to one and, in one notable engagement, three Israeli Centurion tanks succeeded in destroying or immobilizing no fewer than 35 Russian-built T-55s.

Throughout Monday the beleaguered 7th Brigade continued to fight against overwhelming odds. The Syrians' new Soviet T-62 tanks were fitted with what were then sophisticated night vision 'scopes, which gave them an enormous advantage over the ageing Israeli tanks, and by Tuesday morning the 7th had very few serviceable vehicles left. The Syrians then unleashed a massive bombardment with artillery, rockets and ground-attack aircraft, under cover of which the T-62s, supported by infantry, began to inch forward. The Israelis retired a few hundred metres and prepared for the onslaught. As the Syrians breasted the skyline, the remaining 15 Centurions and Pattons opened fire and then, incredibly, counter-attacked. The astonished Syrians fell back momentarily, as a Great Dane will when menaced by a Jack Russell, but within minutes the Israeli force had been depleted to only seven tanks, and they were running out of ammunition. As in a film, the "cavalry" arrived in the nick of time in the form of a scratch force of another 13 tanks, and the demoralized Syrians, who had expected a walkover, began to retire.

By the Wednesday, the delayed Israeli mobilization of the reserves was really taking effect, however, and, despite still being outnumbered, the forces on the Golan Heights turned on the offensive. Although their tank crews continued to put up a stiff fight, the Syrian infantry did not give them the support they deserved and, by midday on 10 October, all Syrian forces had been pushed back behind their original start lines. The road was clear for an Israeli invasion of Syria itself.

D-Day on the Suez Canal

Meanwhile, in Egypt, the Yom Kippur War had begun with an intensive air strike by some 240 aircraft against Israeli anti-aircraft missile batteries, radar stations and strongpoints, accompanied by a massive artillery barrage from some 2000 muzzles against the tiny force of just 436 Israeli soldiers guarding the strongpoints, strung at 11 km (7 mile) intervals along the 175 km (110 mile) canal line. This bombardment was followed by an assault by 8000 Egyptian infantry, who carefully selected landing sites in the gaps between the Israeli blockhouses. They were followed by special assault teams whose assignment was to eliminate the blockhouses while Egyptian Army engineers began construction of ten bridges across the canal.

The task of the Israeli commander in charge of the armoured brigades east of the canal was not an enviable one. General Abraham Mandler was aware that the Egyptians were attacking, but he did not know where to concentrate his forces for a counter-thrust. Should he try to destroy the bridges which the enemy was building, or should he attempt to join up with surviving forces in the blockhouse line? It was a situation at which many top-rate commanders would have balked but, unfortunately, General Mandler made the mistake of deciding to commit his tanks in small groups in order to find out exactly what was happening. They were met enthusiastically by Egyptian soldiers armed with new Soviet wire-guided anti-tank missiles, and were destroyed piecemeal. By nightfall, Mandler had lost nearly two-thirds of his original force of 280 tanks.

At 09:00 on Sunday the 7th, the first Egyptian armoured units began swarming across the newly built bridges over the canal. The plight of the surviving defenders in the Israeli strongpoints was desperate, but Mandler had been ordered to let them fend for themselves and to concentrate his remaining armour against the Egyptian tanks. There are many tales of heroism from this period of the war, but one of the most outstanding must be that of the southernmost Israeli garrison at Port Tewfik, where 42 defenders held out for an entire week against a whole Egyptian army, defying all attempts to enter their position and finally surrendering only when all their medical supplies and ammunition were exhausted.

At 11:40 on Sunday, Dayan himself arrived to review the situation in the Sinai, and he took the immediate decision to withdraw from the canal zone to the high ground east of it. The next few days witnessed a battle of containment as the Egyptians fought to break out into the Sinai, and the Israelis doggedly held them back. Egyptian tactics during this phase of the war can only be described as suicidal. They would prepare for an attack under cover of darkness, sending their infantry forward to within 1800 m (2000 yd.) of the Israeli defences. At dawn, a short but intense artillery barrage would announce the assault, and then the infantry, supported by tanks, would move forward. Only one such attack, on Tuesday the 9th, achieved partial success, before being thrown back by an armoured Israeli counter-thrust. By Wednesday (at which time the Israelis were pushing off the Golan Heights), the Egyptians had run out of steam, and it was the Israelis' turn to attack.

Counter-attack

The basic plan was for a two-division assault across the canal at the junction of the Egyptian 2nd and 3rd Armies, for which a special prefabricated bridge had been prepared. This was a dangerous scheme, because the bulk of the Egyptian armoured reserves were on the west bank of the canal, but, as we have seen elsewhere, "who dares, wins."

Coincidentally, the Egyptians were also summoning their strength for another attempt at breaking out and, unknown to each other, both sides chose 14 October as the day of attack. The Egyptians attacked first in four columns, one in the north from Qantara, one from Ismailia, one towards the Mitla Pass, and one in the south along the Gulf of Suez. However, the Israelis were fully prepared and had learned the danger of the Egyptian anti-tank wire-guided missiles. Keeping to the high ground, they used the highly accurate 105 mm guns on their Centurion and Patton tanks to knock out the Egyptian missile operators, moving rapidly from one position to another in order to spoil the Egyptians' aim.

The Israelis revised their basic plan, to take advantage of the situation. Instead of crossing the canal opposite Ismailia, as originally envisaged, the attack would now take place further south at Deversoir, just north of the Great Bitter Lake. The offensive began to roll late in the afternoon of the 15th, three armoured columns supported by paras and a rolling artillery bombardment moving rapidly towards the canal, while a diversionary attack pinned down the Egyptians in front of Ismailia. Heavy resistance was encountered in the Chinese Farm area, but Israeli "watch and dodge" tactics, in which one tank moved while a second spotted for anti-tank missiles, were largely successful in minimizing casualties from these missiles.

The Israelis were handed one present on a plate, when the brigade commanded by Colonel Amnon suddenly found that it had broken through in the junction between the Egyptian 2nd and 3rd Armies, and was actually behind the lines. Pandemonium broke out among the Egyptians. Soldiers and tanks raced hither and thither in total confusion, while Amnon's tanks coolly blasted away at ammunition dumps, fuel depots, radar and missile sites, tanks and trucks. By the early morning of the 16th, the brigade entrusted to secure a foothold across the canal was on the west bank, the infantry crossing on rafts which were then sent back for the tanks. Israeli reinforcements, who were bringing pontoons in order to build bridges, pushed forward through the gap in the Egyptian lines created by Colonel Amnon's brigade, but were unable to reach the bank of the canal before dawn, and it would have been suicidal to try to build bridges in daylight.

Inevitably, the Egyptians counter-attacked on the 17th, but their attempt to throw the Israelis back from the canal failed, with the loss of 86 T-62 tanks against a mere 4 Israeli tanks destroyed. Thus, during the night of 18/19 October, Israeli engineers assembled the pontoon bridge in position and their tanks pressed across, splitting into two columns heading northwards and southwards along the west bank. By the evening of the 18th, the southern force had secured the strategically important Geneifa Hills and, on the following day, they seized Fayid airport.

However, Soviet Premier Kosygin telephoned President Sadat on the evening of the 20th and persuaded him to agree to a cease-fire, while American envoy Henry Kissinger convinced the Israelis.

Towards Damascus

Back in the east, on 11 October, Israeli forces had begun a major counter-attack in the northern sector of the Golan Heights, but the terrain and the multiplicity of Syrian anti-tank missiles held them up, and they could only make slow progress. Further south, another Israeli division launched an attack straight down the Damascus road, but it too ran into stiff opposition, and an entire armoured brigade was surrounded and virtually annihilated before being relieved by horrified paras the following morning. However, the Syrians were virtually at the end of their strength, and the

Egyptian attack on the 14th has often been interpreted as an attempt to take Israeli pressure off them while reinforcements, in the form of an Iraqi armoured division, could be brought forward. However, this fared no better than the Syrian armoured formations had. The build-up was spotted by the Israeli commander on the southern flank, General Laner, and he prepared a classic trap: a three-sided killing-ground into which the oblivious Iraqi tanks obligingly trundled. Battle was joined at a distance of only 50 m (55 yd.) and, hit in both flanks, the Iraqi forces reeled back in disorder, losing 80 tanks. Israeli casualties were zero.

The next attack came from Jordanian Centurion tanks every bit as good as the Israelis' own. They moved forward with determination but did not receive coordinated support from their Syrian and Iraqi allies, and were unable to make any headway against the Israeli bridgehead. A final attack by Iraqi forces against the northern flank of the bridgehead resulted in a seven-hour battle, again often at point-blank range, until an Israeli assault on the Iraqis' flank finally won the day. Meanwhile, Mount Hebron had been taken by the Golani Brigade, which advanced frontally, while Israeli paras were dropped by helicopter behind the Syrian lines. On 22 October, the Syrian government agreed to the cease-fire and the war was over.

THE LEBANON

Denied of their bases in Jordan after King Hussein expelled them just prior to the Yom Kippur War, the Palestine Liberation Organization guerrillas established their headquarters in Beirut. Following the Arab defeat in that campaign, the PLO intensified its raids across the border as well as other terrorist activities, which came to a head with the shooting of the Israeli ambassador in London in June 1982. The Israelis retaliated with an air strike on the PLO arms depot in Beirut's sports stadium, and the PLO escalated the conflict by means of an artillery bombardment of Israeli border settlements. Prime Minister Begin's patience finally snapped, and Israeli tanks were ordered into Lebanon, where the situation was already confused because of the internecine war which had been going on for some years between Lebanese Christians and Muslims. To begin with, the Israeli attack was purely defensive, being aimed at clearing a 40 km (25 mile) strip of southern Lebanon in order to push the PLO artillery back out of range of the northern settlements in Israel. However, the war soon escalated into more than this for, while Israeli sympathies largely lay with the Christian faction in Lebanon, Syria supported the Muslim cause and had maintained a strong military presence in the country ever since 1976.

Sunday, 6 June 1982. The war in the Falkland Islands was drawing to a close, but Colonel Eli Geva's thoughts were elsewhere as his armoured brigade rolled across the Lebanese border, heading for the line of the El Awali River which the Israelis had decided upon as a useful physical border to their planned demilitarized zone. Another column advanced through Metulla and seized Beaufort Castle which had been built by the Crusaders and which, standing on high ground, had for years served as a PLO fortress from which they could launch rocket attacks on the Israeli villages below. During the evening, Israeli paras landed in assault craft at the mouth of the El Awali River, and, on Monday, a third Israeli armoured column began moving towards the Al-Shouf Mountains.

Palestinian forces fought back viciously, killing large numbers of their own people—innocents held hostage by the terrorist forces who were supposed to be acting on their behalf. But, by the end of the first week of fighting, Israeli troops were in the suburbs of Beirut and had linked with the Christian Phalangists in cutting the road from Beirut to Damascus.

General Sharon, who had commanded the Israeli centre on the Suez front during the Yom Kippur War, was itching to get to grips with the Syrians in Lebanon, who were maintaining a distinctly low profile at this stage. His chance came when the Syrians sent tanks to reinforce a PLO unit. Putting Major-General "Yanosh" Bengal in charge of the retaliatory force was no accident: Bengal had commanded the 7th Armoured Brigade on the Golan Heights in 1973, and his thirst for revenge against the Syrians was not yet quenched. Let off the leash, Bengal pursued the Syrians with vigour and, within two days of intense fighting, had killed at least 1000 men and had destroyed approximately 300 enemy tanks. By the weekend following that on which the invasion began, the Israelis had destroyed the heart of the PLO resistance, given the Syrians a sound thrashing, and established sound links with the Phalangist forces in Beirut.

Now the war entered a new phase as PLO guerrillas established fresh strongpoints, usually around or in the middle of harmless civilian buildings, not excluding hospitals. Intensive street-fighting was the inevitable result as the campaign waxed and waned over the long, hot days of that summer of 1982. The PLO dug in more firmly, while the Israelis were inhibited in their use of aircraft and artillery by the danger to countless innocent lives. During July, *Zahal* succeeded in capturing Beirut airport and various PLO camps in the vicinity, but Palestinian reinforcements were still flooding through from Syria and, on the 22nd of that month, the Israelis responded with a furious artillery bombardment which destroyed a further 70 Syrian tanks— many of them the new Russian T-72s which were pitched into battle in the Lebanon for the first time against the Israeli-designed and -built Merkava (which proved itself superior).

At the end of July, all Israeli reserves were mobilized

Israeli paras ('The Guys') shuffle forward in the cramped confines of their transport aircraft prior to a drop.

and, on 1 August, began tightening a ring of steel around Beirut. The PLO had had enough by this time and wanted nothing more than a cease-fire which would allow them to escape. This Arik Sharon would not permit, and he called up air strikes which for two days pounded every known or suspected PLO strongpoint, leaving Beirut in rubble. Reprisals inside Israel caused Prime Minister Menachem Begin to resign. Although it had administered a severe blow to both the PLO and Syria, the Israeli offensive failed in its ultimate objective of creating a new and peaceful state in the Lebanon, and the after-effects of the war are still being felt to this day.

The Israeli Army today

Surrounded by potential enemies, Israel is the most security-conscious country in the world outside the Soviet Union, and is constantly altering the composition of its forces, their designations, locations and commanders, with the result that, for example, different accounts of the Six-Day War can put one unit in two different places at the same time, or give the same unit two different designations. Israeli vehicles carry none of the divisional or regimental insignia beloved by other armies, but just individual numbers, and repeated efforts by foreign observers and journalists to crack the "code" have produced even more discrepancies. Thus, it is impossible to say that unit X comprises Y number of men trained in parachute jumping and amphibious warfare, or whatever, as is possible with the élite forces of most other countries in this book. What *can* be said is that *Zahal* possesses airborne, mountain and armoured brigades which have proved their élite status time and time again, and which are believed to be organized as follows.

A parachute or mountain brigade will consist of three combat battalions, one artillery regiment, one reconnaissance company, and supporting signals and engineering units. Each battalion in turn consists of three rifle companies plus a headquarters company which doubles as the support company. The tripod arrangement continues downwards with three platoons to a company and three sections, each of ten men in two squads, to a platoon. An armoured brigade similarly will consist of three battalions, but, depending on its intended role, there may be three or four tank companies to a battalion, together with reconnaissance and self-propelled mortar platoons. Each tank company consists of three troops, each with three tanks, plus an HQ section with three tanks and two armoured personnel carriers.

Conscription in Israel is universal, with men serving for three years and women for two, after which soldiers revert to the reserve, which currently comprises a quarter of a million men and women on permanent 12-hour standby out of a population of only four million! The regular standing army consists of approximately 18,000 soldiers backed by 120,000 conscripts, in addition to which there is a small battalion of approximately 300 naval commandos trained in amphibious assault operations. Specialist trade training in the Israeli army lasts for the remarkably short period of three months, but is "hi-tech" and intensive.

In any war, Israel's policy—because of the small size of the country—has to be to carry the fighting to the enemy, and *Zahal's* objective has always been to achieve a quick result, because a prolonged war would bankrupt the country. Leadership from the front is not only encouraged but expected, and this has led to some of *Zahal's* most spectacular successes, even though it means that the casualty rate among combat officers is higher than in most other countries. Due to their experience, though, the Israeli defence forces today are among the most highly skilled in the world.

VII

WARSAW PACT & IRREGULAR FORCES

While "never mind the quality, feel the width," may be an old joke, there are few Western observers who would see this expression as a laughing matter when it is used to describe the military forces of Soviet Russia and their allies. The USSR defeated Nazi Germany in World War 2 strictly through numerical superiority in both men and weapons (and would have won the war even without American, British and Allied assistance), and their whole thinking on future global conflict remains the same. The Soviet and Warsaw Pact forces facing Western Europe could overrun a minimum of 30 km (19 miles) a day on an 800 km (500 mile) front by sheer weight of numbers, regardless of tactics, *if* the NATO countries hesitated to use tactical nuclear weapons; two-thirds of their first-wave assault troops are, with oriental casualness, regarded as expendable. The balance would be sufficient to overrun and occupy the Continent.

If this is genuinely the case—as can be proved—then why, it may well be asked, do the Soviets and their allies bother with special forces at all? The answer is simple: although an accomplishment may be militarily possible, it is not necessarily desirable.

Speed, secrecy and surprise

Speed, secrecy and surprise have for millennia been regarded as the key ingredients in military success, and, as we have already seen, these goals are pursued assiduously by the élite forces of many nations. For the Russians, however, they have a special meaning as their whole military posture is based upon an offensive strategy, as compared with NATO's, which places its emphasis on defence and deterrence.

Despite their two-to-one superiority in men, tanks, guns and aircraft in Europe, Soviet forces would rely heavily on the preparatory work of "desant" units to weaken the West's defence and to create confusion and disorganization. The word "desant" itself does not have a precise parellel in Western military terminology, combining elements of both "landing" and "assault." It is best described by example, although here we are handicapped by the fact that Soviet soldiers are not free to give press interviews! However, in an SAS-style "desant" operation, men of the VDV (*Vozdushno-Desantnyye-Voyska*, or airborne troops, most probably comprised largely of *Vysotniki* or *Raydoviki*, the Russian equivalents of the SAS or Rangers) would be dropped by MI-8 *Hip* battlefield assault helicopters, or by parachute from I-76 *Candid* four-jet transports, in small groups of about twenty men behind enemy lines.

Their targets would be very much the same as those of

the SAS under similar circumstances, and were described in a Royal United Services Institute (RUSI) bulletin. The principal objective of each group would be to reconnoitre an area for a later, large-scale, airborne assault, sounding out enemy positions and noting optimum sites for the invaders to occupy. Once this had been accomplished and the information radioed back, each team's task would become one of sabotage.

In one typical exercise, teams were parachuted by night into a "defended" zone. Dressed in lightweight camouflage smocks, and carrying silenced assault rifles, they would melt into the background if they encountered substantial opposition, since full-scale firefights would have hindered them from reaching their prime objectives. However, reports of such obstructions would be radioed back immediately. (Here, the Russian reliance on quantity rather than quality would prove a hindrance because, compared with the sophisticated, miniaturized and computerized battlefield radios used by the Americans and British, the Soviet radio operators would have to change frequencies manually, and to a pre-arranged schedule, to avoid interception.)

Sabotage

Having reconnoitred their designated area, surviving members of the "desant" team would begin sabotaging vital Western installations, in particular communications posts; laying landmines to disrupt counter-offensives; and placing markers on suitable landing zones for the far larger back-up force. A typical target—a tactical nuclear weapon site—could be "taken out" by a mere half-dozen men of the *Vysotniki*, and the fact that Russian exercises emphasize such objectives shows clearly that the Soviet Union knows that NATO would have to resort to nuclear defence

Desant from the sea: Soviet amphibious vehicles, supported by helicopters, come ashore from a tank landing ship.

within a maximum of five days following a full-scale conventional attack.

One major difference between the Soviet "desant" teams and their American or British counterparts is that they are only intended to operate in isolation for short periods of time—hours rather than days—and are regarded very much as small cogs in a large machine rather than as units able to act intelligently and damagingly on their own, as the SAS teams did so convincingly in the Falklands. The main assault would follow the *Vysotniki* operations at daybreak, huge AN-12 *Cub* transports dropping whole divisions of airborne troops and support equipment, including armoured personnel carriers and assault guns. Alternatively, especially in difficult terrain such as that to be found on the north of NATO's flank in Norway, heavy-duty helicopters would be deployed.

A measure of the Soviets' dependence on their "desant" troops to crack open the front line in Europe is demonstrated by the fact that, of nine whole divisions in the VDV, each comprising some 8500 men, no fewer than seven are kept at constant readiness *in peacetime,* even though the number of aircraft available (approximately 1500) means that only two divisions could be deployed at a time.

Russian "desant" troops have been actively engaged in recent years, the 105th Airborne Division spearheading the invasion of Afghanistan in 1979, while the 103rd—which had captured Prague airport during the Dubcek crisis of 1968—was on instant alert standby to be flown out to Egypt in 1973, had the Israelis not stopped their advance at the Suez Canal.

"Desant" from the sea

Following, or launched simultaneously with, a Soviet attack via Finland into the northern flank of Norway, would almost certainly come a naval pincer movement out of the Baltic and Black Seas to hit Denmark and West Germany on the one hand, and Greece and Turkey on the other. For this reason the Russians maintain strong Marine Infantry formations as well as specially trained small assault teams akin to the SBS. In most respects, however, their philosophy concerning naval "desant" operations is the same as it is for their application of airborne troops. Small units would be landed, usually and preferably by night, to assess the opposition, reconnoitre strongpoints, mark safe lines of approach and, if necessary, help to safeguard the bridgehead until the main wave of troops arrived at daylight.

A Russian assault from the sea is impressive in the extreme. Landing craft pour inshore, halting at a safe distance, if necessary, to disgorge their waves of amphibious tanks and armoured personnel carriers, while helicopters from ships such as the *Moskva* and *Leningrad* drop yet more troops right on top of the beach defences. "Jump jets," Yak-36MPs, copied from the Harrier, provide overhead protection while also being able to give ground support fire and, in particular, take out radar and missile installations.

An ominous statistic to consider is that three out of every four Soviet "desant" exercises against simulated NATO opposition are successful.

Soviets abroad

Russian special forces, including clandestine members of the GRU—the Army Secret Police—are widely known to have served, and to be serving still, as military advisers and actual fighting troops in many Middle Eastern and

WEAPONS OF THE SOVIET UNION AND RUSSIAN-EQUIPPED REGULAR AND IRREGULAR FORCES

Designation	Type	Calibre	Magazine	Rate of fire	Range	Remarks
AK47M	Assault rifle	7.62 mm	30 rounds	600 rpm cyclic	300–400 m	Most widely used assault rifle in the world
AK574	Assault rifle	5.45 mm	30 rounds	650 rpm cyclic	400 m	New replacement for the AK47
RPK	Light machine-gun	7.62 mm	30, 40 or 75 rounds	660 rpm cyclic	800 m	Standard support weapon used at section level
PKM	Machine-gun	7.62 mm	100-, 200-, or 250-belt	690–720 rpm	1000 m	
M41	Mortar	60 mm	Single-shot	20 rpm	800 m	
M37	Mortar	82 mm	Single-shot	15 rpm	3000 m	
Sagger	Anti-tank missile	120 mm	Single-shot	Not applicable	3000 m	
RPG7	Anti-aircraft missile	85 mm	Single-shot	Not applicable	300 m	

"Third World" countries—particularly Cuba—and Russian-trained Cuban advisers and troops have been active in many of the world's trouble spots, notably Angola, during the 1970s.

The Soviet Army also keeps a very strong presence within the countries of the Warsaw Pact alliance, just as America and Britain do in West Germany. The main concentration is obviously in East Germany where, in addition to six German divisions, the Russians maintain no fewer than 9 armoured and 13 mechanized rifle divisions. Similarly, alongside the ten Czech divisions, the Russians field two tank and three mechanized rifle divisions. Only two of the Warsaw Pact countries other than Russia have special forces: Czechoslovakia, which has a long and illustrious military history as well as a sophisticated indigenous armaments industry, has an airborne brigade, including self-propelled armoured assault and anti-aircraft guns; while Poland has both an airborne division and an amphibious assault division. In all the Warsaw Pact countries, there is far greater standardization of both organization and equipment than exists within NATO, so these forces may safely be assumed to be constructed on the Soviet model, with the exception of some home-built weapons and vehicles such as the Czech OT-64 and OT-65 armoured personnel and reconnaissance vehicles, plus Czech Tatra and Polish Star trucks.

Apart from repressing democratic movements in the Warsaw Pact countries of their supposed allies, such as Hungary in 1956, Czechoslavakia in 1967 and Poland in recent years; and aiding and abetting left-wing nationalist movements in Third World countries and terrorist movements everywhere; and from propping up, usually through economic and military aid, various non-aligned countries; Soviet forces had not seen genuine warfare until they invaded Afghanistan in December 1979. "Advisors" and "technicians" have seen plenty of action, of course, from Korea and Vietnam to the Middle East, Africa, the Caribbean and Central and South America, but Afghanistan was the first real encounter for regular Soviet troops.

The Russians were no strangers to the country. After Mohammed Daud Khan was overthrown by Nur Mohammed Taraki and Hafizullah Amin in the *coup d'état* of April 1978, the new rulers welcomed further Soviet aid to boost the country's weak and predominantly feudal economy and to assist in the agrarian and other reforms which they were planning. However, Afghanistan is not only one of the poorest, but it is also one of the most medievally conservative countries in the world, and Taraki's reform programme met with considerable opposition, particularly from the landowning classes. Dissent produced repression in a familiar escalating spiral. In February 1979, the American ambassador was kidnapped by an extremist group and later killed, along with his captors, when Afghan security forces attempted to rescue him. A month later, a garrison of Afghan troops murdered all the Russian advisors in Herat, a town near the Iranian border. Amin's secret police stepped up their activities, the country's regular soldiers were confined to their barracks, and an increasing flood of Russian military equipment, including helicopters, began to arrive in the country. At the same time, the number of Afghan civilians leaving their homeland swelled in proportion and, by the time of the formal Russian invasion of Afghanistan in December, some 400,000 had fled over the mountains into Pakistan. Of more military significance is the fact that, by the same time, more than half of Afghanistan's regular troops had deserted and, literally, headed for the hills, where they continue to form the hard core of the resistance movement.

In desperation, Taraki requested—and received—more and more Soviet military aid in order to put down mutinies among the surviving troops and riots among the civilian population, while Amin gradually emerged as the real strong man of the regime. Taraki visited Moscow and asked Leonid Brezhnev's help in removing this thorn in his flesh, but an agent in his staff reported events to Amin, who had Taraki arrested and later executed. The country was in turmoil and Amin was hated by the vast majority of the population. However, he still had a 20-year treaty with the Soviet Union.

The Russians rewarded Amin by invading Afghanistan on 27 December 1979. Tanks and armoured personnel carriers, supported in the air by MiG ground-attack fighters and helicopter gunships, swiftly surrounded the country's capital, Kabul, and ruthlessly suppressed all attempts at opposition. Amin himself was executed.

The Afghan war

As ignorant and conservative as their forefathers, who denied the Khyber Pass to the British Army in the 19th century, the Afghan hill-farmers, who now constitute the heart of Afghan resistance to the Soviet invaders, still look like the mountain bandits from whom they are descended, with their flowing moustaches, billowing trousers, loose shirts and turbans. Unlike the Palestinians, whom they resemble in so many ways, however, the Afghan freedom fighters lack any unified political goal other than that of expelling the invaders, and are even divided into a variety of religious factions. Their advantage lies in the fact that, whereas the Russians have largely been able to secure the towns and cities, the guerrillas control the countryside— and Napoleon lost his war in Spain for exactly the same reason.

As did the Americans in Vietnam, the Russians invaded Afghanistan full of confidence and with the most modern

A Russian T-72 tank stands guard in a Kabul street. While the Soviets control the towns, the guerrillas hold the country.

military equipment, spearheaded by élite airborne troops. Like the Vietcong, the Afghan guerrillas have the support of the majority of the local populace and are able to blend innocently into the background, when they are not trekking across the remote mountains in search of a target to ambush. They have more enthusiasm than skill, although their knowledge of the terrain helps them, while the Russian armoured vehicles must keep to the main roads, such as they are. Soviet armoured columns roam the country in huge convoys, protected from above by helicopter gunships eager to take off against the first hint of armed resistance, while élite airborne troops parallel SAS and Green Beret operations in Vietnam, being dropped secretly to sabotage guerrilla camps and set up ambushes. In some parts of the country, the Russians have deliberately driven people from their homes in an effort to create an inhospitable wasteland out of which the Afghan resistance cannot operate. In other areas, they have seeded tracts of farmland with small and virtually undetectable anti-personnel mines. The Soviets have also taken advantage of the fierce tribal vendettas existing between many members of the resistance groups, winning some to their side by the promise of vengeance against their enemies.

In return, although untutored in modern warfare, the Afghan guerrillas have resorted to the classic tactics of mining roads along which Soviet patrols are known to pass; of attacking isolated military and government posts; and of bomb attacks and assassinations in the towns and cities. The situation has so many military parallels with that prevailing in Northern Ireland that one final question has to be asked:

Freedom fighter or terrorist?

The bulk of this book has been devoted to what the people of most Western countries regard as the guardians of their freedom: the élite military forces of the democratic nations. To others, however, these same forces are the mailed fist of repression, and it must not be forgotten that many of the terrorist groups are as well armed and, in many cases, as well trained and dedicated to a cause as are the marines, paras and special forces of America, Britain or other countries.

At the heart of the terrorist movement lies the Palestine Liberation Organization which, through Moscow, has for at least two decades led the way in financing and training other groups dedicated to the overthrow of existing Western governments, to providing them with intelligence aid, documentation, weapons and ammunition, and to establishing infiltration and escape routes. Such assistance has been particularly prevalent in Latin America and, at the time of writing this book, seems likely to bring upon the people of Nicaragua the same type of American response as befell Grenada.

The PLO is financed today mainly by Saudi Arabia and Kuwait, but still relies heavily on Soviet assistance, particularly in the matter of arms and ammunition. In turn, the PLO trains guerrillas from other countries in camps in the

Middle East. In any one year, more than 2000 terrorists take the four-month training courses in Syria, South Yemen and, until recently, Lebanon. They come from Argentina, Brazil, Chile, Uruguay, Mexico and El Salvador in Latin America; from Turkey, Spain, West Germany, Italy and Ireland in Europe; from Pakistan, Bangladesh, Iran, Armenia, the Philippines, Japan and Sri Lanka in Asia; and from South Africa, Zimbabwe, Niger, Somalia, Ghana, Nigeria, Tunisia, Egypt, Togo and Mali in Africa. Simultaneously, PLO veterans are frequently dispatched as advisers in the field to other terrorist organizations around the world. Their affiliations include the Italian *Operaia Autonomia* and *Brigada Rossa* (Red Brigade), the Spanish *Euzcadi Ta Askatauna* (Basque separatists), the Moro National Liberation Front in the Philippines, the Baader-Meinhof Red Army Faction in Germany, the Irish Republican Army, the Japanese Red Army and the Dutch Red-Aid, among others.

What, the objective reader must ask, differentiates these groups from the Afghans? In all cases the ultimate aim is the abolition of what a particular guerrilla group considers a repressive regime, or the establishment of an independent state for an ethnic or religious faction. In the West, it is popular to think of the Russians as the "bad guys," and therefore their invasion of Afghanistan—regardless of their mutual aid treaties with the two preceding governments—is seen as unnecessary intervention in the affairs of an autonomous state, and the Afghan guerrillas are therefore regarded as "freedom fighters." But the Palestinians or the IRA see themselves as fighting for exactly the same reasons. The whole question, "freedom fighter or terrorist?" is decided by a value judgement, depending on individual circumstances, education, political inclination, geography and a multitude of other factors.

INDEX

245